Java™

An Introduction to Computer Science and Programming

Walter Savitch

Taken from

Java™: An Introduction to Computer Science and Programming, Third Edition
by Walter Savitch

Custom Edition for University of Victoria

Cover Art: *Untitled 3*, by Armstrong.

Taken from:

Java™: An Introduction to Computer Science and Programming, Third Edition
by Walter Savitch

Published by Pearson Prentice Hall
Upper Saddle River, New Jersey 07458

This special edition published in cooperation with Pearson Custom Publishing.

Printed in Canada

10 9 8 7 6 5 4 3 2 1

ISBN 0-536-80573-3

BA 998851

LR

Please visit our web site at *www.pearsoncustom.com*

PEARSON CUSTOM PUBLISHING
75 Arlington Street, Suite 300, Boston, MA 02116
A Pearson Education Company

TABLE OF CONTENTS

Chapter 1

Intro to Computers and Java

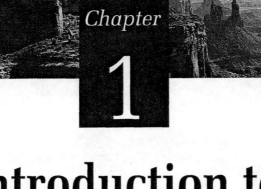

Introduction to Computers and Java

chapter

It is by no means hopeless to expect to make a machine for really very difficult mathematical problems. But you would have to proceed step-by-step. I think electricity would be the best thing to rely on. -Charles Sanders Peirce (1839–1914)

This chapter gives you a brief overview of computer hardware and software. Our discussion of software will include a description of a methodology for designing programs known as object-oriented programming. Much of this introductory material applies to programming in any language, not just to programming in Java. Section 1.3 introduces the Java language and explains two simple Java programs. An optional section at the end of this chapter gives some sample applets, which are Java programs that can be run from an Internet Website.

OBJECTIVES

Give you a brief overview of computer hardware and software.

Introduce you to the basic techniques of program design in general and object-oriented programming in particular.

Give you an overview of the Java programming language.

PREREQUISITES

This first chapter does *not* assume that you have had any previous programming experience, but it does assume that you have access to a computer. To get the full value from the chapter, and from the rest of this book, you should have a computer that has the Java language installed, so that you can try out what you are learning. The Preface discusses some ways to obtain a free copy of the Java language for your computer.

If you prefer, you may intersperse the reading of this first chapter with your reading of the next five chapters of the book. However, you should read at least Section 1.3 before moving on to Chapter 2. You can read Section 1.3 before reading Sections 1.1 and 1.2. (In fact, you can read Sections 1.1, 1.2, and 1.3 in any order.)

1.1 COMPUTER BASICS

The Analytical Engine has no pretensions whatever to originate anything. It can do whatever we know how to order it to perform. It can follow analysis; but it has no power of anticipating any analytical relations or truths. Its province is to assist us in making available what we are already acquainted with. -Ada Augusta, Countess of Lovelace (1815–1852)

r systems consist of **hardware** and **software.** The hardware is the physical A set of instructions for the computer is called a **program.** All the different kinds of programs used to give instructions to the computer are referred to as software. In this book, we will be discussing software, but in order to understand the software, it does help to know a few basic things about computer hardware.

Hardware and Memory

Most computers available today have the same basic components, configured in basically the same way. They all have input devices, such as a keyboard and a mouse. They all have output devices, such as a display screen and a printer. They also have two or three other basic components, usually housed in some sort of cabinet, where they are not so obvious. These other components are a processor and two kinds of memory, known as main memory and auxiliary memory.

processor
CPU
chip

The **processor** is the device inside your computer that follows a program's instructions. (The processor is also called the **CPU,** which stands for **central processing unit.**) If you buy a PC, you will be told what kind of chip it has. The **chip** is the processor. Currently, one of the better-known chips is the Pentium processor. The processor follows the instructions in a program, but it can carry out only very simple instructions, such as moving numbers or other items around from one place in memory to another and performing some simple arithmetic operations like addition and subtraction. The power of a computer comes from its speed and the intricacies of its programs. The basic design of the hardware is relatively simple.

memory

A computer's **memory** holds data for the computer to process, and it holds the result of the computer's intermediate calculations. The computer has two basic kinds of memory, known as main memory and auxiliary memory. All of the various kinds of disk drives, diskettes, and compact discs that are used with computers are types of **auxiliary memory.** They are the (more or less) permanent memory. (Auxiliary memory is also called **secondary memory.**) The working memory that your program uses for intermediate calculations (and for holding the program you are currently running) is called the **main memory.** It is the character of the main memory that you most need to be aware of when you are writing programs. Main memory holds the current program and much of the data that the program is manipulating.

auxiliary memory

main memory

To make this more concrete, let's look at an example. You may have heard a desktop computer (PC) described as having, say, 256 megabytes of RAM and a 20-gigabyte hard drive (or some other numbers for RAM and hard drive storage). **RAM** (short for random access memory) is the main memory, and the hard drive is the principal (but not the only) form of auxiliary memory. A byte is a quantity of memory. So 256 megabytes of RAM is approximately 256 million bytes of memory, and a 20-gigabyte hard drive has approximately 20 billion bytes of memory. So what exactly is a byte? Read on.

RAM

A **bit** is a digit that can assume only the two values 0 and 1. (Actually, any two values will do, but the two values are typically written as 0 and 1.) A **byte** is eight bits of memory—that is, a quantity of memory capable of holding eight digits, each either 0 or 1. Both main memory and auxiliary memory are measured in bytes. In main memory, the organization of the bytes is very important. The computer's main memory consists of a long list of numbered locations, each of which can hold one byte of information. The number of a byte is called its **address.** A piece of data, such as a number or a keyboard character, can be stored in one of these bytes. When the computer needs to recover the data later, it uses the address of the byte to find the data item.

bit

byte

address

Data of various kinds, such as letters, numbers, and strings of letters, are encoded as a series of zeros and ones and placed in the computer's memory. As it turns out, one byte is just large enough to store a single keyboard character. This is one of the reasons that a computer's memory is divided into these 8-bit bytes, instead of into pieces of some other size. However, in order to store a large number or a string of letters, the computer needs more than a single byte. When the computer needs to store a piece of data that cannot fit into a single byte, it uses a number of adjacent bytes. These adjacent bytes are then considered to be a single, larger **memory location,** and the address of the first byte is used as the address of the entire larger memory location. Display 1.1 shows how a typical computer's main memory might be divided into memory locations. The boundaries between these locations are not fixed by the hardware. The size and location of the boundaries will be different when different programs are run.

memory location

Recall that main memory is used only when the computer is running a program. Auxiliary memory is used to hold data in a more or less permanent form. Auxiliary memory is also divided into bytes, but these bytes are then grouped into much larger units known as **files.** A file may contain (in an encoded form) almost any sort of data, such as a program, a letter, a list of numbers, or a picture. The important characteristics of a file are that it has a name and that it can hold data. When you write a Java program, you will store the program in a file. The file is stored in auxiliary memory (typically some kind of disk storage), and when you want to run the program, the program is copied from auxiliary memory to main memory.

file

DISPLAY 1.1 Main Memory

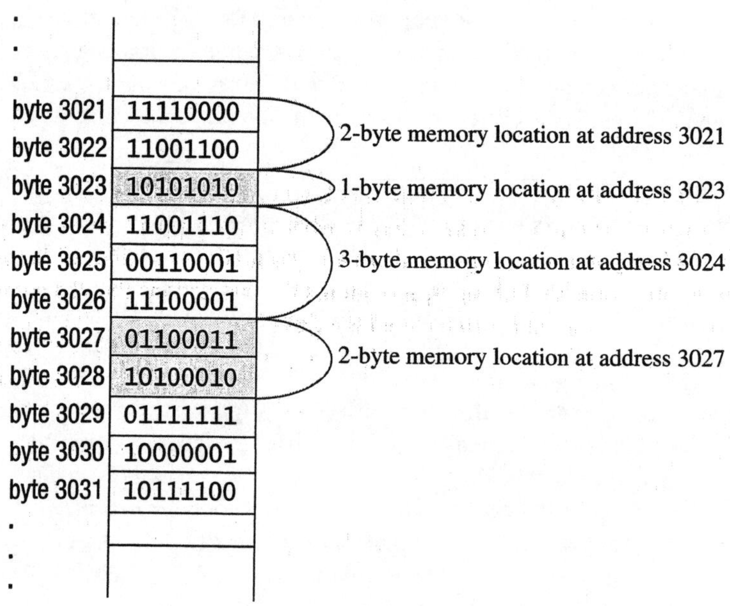

Files are often organized into groups of files known as **directories** or **folders.** *Folder* and *directory* are two names for the same thing. Some computer systems use one name, and some use the other.

directory
folder

FAQ:[1] Why Just Zeros and Ones?

Computers use zeros and ones because it is easy to make a physical device that has only two stable states. However, when you are programming, you normally need not be concerned about the encoding of data as zeros and ones. You can program as if the computer directly stored numbers, letters, or strings of letters in memory.

There is nothing special about the digits zero and one. We could just as well use any two names, such as *A* and *B* or *true* and *false*, instead of *zero* and *one*. The important thing is that the underlying physical device has two stable states, such as on versus off or high versus low voltage. Calling these two states *zero* and *one* is simply a convention, but it's one that is almost universally followed.

Quick Reference: Bytes and Memory Locations

A **byte** is a memory location that can hold eight digits, each either 0 or 1. A computer's main memory is divided into numbered bytes. The number of a byte is called its **address.** To store a piece of data that is too large to fit into a single byte, the computer uses a number of adjacent bytes. These adjacent bytes are considered to be a single larger memory location, and the address of the first byte is used as the address of the entire larger memory location.

Programs

You probably have some idea of what a program is. You use programs all the time. For example, text editors and word processors are programs. A bank ATM machine is really a computer that is running a program. A **program** is simply a set of instructions for a computer to follow.

program

Display 1.2 shows two ways to view the running of a program. To see the first way, forget the dashed lines that form a box. What's left is what really happens when you run a program. Note that when you run a program, there are (normally) two kinds of input to a computer. The program is one kind of input; it contains the instructions that the computer will follow. The other kind of input is often called the **data** for the program. It is the information that the computer program will process. For example, if the program is a simple spelling check program, the data would be the text that needs to be checked. As far as the computer is concerned, both the data and the program itself are input. The output is the result (or results) produced when the computer follows the program's instructions. If the program checks the spelling of some text, the output might be a list of words that are misspelled. When you give the computer a program and some data and tell the computer to follow the instructions in the program, that is called **running** the program on the data, and the computer is said to **execute** the program on the data.

data

running or
executing

---

1. FAQ stands for frequently asked question.

DISPLAY 1.2 Running a Program

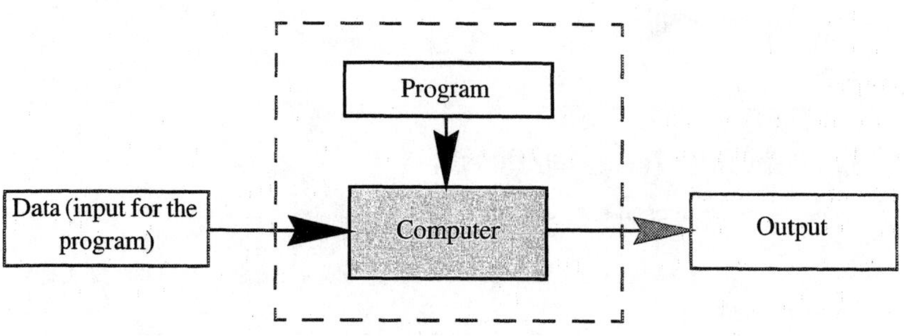

This first view of running a program is what really happens, but it is not always the way we think about running a program. Another view is to think of the data as the input to the program. In this second view, the computer and the program are considered to be one unit that takes the data as input and produces the output. In this view, the combined program–computer unit is indicated by the box with the dashed outline. When we take this view, we think of the data as input to the program and the output as output from the program. Although the computer is understood to be there, it is presumed just to be something that assists the program. Programmers find this second view to be more useful when they design a program.

operating system

There are more programs on your computer than you might think when you first begin using your computer. Much of what you think of as "the computer" is actually a program rather than hardware. When you first turn on a computer, you are already running and interacting with a program. That program is called the **operating system.** The operating system is a kind of supervisory program that oversees the entire operation of the computer. If you want to run a program, you tell the operating system what you want to do. The operating system then retrieves and starts the program. The program you run might be a text editor, a program to surf the World Wide Web, or some program that you wrote using the Java language. You might tell the operating system to run the program by clicking an icon with your mouse, by choosing a menu item, or by typing in a simple command. Thus, what you probably think of as "the computer" is really the operating system. Some common operating systems are DOS, Microsoft Windows, Apple's (Macintosh) Mac OS, Linux, and UNIX.

FAQ: What Exactly Is Software?

The word *software* simply means programs. Thus, a software company is a company that produces programs. The software on your computer is just the collection of programs on your computer.

Programming Languages and Compilers

Most modern programming languages are designed to be (relatively) easy for people to write and to understand. These programming languages that are designed for people to use are called **high-level languages.** Java is a high-level language. Most of the programming languages you are likely to have heard of, such as Pascal, FORTRAN, C, C++, BASIC, and Visual Basic, are also high-level languages. Unfortunately, computer hardware does not understand high-level languages. Before a program written in a high-level language can be run, it must be translated into a language that the computer can understand. The languages that the computer can (more directly) understand are called **low-level languages.** The translation of a program from a high-level language, like Java, to a low-level language is performed by another program known as a **compiler.**

high-level language

low-level language

compiler

When you run a program written in a high-level language, such as a Java, you are actually running a low-level-language translation of that program. Thus, before you run a high-level-language program, you must first run the compiler on the program. When you do this, you are said to **compile** the program.

compile

The low-level languages produced by compilers are usually referred to as **machine languages** or **assembly languages.** The language that the computer can directly understand is called machine language. Assembly language is almost the same thing as machine language, but it needs some minor additional translation before it can run on the computer. Normally, this additional translation is done automatically and need not be of concern to you. In practice, it will look as though you are running the program produced by the compiler.

machine language

One disadvantage of the translation process we just described for high-level languages is that, with most programming languages, you need a different compiler for each type of computer and each operating system. If you want to run your high-level-language program on three different types of computers, you need to use three different compilers and must compile your program three different times. Moreover, if a manufacturer comes out with a new type of computer, a team of programmers must write a new compiler for that computer. This is a problem because compilers are very large programs that are expensive and time consuming to produce. Despite this cost, this is the way most high-level-language compilers work. Java, however, uses a slightly different and much more versatile approach to compiling. We discuss the Java approach to compiling in the next subsection.

When you use a compiler, the terminology can get a bit confusing, because both the input to the compiler program and the output from the compiler program are programs. Everything in sight is a program of some kind or other. To help avoid confusion, we call the input program, which in our case will be a Java program, the **source program,** or **source code.** The translated low-level-language program that the compiler produces is often called the **object program,** or **object code.** The word **code** just means a program or a part of a program.

source code
object code

code

Quick Reference: **Compiler**

A **compiler** is a program that translates a high-level-language program, such as a Java program, into a program in a simpler language that the computer can more or less directly understand.

Java Byte-Code

The Java compiler does not translate your program into the machine language for your particular computer. Instead, it translates your Java program into a language called **byte-code.**

byte-code

Java Virtual Machine

interpreter

Byte-code is not the machine language for any particular computer. Byte-code is the machine language for a hypothetical computer that is something like the average of all computers. This hypothetical computer is called the **Java Virtual Machine.** The Java Virtual Machine is not exactly like any particular computer, but it is similar to all typical computers. Thus, it is very easy to translate a program written in byte-code into a program in the machine language for any particular computer. The program that does this translation is called an **interpreter.** The interpreter works by translating each instruction of byte-code into instructions expressed in your computer's machine language and then executing those instructions on your computer. Thus, an interpreter translates and executes the instructions in the byte-code one after the other, rather than translating the entire byte-code program at once. However, the only detail that you really need to know is that the interpreter somehow allows your computer to run Java byte-code.[2]

In order to run your Java program on your computer, you proceed as follows: First, you use the compiler to translate your Java program into byte-code. Then you use the byte-code interpreter for your computer to translate each byte-code instruction to machine language and to run the machine-language instructions. The whole process is diagrammed in Display 1.3.

It sounds as though Java byte-code just adds an extra step in the process. Why not write compilers that translate directly from Java to the machine language for your particular computer? That could be done, and it is what is done for most other programming languages. Moreover, that technique would produce machine-language programs that typically run faster. However, Java byte-code gives Java one important advantage, namely, portability. After you compile your Java program into byte-code, you can use that byte-code on any computer. When you run your program on another type of computer, you do not need to recompile it. This means that you can send your byte-code over the Internet to another computer and have it run easily on that computer. That is one of the reasons Java is good for Internet applications.

Portability has other advantages as well. When a manufacturer comes out with a new type of computer, the creators of Java do not have to design a new Java compiler. One Java compiler works on every computer. This means that Java can be added to a new computer very quickly and very economically. Of course, every type of computer must have its own byte-code interpreter in order to translate byte-code instructions into machine-language instructions for that particular computer, but these interpreters are simple programs compared to a compiler.

Quick Reference: Byte-Code

The Java compiler translates your Java program into a language called **byte-code.** This byte-code is not the machine language for any particular computer, but is a language that is similar to the machine language of most common computers and that is very easy to translate into the machine language of any particular computer. Each type of computer will have its own translator (called an interpreter) that translates from byte-code instructions to machine-language instructions for that particular computer.

2. Sometimes people use the term *Java Virtual Machine* (JVM) to refer to the Java byte-code interpreter (as well as to refer to the underlying hypothetical machine that the interpreter is based on).

DISPLAY 1.3 Compiling and Running a Java Program

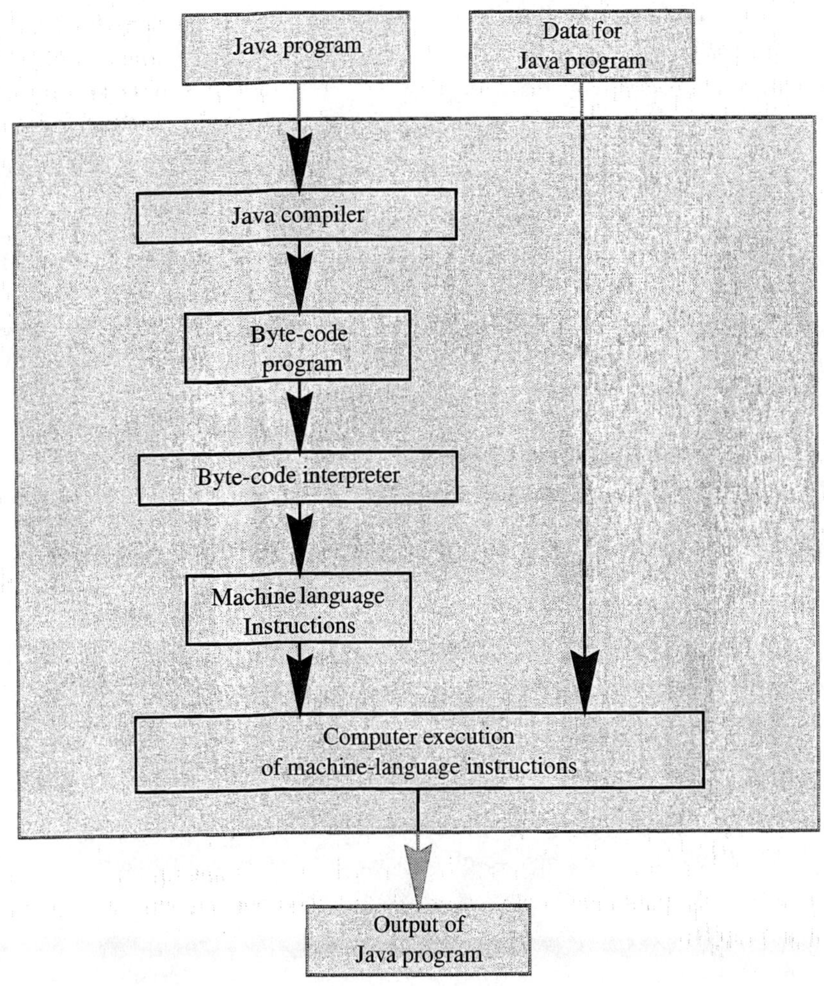

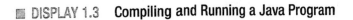

It is important to know about Java byte-code, but in the day-to-day business of programming, you will not even be aware of the fact that there is byte-code for your program. You normally give two commands, one to compile your program (into byte-code) and one to run your program. The **run command** executes the Java byte-code interpreter on the byte-code. This run command might be called "run" or something else, but is unlikely to be called "interpret." You will come to think of the run command as running whatever the compiler produces, and you will not even think about the fact that it is byte-code rather than machine language.

run command

FAQ: Why Is It Called "Byte-Code"?

Programs in low-level languages, such as byte-code and machine-language code, consist of instructions, each of which can be stored in a few bytes of memory. This is presumably why byte-code was given its name. To the designers of Java, byte-code must have looked like "a bunch of bytes."

Linking

linking

A Java program is seldom written as one piece of code all in one file. Instead, it typically consists of different pieces, often written by different people, and each of these pieces is compiled separately. Thus, each piece is translated into a different piece of byte-code. In order to run your program, you need to connect the pieces together. The process of connecting them is called **linking,** and the program that does the linking is called a **linker.** Even the simplest of Java programs will use some standard pieces of byte-code written by somebody else and so will need the linker. These standard pieces of byte-code come with the Java system. On the bright side linking is typically done automatically, so you usually need not be concerned with it.

? Self-Test Questions

Answers to Self-Test Questions appear at the end of each chapter.

1. What are the two kinds of memory in a computer?
2. What is software?
3. What would be the data for a program that computes the sum of two numbers?
4. What would be the data for a program that computes the average of all the quizzes you have taken in a course?
5. What is the difference between a machine-language program, a high-level-language program, and a program expressed in Java byte-code?
6. Is Java a high-level language or a low-level language?
7. Is Java byte-code a high-level language or a low-level language?
8. What is a compiler?
9. What is a source program?
10. What do you call a program that translates Java byte-code instructions into machine-language instructions?

1.2 DESIGNING PROGRAMS

'The time has come,' the Walrus said,
'To talk of many things:
Of shoes–and ships–and sealing wax–
Of cabbages–and–kings...' -Lewis Carroll, *Through the Looking Glass*

Programming is a creative process. We cannot tell you exactly how to write a program to do whatever task you may want it to perform. However, we can give you some techniques that experienced programmers have found to be extremely helpful when designing programs. In this section, we discuss some of these techniques. The techniques are applicable to programming in almost any programming language and are not particular to Java.

Object-Oriented Programming

Java is an **object-oriented programming** language, abbreviated **OOP.** What is an OOP? The world around us is made up of objects, such as people, automobiles, buildings, trees, shoes, ships, sealing wax, cabbages, kings, and so forth. Each of these objects has the ability to perform certain actions, and each of the actions has some effect on some of the other objects in the world. OOP is a programming methodology that views a program as similarly consisting of objects that interact with one another by means of actions.

OOP

This approach is easier to understand if the program simulates something in the real world. For example, consider a program that simulates a highway interchange in order to analyze traffic flow. The program would have an object to simulate each of the automobiles that enter the interchange, perhaps other objects to simulate each lane of the highway, and so forth.

Object-oriented programming comes with its own terminology. The objects are called, appropriately enough, **objects.** The actions that an object can take are called **methods.** Objects of the same kind are said to have the same *type* or, more often, are said to be in the same **class.** For example, in a simulation program, all the simulated automobiles might belong to the same class, probably called the `Automobile` class. All objects within a class have the same methods. Thus, in a simulation program, all automobiles have the same methods (or possible actions), such as moving forward, moving backward, accelerating, and so forth. This does not mean that all simulated automobiles are identical. They can have different characteristics, which the program indicates by associating some data (that is, some information) with each particular automobile object. For example, the data associated with an automobile object might consist of a word telling the make of the automobile and a number indicating its current speed. (All this will become clearer when you start to define classes yourself, using the Java programming language.)

object

method

class

Quick Reference: Objects, Methods, and Classes

An **object** is a program construction that has data (that is, information) associated with it and that can perform certain actions. When the program is run, the objects interact with one another in order to accomplish whatever the program is designed to do. The actions performed by objects are called **methods**. A **class** is a type or kind of object. All objects in the same class have the same kinds of data and the same methods.

As you will see, this same object-oriented methodology can be applied to any sort of computer program and is not limited to simulation programs. Object-oriented programming is not a new methodology, but its use in applications outside of simulation programs did not become popular until the early 1990s.

Object-oriented programming uses classes and objects, but it does not use them in just any old way. It uses them while following certain design principles. The following are three of the main design principles of object-oriented programming:

Encapsulation

Polymorphism

Inheritance

We will discuss each of these principles briefly in this chapter and more fully at appropriate places later in the book.

Quick Reference: Object-Oriented Programming

Object-oriented programming (OOP) is a programming methodology that views a program as consisting of objects that interact with each other by means of actions (known as **methods**). Object-oriented programming uses objects while following certain design principles. The main design principles of object-oriented programming are encapsulation, polymorphism, and inheritance.

Encapsulation

encapsulation

Encapsulation sounds as though it means putting things into a capsule, or, to say it another way, packaging things up. This intuition is correct as far as it goes. The most important part of encapsulation, however, is not simply that things are put into a capsule, but that only part of what is in the capsule is visible. Let's look at an example.

Suppose you want to drive an automobile. What is the most useful description of the automobile? It clearly is not a description of how many cylinders the automobile has and how they go through a cycle of taking in air and gasoline, igniting the gasoline–air mixture, and expelling exhaust. You don't need such details to learn how to drive an automobile. Indeed, knowing those details would be of no real help.

To a person who wants to learn to drive, the most useful description of an automobile consists of information such as the following:

If you press your foot on the accelerator pedal, the automobile will move faster.

If you press your foot on the brake pedal, the automobile will slow down and eventually stop.

If you turn the steering wheel to the right, the automobile will turn to the right.

If you turn the steering wheel to the left, the automobile will turn to the left.

There are other details to describe, but these are perhaps the main ones and are enough to illustrate the concept of encapsulation.

The principle of encapsulation says that, when describing an automobile to somebody who wants to learn to drive, you should provide something like the previous list. In the context of programming, encapsulation means the same thing. It means that when you produce a piece of software, you should describe it in a way that tells other programmers how to use your piece of software, but that omits all the details of how the software works. In particular, if your piece of software is 10 pages long, the description given to another programmer who uses the software should be much shorter than 10 pages, perhaps only a half page long. Of course, that is possible only if you write your software in such a way that it lends itself to this sort of short description.

Note that encapsulation hides the fine detail of what is inside the "capsule." For this reason, encapsulation is often called **information hiding.**

information hiding

Another analogy that may help is that an automobile has certain things that are visible, like the pedals and steering wheel, and other things that are hidden under the hood. The automobile is encapsulated so that the details are hidden under the hood and only the controls needed to drive the automobile are visible. Similarly, a piece of software should be encapsulated so that the details are hidden and only the necessary controls are visible.

Encapsulation is important because it simplifies the job of the programmer who uses the encapsulated software to write more software.

Quick Reference: **Encapsulation**

Encapsulation is the process of hiding (encapsulating) all the details of how a piece of software was written and telling only what a programmer needs to know in order to use the software. Put another way, encapsulation is the process of describing a class or object by giving only enough information to allow a programmer to use the class or object.

Polymorphism

polymorphism

Polymorphism comes from a Greek word meaning "many forms." The basic idea of polymorphism is that it allows the same program instruction to mean different things in different contexts. Polymorphism commonly occurs in English, and its use in a programming language makes the programming language more like a human language. For example, the English instruction "Go play your favorite sport" means different things to different people. To one person, it means to go play baseball. To another person, it means to go play soccer.

In a programming language such as Java, polymorphism means that one method name, used as an instruction, can cause different actions, depending on the kind of objects that perform the action. For example, there can be a method named `output` that will output the data in an object. But which data and how many data items it outputs depend on the kind of object that carries out the action. There is a bit more to explain about polymorphism, but this brief introduction will give you the general idea. (We will explain polymorphism more fully in Chapter 7.)

If polymorphism is an everyday occurrence in languages like English, why is it a big deal in programming languages? The reason is that early programming languages had very little polymorphism. When it was introduced into programming languages, polymorphism was a big deal because it made programs easier to read and understand.

Quick Reference: **Polymorphism**

In a programming language such as Java, **polymorphism** means that one method name, used as an instruction, can cause different actions, depending on the kind of object that performs the action.

Inheritance

inheritance

Inheritance refers to a way of organizing classes. The name comes from the notion of inheritance of traits like eye color, hair color, and so forth, but it is perhaps clearer to think of it in terms of a classification system. An example of such a system is shown in Display 1.4. Note that at each level the classifications become more specialized: The class Vehicle includes the classes Automobile, Motorcycle, and Bus; the class Automobile includes the classes Family Car and Sports Car.

The class Vehicle has certain properties, like possessing wheels. The classes Automobile, Motorcycle, and Bus "inherit" the property of having wheels, but add more properties or restrictions. For example, an Automobile has four wheels, a Motorcycle has two wheels, and a Bus has at least four wheels.

Note that as you go higher in the diagram, the classes are more inclusive. A School Bus is a Bus. Since it is a Bus, a School Bus is also a Vehicle. However, a Vehicle is not necessarily a School Bus. A Sports Car is an Automobile and is also a Vehicle, but a Vehicle is not necessarily a Sports Car.

In programming languages like Java, inheritance is used to organize classes in the manner just described. This type of organization has the advantage of allowing the programmer to avoid repeating the same set of programming instructions for each class. For example, everything that is true of every Vehicle, such as "has a motor," is described only once, and it is inherited by the classes Automobile, Motorcycle, and Bus. Without inheritance, descriptions like "has a motor" would have to be repeated for each of the classes Automobile, Motorcycle, Bus, School Bus, Luxury Bus, and so forth.

Inheritance is very important to object-oriented programming and to the Java language. However, it is a bit difficult to understand without concrete programming examples. We will discuss inheritance in the Java language in Chapter 7. At that point, we will explain the notion of inheritance more fully and more clearly.

DISPLAY 1.4 An Inheritance Hierarchy

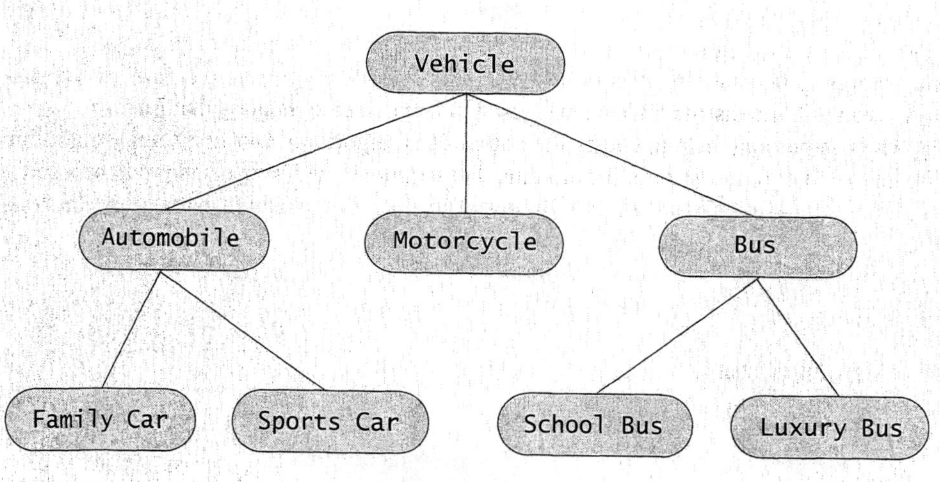

Quick Reference: Inheritance

In a programming language such as Java, **inheritance** is a way of organizing classes so that properties can be defined only once and yet apply to a whole collection of classes.

If You Know Some Other Programming Language

If Java is your first programming language, you should skip this subsection. If you know some other programming language, the discussion that is to follow may help you understand objects in terms of things you already know about. If you are already familiar with some other object-oriented programming language, such as C++, Smalltalk, or Borland's Turbo Pascal or Delphi, then you have a good idea of what objects, methods, and classes are. They are basically the same in all object-oriented programming languages, although some other languages use the words *function* or *procedure* to mean the same thing as *method.* You may be familiar with an older programming language that does not use objects and classes, in which case objects can be described in terms of other, older programming constructs. If you know about variables and functions, you can think of an object as a variable that has multiple pieces of data and its own functions. Methods are really the same thing as what are called *procedures* or *functions* in older programming languages.

Algorithms

Objects interact with one another by performing actions (called methods). You as a programmer need to design these actions by giving instructions for carrying out the actions. The hardest part of designing the actions is not figuring out how to express your solution in Java (or whatever programming language you are using). The hardest part is coming up with a plan or strategy for carrying out the action. This strategy is often expressed as something called an algorithm.

An **algorithm** is a set of instructions for solving a problem. To qualify as an algorithm, the instructions must be expressed so completely and so precisely that somebody could follow the instructions without having to fill in any details or make any decisions that are not fully specified in the instructions. An algorithm can be expressed in English or in a programming language such as Java. However, when we use the word *algorithm,* we usually mean that the instructions are expressed in English or something like English.

algorithm

An example may help to clarify the notion of an algorithm. Our first sample algorithm determines the total cost for a list of items. For example, the list of items might be a shopping list that includes the price of each item. The algorithm would then determine the total cost of all the items on the list. The algorithm is as follows:

Algorithm that determines the total cost of a list of items

1. Write the number 0 on the blackboard.
2. Do the following for each item on the list:

    Add the cost of the item to the number on the blackboard.

    Replace the old number on the blackboard with the result of this addition.
3. Announce that the answer is the number written on the blackboard.

This algorithm uses a blackboard to store intermediate results. Most algorithms need to store some intermediate results. If the algorithm is written in the Java language and run on a computer, intermediate results are stored in the computer's main memory.

Quick Reference: **Algorithm**

An **algorithm** is a set of instructions for solving a problem. To qualify as an algorithm, the instructions must be expressed so completely and precisely that somebody could follow the instructions without having to fill in any details or make any decisions that are not fully specified in the instructions.

? Self-Test Questions

11. What is a method?
12. What is the relationship between classes and objects?
13. Do all objects of the same class have the same methods?
14. What is encapsulation?
15. What is information hiding?
16. What is polymorphism?
17. What is an algorithm?

Reusable Components

When you first start to write programs, you can easily get the impression that each program that is produced is a completely separate project that is designed from scratch. That is not the way good software is produced, however. Most programs are created by combining components that already exist. Doing so saves time and money. Also, since the software being reused has probably been used many times, it is likely to be better tested and therefore more reliable than newly created software.

For example, a highway simulation program might include a new highway object to model a new highway design, but would probably model automobiles by using an automobile class that was already designed for some other program. To ensure that the classes you use in your programs are easily reusable, you must design them to be reusable. You must specify exactly how objects of that class interact with other objects. This is the principle of encapsulation that we discussed earlier. But encapsulation is not the only principle you must follow. You must also design your class so that the objects are general and not designed in an ad hoc way for one particular program. For example, if your program requires that all simulated automobiles move only forward, you should still include a reverse in your automobile class, because some other simulation may require automobiles to back up. (We will return to the topic of reusability after we learn some details about the Java language and have some examples to work with.)

Testing and Debugging

The best way to write a correct program is to carefully design the objects your program will need and the algorithms for the methods the objects will use and then to carefully translate everything into Java code (or into whatever programming language you are using). In other words, the best way to eliminate errors is to avoid them in the first place. However, no matter how carefully you proceed, your program might still contain some errors. When you finish writing a program, you should test it to see whether it performs correctly and then fix any errors you may find.

A mistake in a program is called a **bug.** For this reason, the process of eliminating mistakes in your program is called **debugging.** There are three commonly recognized types of bugs or errors: syntax errors, run-time errors, and logic errors. Let's consider them in that order.

bug

debugging

A **syntax error** is a grammatical mistake in your program. There are very strict grammar rules for how you write a program. If you violate one of these rules—for example, by omitting a required punctuation mark—that is a syntax error. The compiler will catch syntax errors and output an error message telling you that it has found the error and indicating what it thinks the error is. If the compiler says you have a syntax error, you probably do have an error. However, the compiler is only guessing at what the error is, so it could be incorrect in its diagnosis of the problem.

syntax error

Quick Reference: **Syntax**

The rules for the correct way to write a program or part of a program (the grammar rules for a programming language) are called the **syntax** of the language.

An error that is detected when your program is run is called a **run-time error.** If your program contains a run-time error, the computer will output an error message when the program is run. The error message may or may not be easy to understand, but at least it lets you know that something is wrong. Sometimes it can even tell you exactly what the problem is.

run-time error

If there is some mistake in the underlying algorithm for your program, or if you write something in Java that is incorrect, but still valid, your program will compile and run without any error message. You have written a valid Java program, but you have not written the program you want. The program runs and produces output, but the output it produces is incorrect. In this case, your program contains a **logic error.** For example, if you were to mistakenly use the addition sign in place of the subtraction sign, that would be a logic error. You could compile and run your program with no error messages, but the program would give the wrong output. Logic errors are the hardest kind of error to locate, because the computer does not give you any error messages.

logic error

▲ *Gotcha*

Coping with "Gotchas"

gotcha

Any programming language has details that can trip you up in ways that are surprising or hard to deal with. These sorts of problems are often called pitfalls, but a more colorful and more commonly used term is *gotchas*. The term stems from the fact that the problems, or pitfalls, or gotchas, are like traps waiting to catch you. When you get caught in the trap, the trap has "got you," or, as it is more commonly pronounced, "gotcha."

In this book, we have sections like this one, with the heading "Gotcha:" that warn you about many of the most common gotchas and tell you how to avoid them or cope with them. △

▲ *Gotcha*

Hidden Errors

Just because your program compiles and runs without any errors and even gives reasonable-looking output, does not mean that your program is correct. You should always run your program with some test data for which you know what the output is supposed to be. To do this, choose some data for which you can compute the correct output, with pencil and paper, by looking up the answer, or by some other means. Even this testing does not guarantee that your program is correct, but the more testing you do, the more confidence you can have in your program. △

? Self-Test Questions

18. What is a syntax error?
19. What is a logic error?
20. What kinds of errors are likely to produce error messages that will alert you to the fact that your program contains an error?
21. Suppose you write a program that is supposed to compute which day of the week (Sunday, Monday, and so forth) a given date (like December 1, 2004) will fall on. Now suppose that you forget to account for leap years. Your program will then contain an error. What kind of program error is it?

1.3 A SIP OF JAVA

Java. An Island of Indonesia, 48,842 square miles in area, lying between the Indian Ocean and the Java Sea.
java n. Informal. Brewed coffee. [From Java.] - The American Heritage Dictionary of the English Language, First Edition

In this section, we describe some of the characteristics of the Java language and examine a simple Java program.

History of the Java Language

Java is widely viewed as a programming language for Internet applications. However, this book, and many other books and people, view Java as a general-purpose programming language that can be used without any reference to the Internet. At its birth, Java was neither of these things, but it eventually evolved into both.

The history of Java goes back to 1991, when James Gosling and his team at Sun Microsystems began designing the first version of a new programming language that would become Java (though it was not yet called that). The first version of Java was intended to be a programming language for programming home appliances, like toasters and TVs. That sounds like a humble engineering task, but in fact, it's a very challenging one. Home appliances are controlled by a wide variety of computer processors (chips). The language that Gosling and his team were designing needed to work on all these different processors. Moreover, a home appliance is typically an inexpensive item, so the manufacturer would be unwilling to invest large amounts of time and money into developing complicated compilers (programs that would translate the appliance language programs into a language the processor could understand). In this appliance language that the team was designing, and now in the Java language into which it has evolved, programs are first translated into an **intermediate language** that is the same for all appliances (or all computers). Then a small, easy-to-write, and hence inexpensive program translates the intermediate language into the machine language for a particular appliance or computer. The intermediate language is called Java byte-code or simply byte-code, as we discussed in an earlier section. The plan for programming appliances with this first version of Java never caught on with appliance manufacturers, but that was not the end of the story.

intermediate language

byte-code

In 1994, Gosling realized that his language would be ideal for developing a Web browser that could run (Java) programs over the Internet. The Web browser was produced by Patrick Naughton and Jonathan Payne at Sun Microsystems and has evolved into the browser that is today known as HotJava. That was the start of Java's connection to the Internet. In the fall of 1995, Netscape Incorporated decided to make the next release of its Web browser capable of running Java programs. Other companies associated with the Internet have followed suit and have developed software that accommodates Java programs.

FAQ: Why Is the Language Named "Java"?

The question of how Java got its name does not have a very interesting answer. The current custom is to name programming languages in pretty much the same way that parents name their children. The creator of the programming language simply chooses any name that sounds good to her or him. The original name of the language was "Oak." Later the creators realized that there already was a computer language named Oak, so they needed another name, and "Java" was chosen. One hears conflicting explanations of the origin of the name "Java." One traditional, and perhaps believable, story is that the name was thought of when, after a fruitless meeting in which they tried to come up with a new name, the development team went out for coffee, and the rest is, as they say, history.

Applets

There are two kinds of Java programs: applets and applications. An **application** is just a regular program. An **applet** sounds as though it would be a little apple, but the name is meant to convey the idea of a little application. Applets and applications are almost identical. The difference is that an application is meant to be run on your computer, like any other program, whereas an applet is meant to be sent to another location on the Internet and run there.

applet
application

Once you know how to design and write either applets or applications, it is easy to learn to write the other of these two kinds of programs. This book emphasizes applications rather than applets. The reason is that you need to know a number of things about the World Wide Web and Web sites in order to use applets in the way they were intended to be used, and we did not want to cover that whole other topic here. However, if you want to write applets right away, we've given some sample applets later in this chapter in the subsection entitled "Preview Examples of Applets *(Optional)*." Applets are also covered in detail in Chapter 13 of the book.

A First Java Application Program

Our first Java program is shown in Display 1.5. Below the program, we show two screen dialogs that might be produced when a person runs and interacts with the program. The person who interacts with a program is called the **user.** The text typed in by the user is shown in color. If you run this program (and you should do so), both the text displayed by the program and the text you type will be the same color on your computer screen. The user may or may not be the person who wrote the program. In a programming class, they very often are the same person, but in a real-world application, they are usually different people.

user

programmer

The person who writes the program is called the **programmer.** This book is teaching you to be the programmer, and one of the first things you need to learn is that the user of your program cannot be expected to know what you want her or him to do. For that reason, your program must give the user understandable instructions, as we have done in the sample screen dialogs.

At this point, we just want to give you a feel for the Java language by providing a brief, informal description of the sample program shown in Display 1.5. In Chapters 2 and 3, we will explain the details of the Java features used in the program. *Do not worry if some of the details of the program are not completely clear on this first reading*. They will be clarified in Chapters 2 and 3. This is just a preview of things to come.

For now, ignore the following few lines that come at the start of the program:

```
public class FirstProgram
{
    public static void main(String[] args)
    {
```

These opening lines set up a context for the program, but you need not worry about them yet. Instead, you can think of them as being Java's way of writing "Begin the program named FirstProgram."

The next three lines are the first actions the program performs:

```
System.out.println("Hello out there.");
System.out.println("Want to talk some more?");
System.out.println("Answer y for yes or n for no.");
```

Each of these lines begins with System.out.println. Each one causes the quoted string given within the parentheses to be output to the screen. For example, consider

```
System.out.println("Hello out there.");
```

DISPLAY 1.5 A Sample Java Program

```
public class FirstProgram
{
    public static void main(String[] args)
    {
        System.out.println("Hello out there.");
        System.out.println("Want to talk some more?");
        System.out.println("Answer y for yes or n for no.");

        char answerLetter;
        answerLetter = SavitchIn.readLineNonwhiteChar();
        if (answerLetter == 'y')
            System.out.println("Nice weather we are having.");

        System.out.println("Good-bye.");

        System.out.println("Press Enter key to end program.");
        String junk;
        junk = SavitchIn.readLine();
    }
}
```

In order to run this program, you must have both of the files `FirstProgram.java` *and* `SavitchIn.java` *in the same directory (folder) and must compile them both. Read the subsection "Compiling a Java Program or Class" later in this chapter.*

Sample Screen Dialog 1

```
Hello out there.
Want to talk some more?
Answer y for yes or n for no.
y
Nice weather we are having.
Good-bye.
Press Enter key to end program.
```

Sample Screen Dialog 2

```
Hello out there.
Want to talk some more?
Answer y for yes or n for no.
n
Good-bye.
Press Enter key to end program.
```

This code causes the line

```
Hello out there.
```

to be written to the screen.

For now, you can consider these lines, which begin with `System.out.println`, to be a funny way of saying "Output what is shown in parentheses." However, we can tell you a little about what is going on here.

System.out.
println

As we discussed earlier, Java programs work by having things called objects perform actions. The actions performed by an object are called methods. `System.out` is an object used for sending output to the screen; `println` is the method (that is, the action) that this object carries out in order to send what is in parentheses to the screen. When an object performs an action using a method, it is said to **invoke** the method (or **call** the method). In a Java program, you write such a method invocation by writing the object name, followed by a period (called a **dot** in computer jargon), followed by the method name and some parentheses that may or may not have something inside them. The item or items inside the parentheses are called **arguments** and provide the information the method needs to carry out its action. In each of these first three lines, the method is `println`. The method `println` writes something to the screen, and the argument (a string in quotes) tells it what it should write.

invoke

dot

argument

Quick Reference: Classes, Objects, and Methods

A Java program works by having things called **objects** perform actions. The actions are known as **methods**. All objects of the same kind are said to be in the same class. Thus, a **class** is a category of objects. (If you want to know more details about classes and objects, read the subsection entitled "Object-Oriented Programming," earlier in this chapter.) When the object performs the action for a given method, it is said to **invoke** the method (or **call** the method).

In some special cases, a class can serve the same role as an object—that is, the class can perform the action (invoke the method)—but that level of detail need not worry you yet. Just note that things called objects and things called classes can both perform actions and the actions are called methods.

The next line of the program, shown here, says that `answerLetter` is the name of a variable:

```
char answerLetter;
```

variable
char

A **variable** is something that can store a piece of data. The `char` says that the data must be a single character; `char` is an abbreviation for *character.*

The next line reads a character that is typed in at the keyboard and stores this character in the variable `answerLetter`:

```
answerLetter = SavitchIn.readLineNonwhiteChar();
```

SavitchIn

`SavitchIn` is a class designed for users of this text. The class `SavitchIn` is used to obtain input from the keyboard. This class contains the method `readlineNonwhite-Char`, which reads a single nonblank character from the keyboard. If the user types some input on a single line and presses the Enter key (also called the Return key), the method will read the first nonblank character on that line of keyboard input and discard everything else on the line.

The expression

```
SavitchIn.readLineNonwhiteChar();
```

is a method invocation. This method invocation simply reads the first nonblank character, which is 'y' in the first dialog, and dumps the character at the location of the invocation. The beginning of the line tells what is to happen to this character 'y'. It says to make the character the value of the variable answerLetter:

```
answerLetter = SavitchIn.readLineNonwhiteChar();
```

equal sign

The equals sign is used differently in Java than in everyday mathematics. In the preceding program line, the equals sign does not mean that answerLetter *is equal to* SavitchIn.readLineNonwhiteChar(). Instead, the equals sign is an instruction to the computer to *make* answerLetter *equal to* SavitchIn.readLineNonwhiteChar(); that is, it tells the computer to store the character it has read from the keyboard in the variable answerLetter.

As it turns out, SavitchIn is not really an object, but a class. However, in this context, we are using the class SavitchIn as if it were an object. For some special methods, you can use the name of a class rather than the name of an object when you invoke the method. In Chapter 5, we explain the significance of this distinction, but those details need not concern you now. At this point, you could even consider the following as a peculiarly spelled instruction that tells the computer to read one character and store that character in the variable answerLetter:

```
answerLetter = SavitchIn.readLineNonwhiteChar();
```

As we will explain more fully later, SavitchIn does not automatically come with the Java language. The programmer must define the class SavitchIn (or some similar class). To get you started, however, we have defined it for you and placed it on the CD that comes with this text.

double equal sign

The next two lines of the program make a decision to do or not to do something, on the basis of what the user types at the keyboard. Together, these lines perform a test for equality, using the double equals sign. In Java, the double equals sign acts as what you might think of as an ordinary equals sign. The following two program lines first check to see whether the character stored in the variable answerLetter is equal to the character 'y'. If it is, they write "Nice weather we are having." to the screen.

```
if (answerLetter == 'y')
   System.out.println("Nice weather we are having.");
```

If the character stored in answerLetter is anything other than 'y', these two lines do not write anything to the screen.

Notice that one sample dialog outputs the string "Nice weather we are having." and one does not. That is because, in the first run of the program, the character 'y' is stored in the variable answerLetter, and in the second run of the program, the character 'n' is stored in answerLetter.

The following three lines at the end of the program are there to stop the screen output from going away before you can read it:

```
System.out.println("Press Enter key to end program.");
String junk;
junk = SavitchIn.readLine( );
```

Some systems will erase the screen as soon as the program ends. These three lines make the program, and the screen, wait for the user to press the Enter (Return) key. If pressing the Enter (Return) key one time does not end the program, just press it a second time. This detail can vary a little from one system to another. Although you can use the preceding three lines without understanding them, we should explain a bit more about what they do.

The line

```
String junk;
```

declares a variable named `junk`. The type `String` means that `junk` can hold an entire string of characters. If the user enters a line of text and ends the line by pressing the Enter (Return) key, the following line will read the entire line of text and make it as the value of `junk`:

```
junk = SavitchIn.readLine( );
```

Simply pressing the Enter (Return) key will still cause the computer to read the blank line of input, so all the user needs to do is press the Enter key. The variable is named `junk` because the value stored in it is not used for anything.

The method `readLine` is similar to the method `readLineNonwhiteChar`, except that `readLine` reads in an entire line of input rather than a single character. You could end the program in Display 1.5 by typing in the words

```
So long for now.
```

all on one line and then pressing the Enter key. The entire line of text would be stored in the variable `junk`. However, all we really need the user to do to end the program is press the Enter key.

The only things left to explain in this first program are the final semicolons on each line and the braces } at the end of the program. The semicolon acts as ending punctuation, like a period in an English sentence. A semicolon ends an instruction to the computer. The foregoing instructions are called **statements.** The braces } at the end simply signal the end of the program.

statements

Of course, there are precise rules for how you write each part of a Java program. These rules form the grammar for the Java language, just like the rules for the grammar of the English language, but the Java rules are more precise. The grammar rules for a programming language (or any language) are called the **syntax** of the language.

syntax

Quick Reference: Method Invocation

A **method** is an action that an object is capable of performing. When you ask an object to perform the action of a method, that is called **invoking** or **calling** the method. In a Java program, you invoke a method by writing the object name (or, in some special cases, the class name), followed by a period (called a **dot**), followed by the method name, followed by the arguments enclosed in parentheses. The **arguments** are information given to the method.

Examples:

```
System.out.println("Hello out there.");
answerLetter = SavitchIn.readLineNonwhiteChar();
```

In the first example, `System.out` is the object, `println` is the method, and `"Hello out there"` is the argument. If there is more than one argument, the arguments are separated by commas.

In the second example, the class `SavitchIn` serves the same role as an object, the method is `readLineNonwhiteChar`, and there are no arguments. In some cases, such as the methods of the class `SavitchIn`, you can use a class name in place of an object name when you write a method invocation.

In a program, a method invocation is typically followed by a semicolon.

? Self-Test Questions

22. What would the following statement, used in a Java program, cause to be written to the screen?

```
System.out.println("Java is great!");
```

23. Give a statement or statements that can be used in a Java program to write the following to the screen:

```
Java for one.
Java for all.
```

24. Suppose that `mary` is an object of a class named `Person`, and suppose that `increaseAge` is a method for the class `Person` that uses one argument, an integer. How do you write an invocation of the method `increaseAge` for the object `mary`, using the argument `5`? The method `increaseAge` will change the data in `mary` so that it simulates `mary` aging by five years.

25. What is the meaning of the following line, which appears in the program in Display 1.5?

```
answerLetter = SavitchIn.readLineNonwhiteChar();
```

26. Write a complete Java program that uses `System.out.println` to output the following to the screen when the program is run:

```
Hello World!
```

Your program does nothing else, but, if the output goes away before you get a chance to read it, you should add the following to the end of the program:

```
System.out.println("Press Enter key to end program.");
String junk;
junk = SavitchIn.readLine();
```

Note that you do not need to fully understand all the details of the program in order to write it. You can simply follow the model of the program in Display 1.5. (You do want to understand all the details eventually, but that may take a few more chapters.)

Compiling a Java Program or Class

A Java program is divided into smaller parts called classes, and normally each class definition is in a separate file. Before you can run a Java program, you must translate these classes into a language that the computer can understand. This translation process is called compiling. (There is more information on classes in the subsection "Object-Oriented Programming" earlier in this chapter. There is more information on compiling in the subsection entitled "Programming Languages and Compilers," also earlier in the chapter.)

A Java program can consist of any number of class definitions. The program in Display 1.5 consists of two classes. The first is the class named `FirstProgram`, which is shown in Display 1.5. Every program in Java is a class as well as a program. The other class used in this first program is the class `SavitchIn`, which has already been defined for you. At this point, you would not understand the definition of the class `SavitchIn`, but you can still obtain a copy of the class, compile it, and use it. A copy of the class `SavitchIn` is provided on the CD that accompanies this book, along with the other classes defined in this book.

There are, in fact, two other classes used in the program in Display 1.5: the classes named `System` and `String`. However, these two classes are automatically provided for you by Java, and you need not worry about compiling either of them. As a rule, you do not need to compile the classes that are provided for you as part of Java. You normally need compile only the classes that you yourself write. So why do you have to compile the class `SavitchIn`? The reason is that *you* are supposed to write the definition of the class `SavitchIn`. `SavitchIn` is not provided as part of Java. However, to make things easier for you, we have written the definition of the class `SavitchIn` for you. By the time you finish most of this text, you will be fully capable of writing the definition of classes such as `SavitchIn`.

`.java` files

Before you can compile a Java program, each class definition used in the program (and written by you, the programmer) should be in a separate file. Moreover, the name of the file should be the same as the name of the class, except that the file name has `.java` added to the end. The program in Display 1.5 is a class called `FirstProgram`, so it should be in a file named `FirstProgram.java`. The program in Display 1.5 uses the class `SavitchIn`. Therefore, the class definition of `SavitchIn` should be in a file named `SavitchIn.java`.

Before you can run the program in Display 1.5, you must compile both the class `SavitchIn`, which is in the file `SavitchIn.java`, and the class `FirstProgram`, which is in the file `FirstProgram.java`. (If you are in a course, your instructor may have configured the system so that `SavitchIn` is already compiled for you, but later on, when you define your own classes, you will need to compile the classes.)

If you are using a system that has a special environment for Java, you will have a menu command that can be used to compile a Java class or Java program. (You use the same command to compile any kind of Java file.) You will have to check your local documentation to see exactly what this command is, but it is bound to be simple. (In the TextPad environment, which is provided on the CD that comes with the text, the command is Compile Java on the File menu.)

If your operating system expects you to type in a one-line command, that is easy to do. We will describe the commands for the Java system distributed by Sun Microsystems (usually called "the SDK," "the JDK," or "Java 2"). If you have some other version of Java, these commands might be different.

`javac`

To compile a Java class, the command is `javac`, followed by the name of the file containing the class. Suppose you want to compile a class named `MyClass`. It will be in a file named `MyClass.java`. To compile the class, you simply give the following command to the operating system:

```
javac MyClass.java
```

Thus, to compile all the classes needed to run the program in Display 1.5, you would give the following two commands (on two separate lines):

```
javac SavitchIn.java
javac FirstProgram.java
```

Remember, if you have an environment that lets you compile with a menu command, you will find it easier to use the menu command rather than the preceding commands.

`.class` files

When you compile a Java class, the translated version of the program, produced by the compiler, is called byte-code. The resulting byte-code for that class is placed in a file of the same name, except that the ending is changed from `.java` to `.class`. So when you compile a class named `MyClass` in the file `MyClass.java`, the resulting byte-code is stored in a file named `MyClass.class`. When you compile the class file named `SavitchIn.java`, the resulting byte-code is stored in a file named `SavitchIn.class`. And, of course, when you compile the class file named `FirstProgram.java`, the resulting byte-code is stored in a file named `FirstProgram.class`. (There is more information on byte-code in the subsection entitled "Java Byte-Code" earlier in the chapter.)

Running a Java Program

running a Java program

A Java program can involve any number of classes, but when you run a Java program, you run only the class that you think of as the program. You can recognize this class because it will contain words identical to or very similar to

```
public static void main(String[] args)
```

These words will probably (but not necessarily) be someplace near the beginning of the file. The critical words to look for are `public static void main`. The remaining portion of the line might be spelled slightly differently in some cases.

If you are using a system that has a special environment for Java, you will have a menu command that can be used to run a Java program. You will have to check your local documentation to see exactly what this command is. (In the TextPad environment, which is provided on the CD that comes with this text, the command is Run Java Application on the File menu.)

If your operating system expects you to type in a one-line command, then (on most systems) you can run a Java program by giving the command `java`, followed by the name of the class you think of as the program. For example, to run the program in Display 1.5, you would give the following one-line command:

```
java FirstProgram
```

Note that when you run a program, you use the class name, such as `FirstProgram`, without any `.java` or `.class` ending. And remember that if you have a menu command for running a Java program, then that is an easier way to run your Java program.

(When you run a Java program, you are actually running the Java byte-code interpreter on the compiled version of your program. When you run your program, the system will automatically link in any classes you need and run the byte-code interpreter on those classes as well.)

In the preceding discussion, we assumed that the Java compiler and other system software was already set up for you. We also assumed that all the files were in one directory, or folder. If this is not the case, and you need to set up the Java compiler and system software, consult the manuals that came with the software. If you wish to spread your class definitions across multiple directories, that is possible and not difficult, but we will not concern ourselves with that detail now.

? Self-Test Questions

27. Suppose you define a class named `SuperClass` in a file. What name should the file have?

28. Suppose you compile the class `SuperClass`. What will be the name of the file with the resulting byte-code?

29. Is the class `SavitchIn` part of the Java language, or does the programmer have to define the class?

Preview Examples of Applets *(Optional)*

applet

An **applet** is special kind of Java program that can be displayed as part of an Internet site so that it can be sent across the Internet to another user's computer and run on that user's computer. Applets have windowing interfaces, so they are typically more flashy than the kind of program we created in Display 1.5. In this section, we will give you a brief look at how two Java applets were written. This is just a preview; we will not be able to fully explain the applets we show you. (We discuss applets in detail in Chapter 13.)

Display 1.6 shows a simple applet program and the window display that it produces. Let's look at the details.

Swing

The line

```
import javax.swing.*;
```

says that this program uses the Swing library (package). Applets use software in the Swing library.

`PreviewApplet1` is the name of this applet, and the words `extends JApplet` indicate that we are dealing with an applet.

The part that begins

```
public void init()
```

specifies the way the applet looks. The words `public void` will have to remain a mystery for now, but they are required. The word `init` is an abbreviation for "initialization" and indicates that this part describes how the applet is initialized.

init

The line

```
JLabel myFirstLabel = new JLabel("Hello out there!");
```

creates a label named `myFirstLabel`. A **label** is simply some text that can be added to the applet window. In this case, the text says `"Hello out there!"`. The next line adds the label `myFirstLabel` to the applet window:

label

```
getContentPane().add(myFirstLabel);
```

The portion `getContentPane()` produces the inside of the applet window, so this line says to place the label `myFirstLabel` inside the applet window.

Below the applet code in Display 1.6 is a view of what the applet display looks like when the applet is run. **GUI** stands for **graphical user interface,** the term used for windowing interfaces. So the applet window shown in Display 1.6 is a GUI.

GUI

DISPLAY 1.6 A Sample Java Applet

```
import javax.swing.*;

public class PreviewApplet1 extends JApplet
{
    public void init()
    {
        JLabel myFirstLabel = new JLabel("Hello out there!");
        getContentPane().add(myFirstLabel);
    }
}
```

Resulting GUI

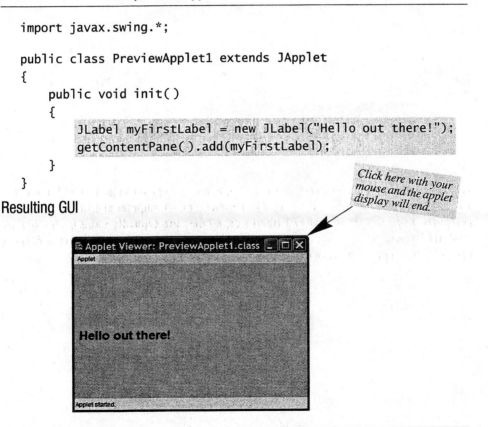

Click here with your mouse and the applet display will end.

Applet Viewer: PreviewApplet1.class
Applet
Hello out there!
Applet started.

Applets can contain pictures. The applet in Display 1.7 is similar to the one in Display 1.6, with two differences, one small and one significant. The label in Display 1.7 has the text `"Java is fun!"` instead of `"Hello out there!"`. That's the small difference. What is really new to this second applet is the addition of a picture, which is done with the following lines:

```
ImageIcon dukeIcon = new ImageIcon("duke_waving.gif");
niceLabel.setIcon(dukeIcon);
```

DISPLAY 1.7 An Applet with an Icon Picture

```
import javax.swing.*;

public class PreviewApplet2 extends JApplet
{
    public void init()
    {
        JLabel niceLabel = new JLabel("Java is fun!");
        ImageIcon dukeIcon = new ImageIcon("duke_waving.gif");
        niceLabel.setIcon(dukeIcon);
        getContentPane().add(niceLabel);
    }
}
```

Resulting GUI[3]

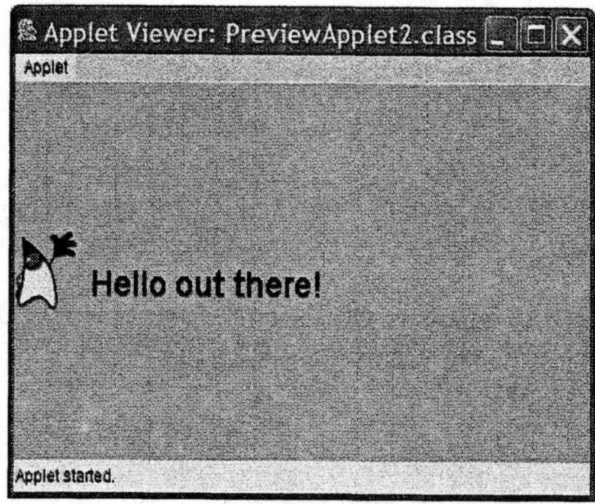

3. Java, Duke, and all Java-based trademarks and logos are trademarks or registered trademarks of Sun Microsystems, Inc. in the United States and other countries. (Duke is the figure waving.)

The first line creates an **icon** (a small picture) from the picture file `duke_waving.gif`. The file `duke_waving.gif` contains a digital version of a picture of Duke, the guy waving in the GUI shown in Display 1.7. The second of the previous two lines adds this icon to the label named `niceLabel`. (Duke is a trademark of Sun Microsystems and serves as a mascot for the Java programming language.)

icon

The preceding two applets simply display something for the user; they do not allow any interaction. Other applets that we will consider in Chapter 13 will interact with the user, but the two we have seen will do as an introduction to applets.

An applet is compiled in the same way as any other Java program, but it is run in a different way.

running an applet

An applet is designed to run from a Web site, but you need not know how to embed an applet in a Web site in order to run it. There are ways to run applets directly. One way is to use an **applet viewer.** The easiest way to do this is to run the applet from an IDE (integrated development environment), such as Forte for Java (also know as Sun ONE Studio) or the TextPad environment, both of which are included on the CD that comes with this text. (In the TextPad environment, the command is Run Java Applet on the Tools menu. If a window pops up asking you to choose a file, answer "No". This environment command will automatically invoke an applet viewer.) If you do not have an IDE or cannot find the right command for the applet viewer, consult a local expert.

applet viewer

The way that you end an applet depends on how you are running it. If you are using an applet viewer (or are running it from an environment), you end the applet display by clicking the close-window button with your mouse. The close-window button will probably be as shown in Display 1.6, but it might be in a different location, depending on your computer and operating system. If the close-window button is not as shown in Display 1.6, it will likely be in the same place as the close-window button on other windows on your computer. If you are running the applet from a Web site, the applet stays until you close or navigate away from the page it is on.

ending an applet

CHAPTER SUMMARY

- A computer's main memory holds the program that is currently being executed, and it also holds many of the data items that the program is manipulating. A computer's main memory is divided into a series of numbered locations called bytes.

- A computer's auxiliary memory is used to hold data in a more or less permanent way.

- A compiler is a program that translates a program written in a high-level language like Java into a program written in a low-level language. The Java compiler translates your Java program into a program in the byte-code language. When you give the command to run your Java program, this byte-code program is translated into machine-language instructions, and the machine-language instructions are carried out by the computer.

- An object is something that has data associated with it and that can perform certain actions. The actions performed by objects are called methods. A class defines a type of object. All objects in the same class have the same methods.

- Three of the main principles of object-oriented programming are encapsulation, polymorphism, and inheritance.
- An algorithm is a set of instructions for solving a problem. To qualify as an algorithm, the instructions must be expressed so completely and precisely that somebody could follow them without having to fill in any details or make any decisions that are not fully specified in the instructions.
- In a Java program, a method invocation is specified by writing the object name (or class name), followed by a period (called a dot), the method name, and, finally, the arguments in parentheses.

✔ Answers to Self-Test Questions

1. Main memory and auxiliary memory.
2. Software is just another name for programs.
3. The two numbers to be added.
4. All the grades on all the quizzes that you have taken in the course.
5. A machine-language program is written in a form the computer can execute directly. A high-level-language program is written in a form that is easy for a human being to write and read. A high-level-language program must be translated into a machine-language program before the computer can execute it. Java byte-code is a low-level language that is similar to the machine language of most common computers. It is relatively easy to translate a program expressed in Java byte-code into the machine language of almost any computer.
6. Java is a high-level language.
7. Java byte-code is a low-level language.
8. A compiler translates a high-level-language program into a low-level-language program such as a machine-language program or a Java byte-code program. When you compile a Java program, the compiler translates your Java program into a program expressed in Java byte-code.
9. The high-level-language program that is input to a compiler is called the source program.
10. A program that translates Java byte-code instructions to machine-language instructions is called an interpreter. It is also often called the Java Virtual Machine.
11. A method is an action that an object is capable of performing. (In some other programming languages, methods are called functions or procedures.)
12. A class is a category of objects. All objects in the same class have the same kind of data and the same methods.
13. Yes, all objects of the same class have the same methods.

14. Encapsulation is the process of hiding all the details of an object that are not necessary to understanding how the object is used. Put another way, encapsulation is the process of describing a class or object by giving only enough information to allow a programmer to use the class or object.

15. "Information hiding" is another term for "encapsulation."

16. In a programming language, such as Java, polymorphism means that one method name, used as an instruction, can cause different actions, depending on what kind of object performs the action.

17. An algorithm is a set of instructions for solving a problem. To qualify as an algorithm, the instructions must be expressed so completely and precisely that somebody could follow the instructions without having to fill in any details or make any decisions that are not fully specified in the instructions.

18. A syntax error is a grammatical mistake in a program. There are very strict grammar rules for how you write a program. If you violate one of these rules—by omitting a required punctuation mark, for example—that is a syntax error.

19. A logic error is a conceptual error in a program's algorithm. If your program runs and gives output, but the output is incorrect, that means you have a logic error.

20. Syntax errors and run-time errors.

21. A logic error.

22. `Java is great!`

23.

```
System.out.println("Java for one.");
System.out.println("Java for all.");
```

24. `mary.increaseAge(5);`

25. This statement skips over blank spaces until it reaches the first nonblank character, and then it reads that nonblank character (`'y'` or `'n'` in the sample dialogs) and stores it in the variable `answerLetter`.

26.

```
public class ExerciseProgram1
{
    public static void main(String[] args)
    {
        System.out.println("Hello World!");

        System.out.println("Press Enter key to end program.");
        String junk;
        junk = SavitchIn.readLine();
    }
}
```

Some details, such as identifier names, may be different in your program. Be sure you compile and run your program.

27. The file with the class named `SuperClass` should be named `SuperClass.java`.

28. `SuperClass.class`.

29. The class SavitchIn is not part of the Java language. The programmer (probably you) is supposed to define a class similar to SavitchIn. To get you started, we have defined it for you, but think of it as a class that you have defined.

Programming Projects

1. Obtain a copy of the file SavitchIn.java, which contains the definition of the class SavitchIn. (It is on the CD that accompanies this book. In a course, your instructor may provide you with a copy. It is also in Appendix 4, but it would be a pain to type the whole thing from there.) Compile the class SavitchIn so that you get no compiler errors. Next, obtain a copy of the Java program shown in Display 1.5. (That program is also on the CD that comes with the book.) Name the file FirstProgram.java. Compile the program so that you receive no compiler error messages. Finally, run the program in FirstProgram.java. If you are in a class and your instructor has already compiled the class SavitchIn for you, you can skip that part.

2. Modify the Java program that you entered in Programming Exercise 1 so that if the user types the letter 'n' in response to the question

```
Want to talk some more?
```

the program will output the phrase

```
Too bad. You seem like such a nice person.
```

The program should behave the same as in Display 1.5 if the user enters 'y' instead of 'n'. Compile and run the modified program. (*Hint:* Include a second statement that begins with if and that tests whether answerLetter is equal to 'n'.)

3. Modify the Java program that you wrote in Programming Exercise 2 to include a third option to the question

```
Want to talk some more?
```

In addition to the responses to 'y' and 'n', if the user enters 'm' for "maybe," the program will output the phrase

```
Sorry, but I can't wait for your decision.
```

4. Both color monitors and your eyes use just three colors—red, blue and green—to create all other colors. In particular, yellow is made by combining red and green, magenta (a shade of purple) by combining red and blue, and cyan by combining green and blue. Write a program that asks the user which of the three colors—yellow, magenta, or cyan—to break down into its two components. If the user enters the letter 'y' for "yellow," the following message is displayed

```
Yellow is made by combining red and green.
```

Similarly, if the letter 'm' for "magenta" is entered, the following message is displayed.

```
Magenta is made by combining red and blue.
```

and if the letter `'c'` for "cyan" is entered, the following message is displayed,

```
Cyan is made by combining green and blue.
```

5. Write a complete Java program that will ask the user for the initials of the user's first and last names and then output a greeting that says "Hello", followed by the user's initials and an exclamation mark. For example, if the user's initials are "J" and "B", then the output greeting would be

```
Hello J B!
```

If the user's initials are stored in the two variables `firstInitial` and `lastInitial`, both of type `char`, the above output can be produced by the following statement:

```
System.out.println("Hello " + firstInitial
                            + ' ' + lastInitial + '!');
```

There is no significance to the fact that we typed the statement on two lines; if it fits on one line, you can type it all on one line. Be sure to note that the blank symbol is output after `firstInitial`. The use of the plus sign in this way is discussed in Chapter 2, but you do not need to read those details before doing this exercise.

Chapter 2

Primitive Types, Strings, and Console I/O

Chapter 2

Primitive Types, Strings, and Console I/O

primitive adj. 1. Not derived from something else; primary or basic. string n. 1. A cord usually made of fiber, used for fastening, tying or lacing. . . . 6. Computer Science. A set of consecutive characters treated by a computer as a single item. -The American Heritage Dictionary of the English Language, Third Edition

In this chapter, we explain enough about the Java language to allow you to write simple Java programs. You do not need any programming experience to understand this chapter. If you are already familiar with some other programming language, such as C, C++, Pascal, BASIC, or FORTRAN, much of what is in Section 2.1 will already be familiar to you. However, even if you know the concepts, you should learn the Java way of expressing them.

OBJECTIVES

Become familiar with the Java data types used for numbers, characters, and similar simple data. These types are called primitive types.

Learn about the assignment statement and expressions.

Find out about the Java data type used for strings of characters and learn how to do simple string processing. This will also serve to familiarize you with the notation used for classes, methods, and objects.

Learn about simple keyboard input and screen output.

PREREQUISITES

If you have not read Chapter 1, you should read at least the subsection of Chapter 1 entitled "A First Java Application Program" to familiarize yourself with the notions of class, method, and object.

As with all optional sections, you do *not* need to cover the subsection of Chapter 1 entitled "Preview Examples of Applets *(Optional)*" before reading this chapter or any other chapter of this book.

2.1 PRIMITIVE TYPES AND EXPRESSIONS

Once a person has understood the way variables are used in programming, he has understood the quintessence of programming. -E. W. Dijkstra, *Notes on Structured Programming*

In this section, we explain how simple variables and arithmetic expressions are used in Java programs.

Variables

variables

Variables in a program are used to store data such as numbers and letters. They can be thought of as containers of a sort, The number, letter, or other data item in a variable is called its **value.** This value can be changed, so that at one time the variable contains, say, 6, and at another time, after the program has run for a while, the variable contains a different value, such as 4. In the program in Display 2.1, `numberOfBaskets`, `eggsPerBasket`, and `totalEggs` are variables. For example, when this program is run with the input shown in the sample dialog, `eggsPerBasket` has its value set to 6 with the following statement, which reads a number from the keyboard.

value of a variable

```
eggsPerBasket = SavitchIn.readLineInt();
```

Later, the value of the variable `eggsPerBasket` is changed to 4 when the program executes the following statement:

```
eggsPerBasket = eggsPerBasket - 2;
```

We will explain these two statements in more detail shortly.

DISPLAY 2.1 A Simple Java Program *(Part 1 of 2)*

```
public class EggBasket
{
    public static void main(String[] args)
    {
        int numberOfBaskets, eggsPerBasket, totalEggs;

        System.out.println("Enter the number of eggs in each basket:");
        eggsPerBasket = SavitchIn.readLineInt();
        System.out.println("Enter the number of baskets:");
        numberOfBaskets = SavitchIn.readLineInt();

        totalEggs = numberOfBaskets * eggsPerBasket;

        System.out.println(eggsPerBasket + " eggs per basket.");
        System.out.println(numberOfBaskets + " baskets.");
        System.out.println("Total number of eggs is " + totalEggs);

        eggsPerBasket = eggsPerBasket - 2;
        totalEggs = numberOfBaskets * eggsPerBasket;

        System.out.println("Now we take two eggs out of each basket.");
        System.out.println(eggsPerBasket + " eggs per basket.");
        System.out.println(numberOfBaskets + " baskets.");
        System.out.println("Total number of eggs is " + totalEggs);

        System.out.println("Press Enter key to end program.");
        String junk;
        junk = SavitchIn.readLine();
    }
}
```

■ DISPLAY 2.1 **A Simple Java Program** *(Part 2 of 2)*

Sample Screen Dialog

```
Enter the number of eggs in each basket:
6
Enter the number of baskets:
10
6 eggs per basket.
10 baskets.
Total number of eggs is 60
Now we take two eggs out of each basket.
4 eggs per basket.
10 baskets.
Total number of eggs is 40
Press Enter key to end program.
```

variables in memory

In Java, variables are implemented as memory locations. (Chapter 1 discussed memory locations.) Each variable is assigned one memory location. When the variable is given a value, this value (encoded as a string of zeros and ones) is placed in the variable's memory location.

The rules for naming variables follow the spelling rules given for Java identifiers in the next subsection. Besides following those rules, you should also choose variable names that are helpful. Variable names should suggest their use or indicate the kind of data they will hold. For example, if a variable is used to count something, you might name the variable `count`. If the variable is used to hold the speed of an automobile, you might call the variable `speed`. You should almost never use single-letter variable names like `x` and `y`. Somebody reading the following would have no idea of what the program is really adding:

```
x = y + z;
```

variable declarations

In order to run your program, the computer must be given some basic information about each variable in your program. It needs to know the name of the variable, how much computer memory to reserve for the variable, and how the data item in the variable is to be coded as strings of zeros and ones. All this information can be obtained, provided that the compiler (and so ultimately the computer) is told the name of the variable and what type of data are stored in the variable. You give this information by **declaring** the variable. Every variable in a Java program must be declared before it is used. For example, the following line from Display 2.1 declares `numberOfBaskets`, `eggsPerBasket`, and `totalEggs` to be variables of type `int`:

declare

```
int numberOfBaskets, eggsPerBasket, totalEggs;
```

A variable declaration consists of a type name, followed by a list of variable names separated by commas. The declaration then ends with a semicolon. All the variables named in the list are declared to have the type given at the start of the declaration.

The type `int` is the most commonly used type for variables that hold whole numbers, such as 42, −99, 0, and 2001. The word `int` is an abbreviation of *integer.*

int

A variable's **type** determines what kind of value the variable can hold. If the type is `int`, the variable can hold whole numbers. If the type is `double`, the variable can hold numbers with a decimal point and a fractional part after the decimal point. If the type is `char`, the variables can hold any one character from the computer keyboard.

type

A variable declaration tells the computer what type of data the variable will hold. Different types of data are stored in the computer's memory in different ways, so the computer must know the type of a variable in order to know how to store and retrieve the value of the variable from the computer's memory.

Quick Reference: Variable Declarations

In a Java program, a variable must be declared before it can be used. Variables are declared as follows:

Syntax:

Type Variable_1, *Variable_2*, . . .;

Examples:

```
int styleNumber, numberOfChecks, numberOfDeposits;
char answer;
double amount, interestRate;
```

There are two main kinds of types in Java: class types and primitive types. As the name implies, a **class type** is a type for a class, that is, a type for objects with both data and methods. A **primitive type** is simpler. Values of a primitive type are simple, indecomposable values, such as a single number or a single letter. The type `SavitchIn` is a class type. `String` is another class type. The types `int`, `double`, and `char` are primitive types. By convention, class type names begin with an uppercase letter and primitive type names begin with a lowercase letter, but variable names of both class and primitive types begin with a lowercase letter. Variable names for class and primitive types are declared in the same way, but there are different mechanisms for storing values in variables of class types and in variables of primitive types. In this and the next chapter, we will confine our attention primarily to primitive types. We will occasionally use variables of a class type, but only in contexts where they behave pretty much the same as variables of a primitive type. In Chapter 4, we will explain class type variables in more detail.

class type

primitive type

Every variable in a Java program must be declared before the variable can be used. Normally, a variable is declared either just before it is used or at the start of a section of your program that is enclosed in braces `{}`. In the simple programs we have seen so far, this means that variables are declared either just before they are used or right after the lines

location of declarations

```
public static void main(String[] args)
{
```

Quick Reference: Syntax

The rules for the correct way to write a program or part of a program (the grammar rules for a programming language) are called the **syntax** of the language.

Many of the boxes in this text describe Java syntax using **syntactic variables**. For example, in the box entitled "Variable Declarations" earlier in this chapter, we used the following:

Syntax:

Type Variable_1, *Variable_2*, . . .;

The words *Type*, *Variable_1*, and *Variable_2* are examples of syntactic variables. They are written in a different font, appear in a special color, and use underscore symbols, so that it will be easy for you to recognize them. Syntactic variables are not meant to be words that might appear in a Java program. Instead, they are a kind of blank that is meant to be filled in by an appropriate Java word (or words). *Type* can be replaced by any Java type. For example, *Type* can be replaced by `int`, `double`, `char`, or any other type name. *Variable_1* and *Variable_2* can each be replaced by any variable name. For example, *Variable_1* can be replaced by `styleNumber`, *Variable_2* can be replaced by `numberOfChecks`, and the . . . indicates that the list of variables can be of any length. Thus,

Type Variable_1, *Variable_2*, . . .;

can, for example, be replaced by

```
int styleNumber, numberOfChecks, numberOfDeposits;
```

to obtain a valid variable declaration that can be used in a Java program. To help clarify these syntax expressions, they are usually followed by one or more examples of the Java item they specify.

Remember: Syntactic Variables

Remember that when you see something in this book like *Type*, *Variable_1*, or *Variable_2*, these words do not literally appear in your Java code. They are syntactic variables, which means that you replace them with something of the category that they describe. For example, *Type* can be replaced by `int`, `double`, `char`, or any other type name. *Variable_1* and *Variable_2* can each be replaced by any variable name.

Java Identifiers

identifier

case sensitive
upper- and lowercase

The technical term for a name in a programming language, such as the name of a variable, is an **identifier.** In Java, an identifier (a name) may contain only letters, digits (0 through 9), and the underscore character (_), but the first character in a name cannot be a digit.[1] In particular, no name can contain a space or any other character such as a dot (period) or an asterisk (*). There is no limit to the length of a name. (Well, in practice, there is always a limit, but there is no official limit, and Java will accept even absurdly long names.) Java is **case sensitive.** This means that uppercase and lowercase letters are considered to be different characters. For example, Java considers `mystuff`, `myStuff`, and `MyStuff` to be

1. Java does allow the dollar sign symbol $ to appear in an identifier, but these identifiers have a special meaning, so you should not use the $ symbol in your identifiers.

three different names, and you could have three different variables (or other items) with these three names. Of course, it is very poor programming practice to have two names that differ only in their capitalization, but the Java compiler would be happy with them. Within these rules, you can use any name you want for a variable or for a class that you define or for any other item you define in a Java program. But there are some style guidelines for choosing names.

Our somewhat peculiar use of uppercase and lowercase letters, such as `numberOfBaskets`, deserves some explanation. It would be perfectly legal to use `NumberOfBaskets` or `number_of_baskets` instead of `numberOfBaskets`, but these other names would violate some well-established conventions about how you should use uppercase and lowercase letters. By convention, we write names using only letters and digits. We "punctuate" multiword names using uppercase letters (since we cannot use spaces). The following are all legal names that also follow this well-established convention:

```
inputStream   YourClass   CarWash   hotCar   theTimeOfDay
```

The following are all illegal names in Java, and the compiler will complain if you use any of them:

```
My.Class   netscape.com   go-team   7eleven
```

The first three contain illegal characters, either a dot or a hyphen. The last name is illegal because it starts with a digit.

Notice that some of the legal names start with an uppercase letter and others, such as `hotCar`, start with a lowercase letter. We will always follow the convention that the names of classes start with an uppercase letter and the names of variables, objects, and methods start with a lowercase letter.

Of course, there are words in a Java program, such as the word `if`, that do not name a variable, a class, or an object. Some words, such as `if`, are called **keywords** or **reserved words.** These keywords have a special predefined meaning in the Java language and cannot be used as the names of classes or objects or anything else other than their intended meaning. A full list of keywords for Java is given in Appendix 1, but it is easier to learn them by use. Beginning in this chapter, keywords, such as `public`, `class`, `static`, and `void`, are in a special color when they appear in displayed code, as you can see in Display 2.1. Some other words, such as `main` and `println`, have a predefined meaning, but are not keywords. That means you can change their meaning, but it is a bad idea to do so, because it could easily confuse you or somebody else reading your program.

keyword
reserved word

Quick Reference: **Names (Identifiers)**

The name of something in a Java program, such as a variable, class, method, or object, must not start with a digit and may contain only letters, digits (0 through 9), and the underscore character (_). Uppercase and lowercase letters are considered to be different characters. (The symbol $ is also allowed, but it is reserved for special purposes, and so you should not use $ in a Java name.)

Names in a program are often called **identifiers.**

Although it is not required by the Java language, the common practice, and the one followed in this book, is to start the names of classes with uppercase letters and to start the names of variables, objects, and methods with lowercase letters. These names are usually spelled using only letters and digits.

▲ *Gotcha*
Java Is Case-Sensitive

Do not forget that Java is case sensitive. If you use an identifier, like `myNumber`, and then in another part of your program you spell the identifier `MyNumber`, Java will not recognize them as being the same identifier. To be seen as the same identifier, they must use exactly the same capitalization. △

Primitive Types

All the Java primitive types are given in Display 2.2. Notice that there are four types for integers, namely, `byte`, `short`, `int`, and `long`. The only differences among the various integer types is the range of integers they can store and the amount of computer memory they use. If you cannot decide which integer type to use, use the type `int`.

integer

floating-point number

A whole number, such as 0, 1, –1, 2, or –2, is called an **integer.** A number with a fractional part, such as 9.99, 3.14159, –5.63, or 5.0 is called a **floating-point number.** Notice that 5.0 is a floating-point number, not an integer. If you ask the computer to include a fractional part and that fractional part happens to be zero, that does not change the type of the number. If it has a fractional part, even if the fractional part is zero, it is a floating-point number. As shown in Display 2.2, Java has two types for floating-point numbers, `float` and `double`. For example, the following code declares two variables, one of type `float` and one of type `double`:

```
float cost;
double capacity;
```

If you cannot decide between the types `float` and `double`, use `double`.

DISPLAY 2.2 Primitive Types

Type Name	Kind of Value	Memory Used	Size Range
`byte`	*integer*	*1 byte*	–128 to 127
`short`	*integer*	*2 bytes*	–32768 to 32767
`int`	*integer*	*4 bytes*	–2147483648 to 2147483647
`long`	*integer*	*8 bytes*	–9223372036854775808 to 9223372036854775807
`float`	*floating-point number*	*4 bytes*	$\pm 3.40282347 \times 10^{+38}$ to $\pm 1.40239846 \times 10^{-45}$
`double`	*floating-point number*	*8 bytes*	$\pm 1.76769313486231570 \times 10^{+308}$ to $\pm 4.94065645841246544 \times 10^{-324}$
`char`	*single character (Unicode)*	*2 bytes*	*all Unicode characters*
`boolean`	`true` *or* `false`	*1 bit*	*not applicable*

The primitive type `char` is used for single characters, such as letters or the percent sign. For example, the following declares the variable `symbol` to be of type `char`, stores the character for uppercase `A` in `symbol`, and then writes that value to the screen so that an `A` would appear on the screen:

```
char symbol;
symbol = 'A';
System.out.println(symbol);
```

Note that when we give a character in a Java program, we enclose the character in single quotes, as in `'A'`. Note also that there is only one single-quote symbol. The same quote symbol is used on both sides of the character. That one symbol serves as both the left and right quote symbol. Finally, remember that uppercase and lowercase letters are different characters. For example, `'a'` and `'A'` are two different characters.

single quotes

The last primitive type we have to discuss is the type `boolean`. There are two values of type `boolean`, namely, `true` and `false`. This means we can use a variable of type `boolean` to store the answer to a true/false question such as "Is `myTime` less than `yourTime`?" We will have more to say about the type `boolean` in the next chapter.

Assignment Statements

The most straightforward way to give a variable a value or to change its value is to use an **assignment statement.** For example, if `answer` is a variable of type `int` and you want to give it the value `42`, you would use the following assignment statement:

assignment statement

```
answer = 42;
```

The equal sign, =, is called the **assignment operator** when it is used in an assignment statement. It does not mean what the equal sign means in other contexts. The assignment statement is an order telling the computer to change the value stored in the variable on the left-hand side of the assignment operator to the value of the expression on the right-hand side. Thus, an assignment statement always consists of a single variable followed by the assignment operator (the equal sign) followed by an expression. The assignment statement ends with a semicolon. So assignment statements take the form

assignment operator

Variable = *Expression*;

The expression can be another variable, a number, or a more complicated expression made up by using arithmetic operators, such as + and *, to combine variables and numbers.

For example, the following are all examples of assignment statements:

```
amount = 3.99;
firstInitial = 'B';
score = numberOfCards + handicap;
eggsPerBasket = eggsPerBasket - 2;
```

(All the names, such as `amount`, `score`, and `numberOfCards`, are variables. We are assuming that the variable `amount` is of type `double`, `firstInitial` is of type `char`, and the rest of the variables are of type `int`.)

When an assignment statement is executed, the computer first evaluates the expression on the right-hand side of the assignment operator (=) to get the value of the expression. It then uses that value to set the value of the variable on the left-hand side of the assignment operator (=). You can think of the assignment operator (=) as saying, "Make the value of the variable equal to what follows."

For example, if the variable numberOfCards has the value 7 and handicap has the value 2, the following makes 9 the value of the variable score:

```
score = numberOfCards + handicap;
```

The following line from the program in Display 2.1 is another example of an assignment statement:

```
totalEggs = numberOfBaskets * eggsPerBasket;
```

* is multiply

This assignment statement tells the computer to set the value of totalEggs equal to the number in the variable numberOfBaskets multiplied by the number in the variable eggsPerBasket. The asterisk character (*) is the symbol used for multiplication in Java.

same variable both sides of =

Note that a variable can meaningfully occur on both sides of the assignment operator (=) and can do so in ways that may at first seem a little strange. For example, consider

```
count = count + 10;
```

This does not mean that the value of count is equal to the value of count plus 10, which, of course, is impossible. Rather, the statement tells the computer to add 10 to the *old* value of count and then make that the *new* value of count, which means that the statement will increase the value of count by 10. Remember that when an assignment statement is executed, the computer first evaluates the expression on the right-hand side of the assignment operator and then makes that value the new value of the variable on the left-hand side of the assignment operator.

As another example, consider the following assignment statement from Display 2.1:

```
eggsPerBasket = eggsPerBasket - 2;
```

This assignment statement will decrease the value of eggsPerBasket by 2.

constant

literals

The number 2 in the preceding assignment statement is called a **constant.** It is called a constant because, unlike a variable such as eggsPerBasket, the value of 2 cannot change. (Constants are sometimes also called **literals.**) Constants need not be numbers. The characters 'A', 'B', and '$' are three constants of type char. Their values cannot change, but they can be used in an assignment statement to change the value of a variable of type char. For example, the following changes the value of the variable firstInitial to 'B':

```
firstInitial = 'B';
```

In this assignment statement, the variable firstInitial would normally be of type char.

Similarly, the following changes the value of the variable price to 9.99:

```
price = 9.99;
```

In this assignment statement, the variable price would normally be of type double (although it could also be of type float). It cannot be of type int or char. As the saying goes, "You can't put a square peg in a round hole," and you can't put a double value in a variable of type int.

Quick Reference: Assignment Statements with Primitive Types

An assignment statement with a variable of a primitive type on the left-hand side of the equal sign causes the following action: First, the expression on the right-hand side of the equal sign is evaluated, and then the variable on the left-hand side of the equal sign is set to this value.

Syntax:

Variable = *Expression*;

Example:

```
score = goals – errors;
interest = rate * balance;
number = number + 5;
```

Specialized Assignment Operators

You can combine the simple assignment operator (=) with an arithmetic operator, such as +, to produce a kind of special-purpose assignment operator. For example, the following will increase the value of the variable `amount` by 5:

```
amount += 5;
```

This statement is really just shorthand for

```
amount = amount + 5;
```

This is hardly a big deal, but it can sometimes be handy.

You can do the same thing with any of the other arithmetic operators: –, *, /, and %. (We cover the % operator later, in the subsection "Arithmetic Operators.") For example, consider the following line:

```
amount = amount*25;
```

This line could be replaced by the following equivalent line:

```
amount *= 25;
```

Simple Input and Output

Now we will give you a brief overview of input and output—just enough to allow you to write and understand programs like the one in Display 2.1. Section 2.3 will continue the discussion of input and output that we start here.

As we noted in Chapter 1, `System.out` is an object and `println` is a method of this object that sends output to the screen. So

```
System.out.println(eggsPerBasket + " eggs per basket.");
```

outputs the value of the variable `eggsPerBasket` (to the screen) followed by the phrase `" eggs per basket."` Notice that the + sign is not being used for arithmetic here. It is a kind of "and." You can read the preceding output statement as an instruction to output the value of the variable eggsPerBasket *and* then to output the string " eggs per basket."

readLineInt

Next, we consider input. In particular, consider the following line from Display 2.1:

```
numberOfBaskets = SavitchIn.readLineInt();
```

This is an assignment statement that sets the value of the variable numberOfBaskets equal to the value returned by the expression

```
SavitchIn.readLineInt()
```

This expression invokes the method readLineInt( ) of the class SavitchIn. As we said in Chapter 1, a method is an action, and invoking a method causes that action to take place. The action performed by the method readLineInt is to read a single integer from a line of input and deliver that value to the program. In this case, the value becomes the new value of the variable numberOfBaskets.

There are a few technical details you need to know when invoking the method readLineInt. First, there should be a pair of empty parentheses after the name readLineInt. Second, the user must input the integer on a line with nothing else on the line, except possibly blank space before or after the number. The value produced by an invocation of the method readLineInt (or any similar method) is usually referred to as the **value returned** by the method invocation.

value returned

readLine-NonwhiteChar

The following line from Display 1.5 in Chapter 1 is similar to the invocation of readLineInt that we just discussed:

```
answerLetter = SavitchIn.readLineNonwhiteChar();
```

The class SavitchIn has a number of different methods for reading different kinds of data. The method readLineNonwhiteChar reads a single nonblank keyboard character, whereas the method readLineInt reads a single integer. Otherwise, the two methods readLineInt and readLineNonwhiteChar are similar. SavitchIn also has a method named readLineDouble that can be used to read a value of type double—that is, to read a number that contains a decimal point.

We will say more about this kind of input and output in Section 2.3 of this chapter.

Quick Reference: Returned Value

An expression like numberOfBaskets * eggsPerBasket produces a value. If numberOfBaskets has the value 2 and eggsPerBasket has the value 10, the number produced is 20. In computer parlance, this is called the **value returned.** So instead of saying, "The number produced is 20.", we would say, "The value returned is 20."

The same terminology is used with method invocations. If a method produces a value, we say that the method returns the value. For example, in the last of the following program statements, the method invocation SavitchIn.readLineInt( ) produces a value—namely, the value read from the keyboard. We refer to this as the value returned by the method invocation SavitchIn.readLineInt( ).

```
int myNumber;
System.out.println("Enter an integer:");
myNumber = SavitchIn.readLineInt();
```

FAQ: What If the Screen Display Goes Away Too Quickly?

Some systems make your program output go away as soon as the program ends. Because computers are fast, this means that the screen dialog can disappear before you get a chance to read it. If this happens on your system, you can add the following to your programs, so the screen display will remain visible until the user presses the Enter (Return) key:

```
System.out.println("Press Enter key to end program.");
String junk;
junk = SavitchIn.readLine();
```

You insert the preceding three lines at the end of your program, as we did in Display 1.5 and Display 2.1. However, we will not add these three lines to programs in the rest of this book. Your program may or may not need the lines, depending on your particular Java environment.

Number Constants

A variable can have its value changed. That is why it is called a variable: its value *varies.* A literal number like 2 cannot change. It is always 2. It is never 3. Literal values like 2 or `3.7` are called **constants** because their values do not change. Literal expressions of types other than number types are also called constants. So, for example, `'Y'` is a constant of type `char`. There is essentially only one way to write a constant of type `char`, namely, by placing the character in single quotes. On the other hand, some of the rules for writing numeric constants are more complicated.

constant

Constants of integer types are written the way you would expect them to be written, such as `2`, `3`, `0`, `-3`, or `752`. An integer constant can be prefaced with a plus or minus sign, as in `+12` and `-72`. Numeric constants cannot contain commas. The number expression `1,000` is *not* correct in Java. Integer constants cannot contain a decimal point. Numbers with a decimal point are floating-point numbers.

integer constant

Floating-point constant numbers may be written in either of two forms. The simple form is like the everyday way of writing numbers with digits after the decimal point. The other, slightly more complicated, form is similar to a notation commonly used in the physical sciences.

floating-point constant

The more complicated notation for floating-point constants is frequently called **e notation, scientific notation,** or **floating-point notation.** For instance, consider the number `865000000.0`. This number can be expressed more clearly in the following notation, which is used in mathematics and physics, but not in Java:

scientific (e) notation

$$8.65 \times 10^8$$

Java has a similar notation, but because keyboards have no way of writing exponents, the 10 is omitted and both the multiplication sign and the 10 are replaced by the letter `e`. So, in Java, 8.65×10^8 is written as `8.65e8` (or in the less convenient form `865000000.0`). The two forms, `8.65e8` and `865000000.0`, are equivalent in a Java program.

Similarly, the number 4.83×10^{-4}, which is equal to `0.000483`, could be written as `4.83e-4` in Java. The `e` stands for *exponent,* since it is followed by a number that is thought of as an exponent of 10.

Because multiplying by 10 is the same as moving the decimal point in a number, you can think of the number after the `e` as telling you to move the decimal point that many digits to the right. If the number after the `e` is negative, you move the decimal point that many digits to the left. For example, `2.48e4` is the same number as `24800.0`, and `2.48e-2` is the same number as `0.0248`.

The number before the `e` may be a number with or without a decimal point. The number after the `e` cannot contain a decimal point

---

FAQ: What Is "Floating" in a Floating-Point Number?

Floating-point numbers got their name because, with the `e` notation we described in this subsection, the decimal point can be made to "float" to a new location by adjusting the exponent. You can make the decimal point in `0.000483` float to after the 4 by expressing this number as the equivalent expression `4.83e-4`. Computer language implementers use this trick to store each floating-point number as a number with exactly one digit before the decimal point (and some suitable exponent). Because the implementation always floats the decimal point in these numbers, they are called floating-point numbers. (The numbers are actually stored in base 2, rather than as the base 10 numerals we used in our example, but the principle is the same.)

Assignment Compatibilities

As we mentioned previously, trying to put a value of one type into a variable of another type is like trying to put a square peg in a round hole. You cannot put an `int` value like `42` in a variable of type `char`. You cannot put a `double` value like `3.5` in a variable of type `int`. You cannot even put the `double` value `3.0` in a variable of type `int`. You cannot store a value of one type in a variable of another type unless the value is somehow converted to match the type of the variable. However, when dealing with numbers, this conversion will sometimes (but not always) be performed automatically for you. The conversion will always be done when you assign a value of an integer type to a variable of a floating-point type, such as

```
double doubleVariable;
doubleVariable = 7;
```

Slightly more subtle assignments, such as the following, also perform the conversion automatically:

```
int intVariable;
intVariable = 7;
double doubleVariable;
doubleVariable = intVariable;
```

More generally, you can assign a value of any type in the following list to a variable of any type that appears further down in the list:

```
byte-->short-->int-->long-->float-->double
```

For example, you can assign a value of type `long` to a variable of type `float` or to a variable of type `double` (or, of course, to a variable of type `long`), but you cannot assign a value of type `long` to a variable of type `byte`, `short`, or `int`. (Note that this is not an arbitrary ordering of the types. As you move down the list from left to right, the types become more complex, either because they allow larger values or because they allow decimal points in the numbers.)

You can assign a value of type `char` to a variable of type `int` or to any of the numeric types that follow `int` in our list of types. However, we do not advise doing so, because the result could be confusing.[2]

If you want to assign a value of type `double` to a variable of type `int`, you must change the type of the value using a type cast, as we explain next.

Quick Reference: Assignment Compatibilities

You can assign a value of any type on the following list to a variable of any type that appears further down on the list:

```
byte-->short-->int-->long-->float-->double
```

In particular, note that you can assign a value of any integer type to a variable of any floating-point type.

Type Casting

The title of this subsection has nothing to do with the Hollywood notion of typecasting. In fact, it is almost the opposite. In Java (and in most programming languages), a **type cast** involves changing the type of a value from its normal type to some other type—for example, changing the type of `2.0` from `double` to `int`. In the previous subsection, we described when you could assign a value of one type to a variable of another type and have the type conversion occur automatically. In all other cases, if you want to assign a value of one type to a variable of another type, you must perform a type cast. Let's see how this is done in Java.

type cast

Suppose you have the following:

```
double distance;
distance = 9.0;
int points;
points = distance;
```

This is an illegal assignment.

2. Readers who have used certain other languages, such as C or C++, may be surprised to learn that you cannot assign a value of type `char` to a variable of type `byte`. This is because Java uses the Unicode character set rather than the ASCII character set, and so Java reserves two bytes of memory for each value of type `char`, but naturally reserves only one byte of memory for values of type `byte`. This is one of the few cases in which you might notice that Java uses the Unicode character set. However, if you convert from an `int` to a `char` or vice versa, you can expect to get the usual correspondence of ASCII numbers and characters.

As the note indicates, the last statement is illegal in Java. You cannot assign a value of type `double` to a variable of type `int`, even if the value of type `double` happens to have all zeros after the decimal point and so is conceptually a whole number.

In order to assign a value of type `double` to a value of type `int`, you must place `(int)` in front of the value or the variable holding the value. For example, you can replace the preceding illegal assignment with the following and get a legal assignment:

```
points = (int)distance;
```

This is a legal assignment.

The expression `(int)distance` is called a type cast. This does not change the value stored in the variable `distance`, but it does change the value returned by the expression. Thus, in the assignment

```
points = (int)distance;
```

neither `distance` nor the value stored in `distance` is changed in any way. But the value stored in `points` is the "`int` version" of the value stored in `distance`. If the value of `distance` is `9.0`, the value of `distance` remains `9.0`, but `9` is the value assigned to `points`.

It is important to note that a type cast does not change the value of the source variable in an expression like `(int)distance`. An expression like `(int)25.36` or `(int)distance` is an expression that *produces* an `int` value. So if the value of `distance` is `25.36`, then the value of `(int)distance` is `25`, but the value of `distance` is still `25.36`. The situation is analogous to computing the number of (whole) dollars you have in an amount of money. If you have $25.36, the number of dollars you have is 25, but the $25.36 has not changed; it has merely been used to produce the whole number 25. For example, consider the following code:

```
double dinnerBill;
dinnerBill = 25.36;
int dinnerBillPlusTip = (int)dinnerBill + 5;
System.out.println(
        "The value of dinnerBillPlusTip is "+dinnerBillPlusTip);
```

The expression `(int)dinnerBill` produces the value `25`, so the output of this code would be

```
The value of dinnerBillPlusTip is 30
```

But the variable `dinnerBill` still contains the value `25.36`.

Be sure to note that when you type cast from a `double` to an `int` (or from any floating-point type to any integer type), the amount is not rounded. The part after the decimal point is simply discarded. This is known as **truncating.** For example, consider the following:

truncating

```
double dinnerBill;
dinnerBill = 26.99;
int numberOfDollars;
numberOfDollars = (int)dinnerBill;
```

This does not set `numberOfDollars` to `27`. It sets `numberOfDollars` to `26`. The result is *not rounded.*

As we mentioned previously, when you assign an integer value to a variable of a floating-point type (such as a variable of type `double`), the integer is automatically type cast to the type of the variable. For example, consider

```
double point;
point = 7;
```

This assignment statement is equivalent to

```
point = (double)7;
```

The type cast `(double)` is implicit in the first version of the assignment.

Quick Reference: Type Casting

In many situations, you are not allowed to store a value of one type in a variable of another type. In these situations, you must use a **type cast** that converts the value to an "equivalent" value of the target type.

Syntax:

(*Type_Name*) *Expression*

Example:

```
double guess;
guess = 7.8;
int answer;
answer = (int)guess;
```

The value stored in `answer` will be 7. Note that the value is truncated, *not rounded.* Note also that the variable `guess` is not changed in any way. The assignment statement affects only the value stored in `answer`.

■ Java Tip
Type Casting a Character to an Integer

Java sometimes treats values of type `char` as integers, but the assignment of integers to characters has no connection to the meaning of the characters. For example, the following type cast will output the `int` value corresponding to the character `'7'`:

```
char symbol;
symbol = '7';
System.out.println((int)symbol);
```

You might expect the preceding to output 7 to the screen, but it does not. It outputs the number 55. Java (and all other programming languages) use an arbitrary numbering of characters so as to produce an integer corresponding to each character. In this correspondence, there is nothing special about the digits; they are just characters the same as the letters or the plus sign. Thus, no effort was made to have the digits correspond to their intuitive values. Basically, they just wrote down all the characters and then numbered them in the order they were written down. The character '7' just happened to get 55. (This numbering system is called the Unicode system, which we discuss later in the chapter. If you have heard of the ASCII numbering system, the Unicode system is the same as the ASCII system for the characters of the English language.) □

Programming Tip

Initialize Variables

uninitialized variable

A variable that has been declared, but that has not yet been given a value by an assignment statement (or in some other way), is said to be **uninitialized.** If the variable is a class variable, it literally has no value. If the variable is a variable of a primitive type, it may have some default value. However, your program will be clearer if you explicitly give the variable a value, even if you are simply reassigning the default value. (The exact details on default values have been known to change and should not be counted on.)

One easy way to ensure that you do not have an uninitialized variable is to initialize it within the declaration. Simply combine the declaration and an assignment statement, as in the following examples:

```
int count = 0;
double taxRate = 0.075;
char grade = 'A';
int balance = 1000, newBalance;
```

Note that you can initialize some variables and not initialize others in a declaration.

Sometimes the compiler may complain that you have failed to initialize a variable. In most cases, that will indeed be true. Occasionally, though, the compiler is mistaken in giving this advice. However, the compiler will not compile your program until you convince it that the variable in question is initialized. To make the compiler happy, initialize the variable when you declare it, even if the variable will be given another value before it is used for anything. In such cases, you cannot argue with the compiler. ○

Quick Reference: Combining a Variable Declaration and an Assignment

You can combine the declaration of a variable with an assignment statement that gives the variable a value.

Syntax:

Type Variable_1 = *Expression_1*, *Variable_2* = *Expression_2*, ...;

Example:

```
int numberSeen = 0, increment = 5;
double height = 12.34, prize = 7.3 + increment;
char answer = 'y';
```

▲ Gotcha

Imprecision in Floating-Point Numbers

Floating-point numbers are stored with a limited amount of accuracy and so are, for all practical purposes, only approximate quantities. For example, the floating-point number `1.0/3.0` is equal to

```
0.3333333...
```

where the three dots indicate that the 3s go on forever. The computer stores numbers in a format somewhat like the decimal representation on the previously displayed line, but it has room for only a limited number of digits. If it can store only 10 digits after the decimal, then `1.0/3.0` is stored as

`0.3333333333` (and no more 3s)

Thus, `1.0/3.0` is stored as a number that is slightly smaller than one-third. In other words, the value stored as `1.0/3.0` is only approximately equal to one-third. In reality, the computer stores numbers in binary notation, rather than in base 10, but the principles are the same and the same sorts of things happen. Some floating-point numbers lose accuracy when they are stored in the computer.

Floating-point numbers (like numbers of type `double`) and integers (like numbers of type `int`) are stored differently. As we indicated in the previous paragraph, floating-point numbers are, in effect, stored as approximate quantities. Integers, on the other hand, are stored as exact quantities. This difference sometimes can be subtle. For example, the numbers `5` and `5.0` are conceptually the same number. But Java considers them to be different. The whole number `5` is of type `int` and is an exact quantity. The number `5.0` is of type `double` because it contains a fractional part (even though the fraction is `0`), and so `5.0` is stored with only a limited degree of accuracy. △

? Self-Test Questions

1. Which of the following may be used as variable names in Java?

   `rate1, 1stPlayer, myprogram.java, long, TimeLimit, numberOfWindows`

2. Can a Java program have two different variables with the names `aVariable` and `avariable`?
3. Give the declaration for a variable called `count` of type `int`. The variable should be initialized to zero in the declaration.
4. Give the declaration for two variables of type `double`. The variables are to be named `rate` and `time`. Both variables should be initialized to zero in the declaration.
5. Write the declaration for two variables called `miles` and `flowRate`. Declare the variable `miles` to be of type `int` and initialize it to zero in the declaration. Declare the variable `flowRate` to be of type `double` and initialize it to `50.56` in the declaration.

6. Write a Java assignment statement that will set the value of the variable `interest` to the value of the variable `balance` multiplied by `0.05`.

7. Write a Java assignment statement that will set the value of the variable `interest` to the value of the variable `balance` multiplied by the value of the variable `rate`. The variables are of type `double`.

8. Write a Java assignment statement that will increase the value of the variable `count` by 3. The variable is of type `int`.

9. What is the output produced by the following lines of program code?

```
char a, b;
a = 'b';
System.out.println(a);
b = 'c';
System.out.println(b);
a = b;
System.out.println(a);
```

10. In the Java Tip entitled "Type Casting a Character to an Integer," you saw that the following does not output the integer 7:

```
char symbol;
symbol = '7';
System.out.println((int)symbol);
```

Thus, `(int)symbol` does not produce the number corresponding to the digit in `symbol`. Can you give an expression that will work to produce the integer that intuitively corresponds to the digit in `symbol` (assuming that `symbol` contains one of the 10 digits `'0'`, `'1'`, . . ., `'9'`)? *Hint*: The digits do correspond to consecutive integers, so if `(int)'7'` is `55`, then `(int)'8'` is `56`.

11. What is the output produced by the following code?

```
int result = 10;
result *= 3;
System.out.println("result is " + result);
```

Arithmetic Operators

In Java, you can form arithmetic expressions involving addition (+), subtraction (–), multiplication (*), and division (/) in basically the same way that you would form them in ordinary arithmetic or algebra. You can combine variables or numbers by using the arithmetic operators +, –, *, and /. The meaning of such an expression is basically what you expect it to be, but there are some subtleties about the type of the result and, occasionally, even about the value of the result. All of the arithmetic operators can be used with numbers of any of the integer types, any of the floating-point types, and even with numbers of differing types. The type of the value produced depends on the types of the numbers being combined.

mixing types

Let's start our discussion with simple expressions that combine only two variables, two numbers, or a variable and a number. If both operands (i.e., each number or variable) are of the same type, then the result is of that type. If one of the operands is of a floating-point type and the other is of an integer type, the result is of the floating-point type. For example, consider the expression

```
amount - adjustment
```

If the variables `amount` and `adjustment` are both of type `int`, the result (the value returned) is of type `int`. If either `amount` or `adjustment`, or both, are of type `double`, then the result is of type `double`. If you replace the operator – with any of the operators +, *, or /, the type of the result is determined in the same way.

Larger expressions using more than two operands can always be viewed as a series of steps, each of which involves only two operands. For example, to evaluate the expressions

```
balance + (balance*rate)
```

you (or the computer) evaluate `balance*rate` and obtain a number, and then you combine that number with `balance`, using addition. This means that the same rule we used to determine the type of an expression with two operands can also be used for more complicated expressions: If all of the items being combined are of the same type, the result is of that type; if some of the items being combined are of integer types and some are of floating-point types, then the result is of a floating-point type.

Knowing whether the value produced is of an integer type or a floating-point type is typically all that you need to know. However, if you need to know the exact type of the value produced by an arithmetic expression, you can determine it as follows: The type of the value produced is one of the types used in the expression. Of all the types used in the expression, it is the last type (reading from left to right) on the following list:

```
byte-->short-->int-->long-->float-->double
```

Note that this is the same sequence as the one used to determine automatic type conversions.

The division operator (/) deserves special attention, because the type of the result can affect the value produced in a dramatic way. When you combine two numbers with the division operator and at least one of the numbers is of type `double` (or of some other floating-point type), the result is what you would normally expect of a division. For example, `9.0/2` has one operand of type `double`, namely, `9.0`. Hence, the result is the type `double` number `4.5`. However, when both operands are of an integer type, the result can be surprising. For example, `9/2` has two operands of type `int`, so it yields the type `int` result `4`, not `4.5`. The fraction after the decimal point is simply lost. Be sure to notice that when you divide two integers, the result *is not rounded*; the part after the decimal point is discarded (truncated), no matter how large it is. So, `11/3` is `3` (not `3.6666`...). If there is nothing but a zero after the decimal point, that decimal point and zero after the decimal point are still lost, and even this seemingly trivial difference can be of some significance. For example, `8.0/2` evaluates to the type `double` value `4.0`, which is only an approximate quantity. However, `8/2` evaluates to the `int` value `4`, which is an exact quantity. The approximate nature of `4.0` can affect the accuracy of any further calculation that is performed with this result.

division

integer division

The % **operator** can be used with operands of integer types to recover something equivalent to the fraction after the decimal point. When you divide one integer by another, you get a result (which some call a quotient) and a remainder. For example, `14` divided by `4` yields `3` with a remainder of `2`. To rephrase it, `14` divided by `4` is `3` with `2` left over. The % operation gives the remainder—that is, the amount left over— after doing the division. So `14/4` evaluates to `3`, and `14%4` evaluates to `2`, because `14` divided by `4` is `3` with `2` left over.

the % operator

The % operator has more applications than you might at first suspect. It allows your program to count by 2s, 3s, or any other number. For example, if you want to do something to every other integer, you need to know whether the integer is even or odd, so you can perform the action on every even integer (or alternatively, on every odd integer). An integer `n` is even if `n%2` is equal to 0, and the integer is odd if `n%2` is equal to 1. Similarly, if you want your program to do something to every third integer, then your program can step through all the integers, using an `int` variable `n` to store the integer, and can test `n%3`. In this case, your program might perform the action only when `n%3` is equal to 0.

Parentheses and Precedence Rules

parentheses

Parentheses can be used to group items in an arithmetic expression in the same way that you use parentheses in algebra and arithmetic. With the aid of parentheses, you can tell the computer which operations are performed first, second, and so forth. For example, consider the following two expressions that differ only in the positioning of their parentheses:

```
(cost + tax) * discount
cost + (tax * discount)
```

To evaluate the first expression, the computer first adds `cost` and `tax` and then multiplies the result by `discount`. To evaluate the second expression, it multiplies `tax` and `discount` and then adds the result to `cost`. If you use some numbers for the values of the variables and carry out the two evaluations, you will see that they produce different results.

If you omit the parentheses, the computer will still evaluate the expression. For example, consider the following assignment statement:

```
total = cost + tax * discount;
```

This is equivalent to

```
total = cost + (tax * discount);
```

When parentheses are omitted, the computer performs multiplication before addition. More generally, when the order of operations is not determined by parentheses, the computer will perform the operations in an order determined by the **precedence rules** shown in Display 2.3. (Display 2.3 shows all the operators we will use in this chapter. More precedence rules will be given in Chapter 3, and an even more complete list of precedence rules is given in Appendix 2.) Operators that are listed higher on the list are said to have **higher precedence.** When the computer is deciding which of two operations to perform first and the order is not dictated by parentheses, it performs the operation of higher precedence before the operation of lower precedence. Some operators have equal precedence, in which case the order of operations is determined by the left-to-right order of the operators. Binary operators of equal precedence are performed in left-to-right order. Unary operators of equal precedence are performed in right-to-left order.

precedence rules

unary operator

A **unary operator** is an operator that has only one argument (one thing that it applies to), like the operator – in the assignment statement

```
bankBalance = -cost;
```

■ **DISPLAY 2.3 Precedence Rules**

Highest Precedence

First: the unary operators: +, –, ++, ––, and !
Second: the binary arithmetic operators: *, /, and %
Third: the binary arithmetic operators: + and –

Lowest Precedence

binary operator

A **binary operator** has two arguments, like the operators + and * in

```
total = cost + (tax * discount);
```

Note that the same operator symbol can sometimes be used as both a unary and a binary operator. For example, the – and + symbols can serve as either binary or unary operators.

These precedence rules are similar to the rules used in algebra classes. However, except for some very standard cases, it is best to include the parentheses, even if the intended order of operations is the one indicated by the precedence rules. The parentheses make the expression clearer to a person reading the program code. One standard case in which it is normal to omit parentheses is a multiplication within an addition. Thus,

```
balance = balance + (interestRate*balance);
```

would usually be written

```
balance = balance + interestRate*balance;
```

Both forms are acceptable, and the two forms have the same meaning.

spacing

When writing arithmetic expressions, you can include spaces before and after operations or you can omit them. Similarly, you can include or omit spaces around parentheses.

Display 2.4 shows some examples of how you write arithmetic expressions in Java and indicates some of the parentheses that you can normally omit.

■ **DISPLAY 2.4 Arithmetic Expressions in Java**

Ordinary Mathematical Expression	Java Expression (Preferred Form)	Equivalent Fully Parenthesized Java Expression
$rate^2 + delta$	`rate*rate + delta`	`(rate*rate) + delta`
$2(salary + bonus)$	`2*(salary + bonus)`	`2*(salary + bonus)`
$\frac{1}{time + 3mass}$	`1/(time + 3*mass)`	`1/(time + (3*mass))`
$\frac{a-7}{t+9v}$	`(a - 7)/(t + 9*v)`	`(a - 7)/(t + (9*v))`

Case Study
Vending Machine Change

task specification

Vending machines often have small computers to control their operation. In this case study, you will write a program that handles one of the tasks that such a computer would need to perform. The input and output will be performed via the keyboard and screen. To integrate this program into a vending machine computer, you would have to embed the code from the program into a larger program that takes its data from someplace other than the keyboard and sends its results to someplace other than the screen, but that's another story. In this case study, the user enters an amount of change from 1 to 99 cents. The program responds by telling the user one combination of coins that equals that amount of change.

For example, if the user enters `55` for 55 cents, the program tells the user that 55 cents can be given as two quarters and one nickel (i.e., two 25-cent coins and one 5-cent coin). You decide that the dialog should read like the following example, which you write out to see how it looks before coding the program:

```
Enter a whole number from 1 to 99.
I will output a combination of coins
that equal that amount of change.
87
87 cents in coins:
3 quarters
1 dime
0 nickels and
2 pennies
```

data

The program will need variables to store the amount of change and the number of each type of coin. So it will need at least the following variables:

```
int amount, quarters, dimes, nickels, pennies;
```

That takes care of some routine matters, and now you are ready to tackle the heart of the problem. You need an algorithm to compute the number of each kind of coin. You come up with the following algorithm:

pseudocode first try

Algorithm to determine the number of coins in `amount` cents:

Read the amount into the variable `amount`.

Set the variable `quarters` equal to the maximum number of quarters in `amount`.

Reset `amount` to the change left after giving out that many quarters.

Set the variable `dimes` equal to the maximum number of dimes in `amount`.

Reset `amount` to the change left after giving out that many dimes.

Set the variable `nickels` equal to the maximum number of nickels in `amount`.

Reset `amount` to the change left after giving out that many nickels.

```
pennies = amount;
```

Output the original amount and the numbers of each coin.

pseudocode

This algorithm is expressed in **pseudocode,** which is any convenient combination of Java and English used to express an algorithm before the algorithm is translated into Java.

When you look at your pseudocode, you realize that the algorithm changes the value of `amount`. However, you want to have the original amount at the end so that you can output it. So you use one more variable, called `originalAmount`, to save the original amount. You modify the pseudocode as follows:

Algorithm to determine the number of coins in `amount` cents:

pseudocode revised

Read the amount into the variable `amount`.

`originalAmount = amount;`

Set the variable `quarters` equal to the maximum number of quarters in `amount`.

Reset `amount` to the change left after giving out that many quarters.

Set the variable `dimes` equal to the maximum number of dimes in `amount`.

Reset `amount` to the change left after giving out that many dimes.

Set the variable `nickels` equal to the maximum number of nickels in `amount`.

Reset `amount` to the change left after giving out that many nickels.

`pennies = amount;`

Output `originalAmount` and the numbers of each coin.

coding

You now need to produce Java code that does the same thing as your pseudocode. Much of it is routine. The first line of your pseudocode simply calls for prompting the user and then reading input from the keyboard. You produce the following Java code for this first line of pseudocode:

```
System.out.println("Enter a whole number from 1 to 99.");
System.out.println("I will output a combination of coins");
System.out.println("that equals that amount of change.");

amount = SavitchIn.readLineInt();
```

The next line of pseudocode, which sets the value of `originalAmount`, is already Java code, so you need not do any translating.

Thus far, the `main` part of your program reads as follows:

```
public static void main(String[] args)
{
    int amount, originalAmount,
        quarters, dimes, nickels, pennies;

    System.out.println("Enter a whole number from 1 to 99.");
    System.out.println("I will output a combination of coins");
    System.out.println("that equals that amount of change.");
```

```
amount = SavitchIn.readLineInt();
originalAmount = amount;
```

Next, you need to translate the following to Java code:

Set the variable `quarters` equal to the maximum number of quarters in `amount`.

Reset `amount` to the change left after giving out that many quarters.

integer division / and %

You give this some thought and decide to try an example. For 55 cents, there are 2 quarters, because 55 divided by 25 is 2 with a remainder of 5. Ah! You realize that the operators / and % can be used for this kind of division. For example,

55/25 is 2 (the maximum number of 25s in 55)
55%25 is 5 (the remainder)

Replacing 55 with `amount` and changing to Java syntax, you produce the following:

```
quarters = amount/25;
amount = amount%25;
```

You realize that dimes and nickels are treated in a similar way, so you next produce the following code:

```
dimes = amount/10;
amount = amount%10;
nickels = amount/5;
amount = amount%5;
```

The rest of the program coding is straightforward. You produce the program shown in Display 2.5 as your final program.

testing

After producing your program, you need to test it on a number of different kinds of data. You decide to test it on each of the following inputs: 0 cents, 4 cents, 5 cents, 6 cents, 10 cents, 11 cents, 25 cents, 26 cents, 35 cents, 55 cents, 65 cents, and a number of other cases. This sounds like a lot of different inputs, but you want to try cases that give zero values for all possible coin values, and you want to test values near change points, like 25 and 26 cents, which changes from all quarters to quarters and another coin. All your tests are successful, but the grammar for the output is not exactly correct. For 26 cents, you get the output

```
26 cents in coins:
1 quarters
0 dimes
0 nickels and
1 pennies
```

The output is correct, but would read a lot better if it said `1 quarter` instead of `1 quarters` and `1 penny` instead of `1 pennies`. The techniques you need to produce this nicer looking output will be presented in the next chapter. For now, let's end this project here. The output is correct and understandable. ■

■ DISPLAY 2.5 Change-Making Program

```
public class ChangeMaker
{
    public static void main(String[] args)
    {
        int amount, originalAmount,
            quarters, dimes, nickels, pennies;

        System.out.println("Enter a whole number from 1 to 99.");
        System.out.println("I will output a combination of coins");
        System.out.println("that equals that amount of change.");

        amount = SavitchIn.readLineInt();
        originalAmount = amount;

        quarters = amount/25;
        amount = amount%25;
        dimes = amount/10;
        amount = amount%10;
        nickels = amount/5;
        amount = amount%5;
        pennies = amount;

        System.out.println(originalAmount
                          + " cents in coins can be given as:");
        System.out.println(quarters + " quarters");
        System.out.println(dimes + " dimes");
        System.out.println(nickels + " nickels and");
        System.out.println(pennies + " pennies");
    }
}
```

25 goes into 87 three times with 12 left over.

87/25 *is* 3.

87%25 *is* 12.

87 cents is three quarters with 12 cents left over.

Sample Screen Dialog

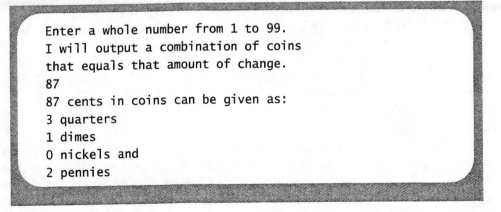

```
Enter a whole number from 1 to 99.
I will output a combination of coins
that equals that amount of change.
87
87 cents in coins can be given as:
3 quarters
1 dimes
0 nickels and
2 pennies
```

? Self-Test Questions

12. What is the output produced by the following lines of program code?

```
int quotient, remainder;
quotient = 7/3;
remainder = 7%3;
System.out.println("quotient = " + quotient);
System.out.println("remainder = " + remainder);
```

13. What is the output produced by the following lines of program code?

```
double result;
result = (1/2) * 2;
System.out.println("(1/2) * 2 equals " + result);
```

14. Consider the following statement from the program in Display 2.5:

```
System.out.println(originalAmount
                   + " cents in coins can be given as:");
```

Suppose that you replaced the preceding line with the following:

```
System.out.println(amount
                   + " cents in coins can be given as:");
```

How will this change the sample dialog in Display 2.5?

15. What is the output produced by the following code?

```
int result = 11;
result /= 2;
System.out.println("result is " + result);
```

Increment and Decrement Operators

The increment and decrement operators can be used to increase or decrease the value of a variable by 1. They are very specialized operators, and you (and Java) could easily get along without them. But they are sometimes handy, and they are of cultural significance because programmers use them. So to be "in the club," you should know how to use them. Even if you do not want to use them yourself, you need to be familiar with these operators so you can understand them when you see them in another programmer's code.

increment operator ++

The **increment operator** is written as two plus signs (++). For example, the following will increase the value of the variable `count` by 1:

```
count++;
```

This is a Java statement. If the variable `count` has the value 5 before this statement is executed, it will have the value 6 after the statement is executed. You can use the increment operator with variables of any numeric type, but they are used most often with variables of integer types (such as the type `int`).

The **decrement operator** is similar, except that it subtracts `1` rather than adds `1` to the value of the variable. The decrement operator is written as two minus signs (−−). For example, the following will decrease the value of the variable `count` by `1`:

decrement operator --

```
count--;
```

If the variable count has the value 5 before this statement is executed, it will have the value 4 after the statement is executed.

Note that

```
count++;
```

is equivalent to

```
count = count + 1;
```

and

```
count--;
```

is equivalent to

```
count = count - 1;
```

As you can see, the increment and decrement operators are really very specialized. Why does Java have such specialized operators? It inherited them from C++ (and C++ inherited them from C). In fact, this increment operator is where the ++ came from in the name of the C++ programming language. Why was it added to the C and C++ languages? Because adding or subtracting `1` is a very common thing to do when programming.

More about the Increment and Decrement Operators

Although we do not recommend doing so, the increment and decrement operators can be used in expressions. When used in an expression, these operators both change the value of the variable they are applied to and return a value.

In expressions, you can place the ++ or −− either before or after the variable, but the meaning is different, depending on whether it is before or after the variable. For example, consider the code

```
int n = 3;
int m = 4;
int result;
result = n * (++m);
```

After this code is executed, the value of `n` is unchanged at `3`, the value of `m` is `5`, and the value of `result` is `15`. Thus, `++m` both changes the value of `m` and returns that changed value to be used in the arithmetic expression.

In the previous example, we placed the increment operator in front of the variable. If we place it after the variable `m`, something slightly different happens. Consider the code

```
int n = 3;
int m = 4;
int result;
result = n * (m++);
```

In this case, after the code is executed, the value of n is 3 and the value of m is 5, just as in the previous case, but the value of result is 12, not 15. What is the story?

The two expressions n * (++m) and n * (m++) both increase the value of m by 1, but the first expression increases the value of m *before* it does the multiplication, whereas the second expression increases the value of m *after* it does the multiplication. Both ++m and m++ have the same effect on the final value of m, but when you use them as part of an arithmetic expression, they give a different value to the expression. If the ++ is *before* the m, then the value of m is increased *before* its value is used in the expression. If the ++ is *after* the m, then the value of m is increased *after* its value is used in the expression.

The -- operator works the same way when it is used in an arithmetic expression. Both --m and m-- have the same effect on the final value of m, but when you use them as part of an arithmetic expression, they give a different value to the expression. If the -- is *before* the m, the value of m is decreased *before* its value is used in the expression. If the -- is *after* the m, the value of m is decreased *after* its value is used in the expression.

The increment and decrement operators can be applied only to variables. They cannot be applied to constants or to more complicated arithmetic expressions.

? Self-Test Questions

16. What is the output produced by the following lines of program code?

```
int n = 2;
n++;
System.out.println("n == " + n);
n--;
System.out.println("n == " + n);
```

2.2 THE CLASS String

Words, words, mere words, no matter from the heart. -William Shakespeare, *Troilus and Cressida*

String

Strings of characters, such as "Enter the amount:", are treated slightly differently from values of the primitive types. There is no primitive type for strings in Java. However, there is a class called String that can be used to store and process strings of characters. In this section, we introduce you to the class String.

String Constants and Variables

You have already been using constants of type String. The quoted string

```
"Enter a whole number from 1 to 99."
```

which appears in the following statement from the program in Display 2.5, is a string constant:

```
System.out.println("Enter a whole number from 1 to 99.");
```

A value of type String is one of these quoted strings. That is, a value of type String is a sequence of characters treated as a single item. A variable of type String can name one of these string values.

The following declares greeting to be the name for a String variable:

```
String greeting;
```

The following sets the value of greeting to the String value "Hello!":

```
greeting = "Hello!";
```

These two statements are often combined into one, as follows:

```
String greeting = "Hello!";
```

Once a String variable, such as greeting, has been given a value, you can write it out to the screen as follows:

```
System.out.println(greeting);
```

If the value of greeting has been set as we just described, this statement will cause

```
Hello!
```

to be written on the screen

Concatenation of Strings

+ operator concatenation

You can connect two strings using the + operator. Connecting ("pasting") two strings together to obtain a larger string is called **concatenation.** So when it is used with strings, the + symbol is sometimes called the **concatenation operator.** For example, consider the following:

```
String greeting = "Hello";
String sentence;
sentence = greeting + "my friend.";
System.out.println(sentence);
```

This will set the variable sentence to "Hellomy friend." and will write the following on the screen:

```
Hellomy friend.
```

Notice that no spaces are added when you concatenate two strings by means of the + operator. If you wanted sentence set to "Hello my friend.", you could change the assignment statement to

```
sentence = greeting + " my friend.";
```

Notice the space before the word "my".

You can concatenate any number of String objects with the use of the + operator. You can even connect a String object to any other type of object via the + operator. The result is always a String object. Java will figure out some way to express any object as a string when you connect it to a string with the + operator. For simple things like numbers, it does the obvious thing. For example,

```
String solution = "The answer is " + 42;
```

will set the String variable solution to "The answer is 42". This is so natural that it may seem as though nothing special is happening, but it does require a conversion from one type to another. The constant 42 is a number, whereas "42" is a string consisting of the character '4' followed by the character '2'. Java converts the number constant 42 to the string constant "42" and then concatenates the two strings "The answer is " and "42" to obtain the longer string "The answer is 42".

Quick Reference: Using the + Sign with Strings

You can concatenate two strings by connecting them with the + sign.

Example:

```
String name = "Chiana";
String greeting = "Hi " + name;
System.out.println(greeting);
```

This sets greeting to the string "Hi Chiana" and then outputs the following to the screen:

```
Hi Chiana
```

Note that we needed to add a space at the end of "Hi".

Classes

class

Classes are central to Java, and you will soon be defining and using your own classes much more than we do in these first few chapters. However, this discussion of the class String gives us an opportunity to introduce some of the notation and terminology used for classes. A **class** is a type whose values are objects. **Objects** are entities that store data and can take actions. For example, objects of the class String store data consisting of strings of characters, such as "Hello". The actions that an object can take are called **methods.** Most of the methods for the class String return, or produce, some value. For example, the method length() returns the number of characters in a String object. So "Hello".length() returns the integer 5 and can be stored in an int variable as follows:

object

method

```
int n = "Hello".length();
```

method call or method invocation

As indicated by the example "Hello".length(), you call a method into action by writing a name for the object, followed by a dot, followed by the method name, and ending with parentheses. When you call a method into action, you are (or your code is) said to **invoke** the method or **call** the method, and the object before the dot is known as the **calling object.**

calling object

Although you can call a method with a constant object, as in "Hello".length(), it is more common to use a variable that names an object as the calling object, as illustrated by the following:

```
String greeting = "Hello";
int n = greeting.length();
```

Information for the method invocation is given in the parentheses. In some cases, such as the method length, no information is needed (other than the data in the calling object), and the parentheses are empty. In other cases, as you will see soon, some information must be provided inside the parentheses. The information in parentheses is known as an **argument** (or arguments).

argument

All objects within a class have the same methods, but each object can have different data. For example the two `String` objects `"Hello"` and `"Good-Bye"` have different data—that is, different strings of characters. However, they have the same methods. Thus, since we know that the `String` object `"Hello"` has the method `length()`, we know that the `String` object `"Good-Bye"` must also have the method `length()`.

Quick Reference: Objects, Methods, and Classes

An **object** is a program construction that has data (that is, information) associated with it and that can perform certain actions. The actions performed by objects are called **methods.** A **class** is a type or kind of object. Different objects in the same class can have different data, but all objects in the same class have the same kinds of data and the same methods. When an object performs the action of a method, the object is said to **invoke** the method or **call** the method. The syntax for a method invocation is to write down a name for the object, followed by a dot, and then ending with a possibly empty set of parentheses. The parentheses enclose some information to use when the method is invoked. This information in parentheses is known as the method's **argument(s)**.

You have now seen two kinds of types in Java: primitive types and class types. The main difference you have seen between these two kinds of types is that classes have methods and primitive types do not have methods. A smaller difference is that all the primitive types are spelled using only lowercase letters, but by convention, class types are spelled with their first letter in uppercase, as in `String`. Later you will see more differences between classes and primitive types.

String Methods

A `String` variable is not just a simple variable, as a variable of type `int` is. A `String` variable is a variable of a class type that can name an object, and an object has methods as well as a value. These `String` methods can be used to manipulate string values. A few of the `String` methods are described in Display 2.6. As with any method, you call (or invoke) a `String` method by writing a dot and the name of the method after the object name. In this section, the object name will always be a variable of type `String`. Any arguments to the method are given in parentheses. Let's look at some examples.

DISPLAY 2.6 Methods in the Class `String` *(Part 1 of 4)*

Method	Description	Example
`length()`	*Returns the length of the* `String` *object.*	`String greeting = "Hello!";` `greeting.length()` *returns* 6.

`equals(`*Other_String*`)`	*Returns* `true` *if the calling object string and the Other_String are equal. Otherwise, returns* `false`.	`String greeting =`
		`  SavitchIn.readLine();`
		`if (greeting.equals("Hi"))`
		`  System.out.println(`
		`    "Informal Greeting.");`

DISPLAY 2.6 Methods in the Class `String` *(Part 2 of 4)*

Method	Description	Example
`equalsIgnoreCase(`*Other_String*`)`	*Returns* `true` *if the calling object string and the* Other_String *are equal, considering uppercase and lowercase versions of a letter to be the same. Otherwise, returns* `false`.	*If a program contains* `String s1 = "mary!";` *then after this assignment,* `s1.equalsIgnoreCase("Mary!")` *returns* `true`.
`toLowerCase()`	*Returns a string with the same characters as the calling object string, but with all characters converted to lowercase.*	`String greeting = "Hi Mary!";` `greeting.toLowerCase()` *returns* `"hi mary!"`
`toUpperCase()`	*Returns a string with the same characters as the calling object string, but with all characters converted to uppercase.*	`String greeting = "Hi Mary!";` `greeting.toUpperCase()` *returns* `"HI MARY!"`
`trim()`	*Returns a string with the same characters as the calling object string, but with leading and trailing whitespace removed.*	`String pause = "   Hmm   ";` `pause.trim()` *returns* `"Hmm"`
`charAt(`*Position*`)`	*Returns the character in the calling object string at* Position. *Positions are counted 0, 1, 2, etc.*	`String greeting = "Hello!";` `greeting.charAt(0)` *returns* `'H'`. `greeting.charAt(1)` *returns* `'e'`.
`substring(`*Start*`)`	*Returns the substring of the calling object string from position* Start *through to the end of the calling object. Positions are counted 0, 1, 2, etc.*	`String sample = "AbcdefG";` `sample.substring(2)` *returns* `"cdefG"`.

DISPLAY 2.6 Methods in the Class `String` *(Part 3 of 4)*

Method	Description	Example
`substring(`*Start*`,` *End*`)`	*Returns the substring of the calling object string from position Start through, but not including, position End of the calling object. Positions are counted 0, 1, 2, etc.*	`String sample = "AbcdefG";` `sample.substring(2, 5)` *returns* `"cde"`.
`indexOf(`*A_String*`)`	*Returns the position of the first occurrence of the string A_String in the calling object string. Positions are counted 0, 1, 2, etc. Returns −1 if A_String is not found.*	`String greeting = "Hi Mary!";` `greeting.indexOf("Mary")` *returns* 3. `greeting.indexOf("Sally")` *returns* −1.
`indexOf(`*A_String*`,` *Start*`)`	*Returns the position of the first occurrence of the string A_String in the calling object string that occurs at or after position Start. Positions are counted 0, 1, 2, etc. Returns −1 if A_String is not found.*	`String name =` `"Mary, Mary quite contrary";` `name.indexOf("Mary", 1)` *returns* 6. *The same value is returned if* 1 *is replaced by any number up to and including* 6. `name.indexOf("Mary", 0)` *returns* 0. `name.indexOf("Mary", 8)` *returns* −1.
`lastIndexOf(`*A_String*`)`	*Returns the position of the last occurrence of the string A_String in the calling object string. Positions are counted 0, 1, 2, etc. Returns* −1 *if A_String is not found.*	`String name =` `"Mary, Mary, Mary quite so";` `name.lastIndexOf("Mary")` *returns* 12.

DISPLAY 2.6 Methods in the Class `String` (Part 4 of 4)

Method	Description	Example
`compareTo(`*A_String*`)`	*Compares the calling object string with A_String to see which comes first in the lexicographic ordering. Lexicographic ordering is the same as alphabetical ordering when both strings are either all uppercase or all lowercase. If the calling string is first,* `compareTo` *returns a negative value. If the two strings are equal, it returns zero. If the argument is first, it returns a positive number.*	`String entry = "adventure";` `entry.compareTo("zoo")` *returns a negative number.* `entry.compareTo("adventure")` *returns zero.* `entry.compareTo("above")` *returns a positive number.*

`length`

As we've already noted, the method `length` can be used to find out the number of characters in a string. For example, suppose we declare `String` variables as follows:

```
String command = "Sit Fido!";
String answer = "bow-wow";
```

Then `command.length( )` returns `9` and `answer.length( )` returns `7`. Notice that spaces, special symbols, and repeated characters are all counted when computing the length of a string.

You can use a call to the method `length` anywhere that you can use a value of type `int`. For example, all of the following are legal Java statements:

```
int count = command.length();
System.out.println("Length is " + command.length());
count = command.length() + 3;
```

position

index

Many of the methods for the class `String` depend on counting **positions** in the string. Positions are counted starting with 0, not with 1. So in the string `"Hi Mom"`, `'H'` is in position 0, `'i'` is in position `1`, the blank character is in position 2, and so forth. A position is usually referred to as an **index** in computer parlance. So it would be more normal to say `'H'` is at index `0`, `'i'` is at index `1`, the blank character is at index `2`, and so forth. Display 2.7 illustrates how index positions are numbered in a string.

The method `indexOf` will return the index of the substring given as its one argument. If the substring occurs more than once, `indexOf` returns the index of the first occurrence of its substring argument. For example, consider

```
String phrase = "Time flies like an arrow.";
```

After this declaration, the invocation `phrase.indexOf("flies")` will return `5` because the `'f'` of `"flies"` is at index `5`. (Remember, the first index is `0`, not `1`.)

DISPLAY 2.7 String Indices

The twelve characters in the string `"Java is fun."` have indices 0 through 11. The index of each character is shown above it.

0	1	2	3	4	5	6	7	8	9	10	11
J	a	v	a		i	s		f	u	n	.

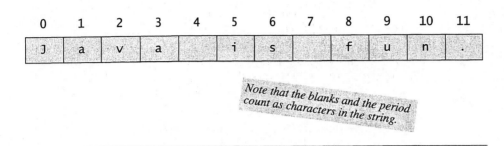

Note that the blanks and the period count as characters in the string.

String Processing

Many reference books on the Java language say that objects of type `String` cannot be changed. In a sense, this is true, but it is a misleading statement. Notice that none of the methods in Display 2.7 changes the value of the `String` object. There are more `String` methods than those shown in Display 2.7, but none of them lets you write statements that say things like "Change the fifth character in the calling object string to `'z'`". This is not an accident. It was done intentionally in order to make the implementation of the `String` class more efficient—that is, to make the methods execute faster and use less computer memory. There is another string class, however, that has methods for altering the string object. It is called `StringBuffer`, but we will not discuss it here because we do not need it.

Although there is no method that allows you to change the value of a `String` object, such as `"Hello"`, you can still write programs that change the value of a `String` variable, which is probably all you want to do anyway. To make the change, you simply use an assignment statement, as in the following example:

```
String name = "D'Aargo";
name = "Ka " + name;
```

The assignment statement in the second line changes the value of the `name` variable from `"D'Aargo"` to `"Ka D'Aargo"`. Display 2.8 shows a sample program that demonstrates how to do some simple string processing that changes the value of a `String` variable. Part of that program is explained in the next subsection.

Escape Characters

quotes in quotes

Suppose you want to output a string that contains quotation marks. For example, suppose you want to output the following to the screen:

```
The word "Java" names a language, not just a drink!
```

The following will not work:

```
System.out.println(
    "The word "Java" names a language, not just a drink!");
```

DISPLAY 2.8 Using the `String` Class

```
public class StringDemo
{
    public static void main(String[] args)
    {
        String sentence = "Text processing is hard!";
        int position;

        position = sentence.indexOf("hard");
        System.out.println(sentence);
        System.out.println("012345678901234567890123");
        System.out.println("The word \"hard\" starts at index "
                                    + position);

        sentence = sentence.substring(0, position) + "easy!";
        System.out.println("The changed string is:");
        System.out.println(sentence);
    }
}
```

The meaning of \" is discussed in the subsection entitled "Escape Characters."

Sample Screen Dialog

```
Text processing is hard!
012345678901234567890123
The word "hard" starts at index 19
The changed string is:
Text processing is easy!
```

This will produce a compiler error message. The problem is that the compiler sees

```
"The word "
```

as a perfectly valid quoted string. Then the compiler sees `Java"`, which is not anything valid in the Java language (although the compiler might guess that it is a quoted string with one missing quote or guess that you forgot a + sign). The compiler has no way to know that you mean to include the `'"'` symbol as part of the quoted string, unless you tell it that you mean to do so. You tell the compiler that you mean to include the quote in the string by placing a backslash (\) before the troublesome character, like so:

backslash \

```
System.out.println(
    "The word \"Java\" names a language, not just a drink!");
```

Display 2.9 lists some other special characters that are indicated with a backslash. These are often called **escape sequences** or **escape characters,** because they escape from the usual meaning of a character, such as the usual meaning of the double quote.

escape sequence or character

It is important to note that each escape sequence is a single character, even though it is written as two symbols. So the string `"Say \"Hi\"!"` contains 9 characters (`'S'`, `'a'`, `'y'`, the blank character, `'\"'`, `'H'`, `'i'`, `'\"'`, and `'!'`), not 11 characters.

Including a backslash in a quoted string is a little tricky. For example, the string `"abc\def"` is likely to produce the error message "Invalid escape character." To include a backslash in a string, you need to use two backslashes. The string `"abc\\def"`, if output to the screen, would produce

```
abc\def
```

The escape sequence `\n` indicates that the string starts a new line at the `\n`. For example, the statement

```
System.out.println("The motto is\nGo for it!");
```

will write the following to the screen:

```
The motto is
Go for it!
```

It may seem that there is no need for the escape sequence `\'`, since it is perfectly valid to include a single quote inside a quoted string, such as `"How's this?"`. But you do need to use `\'` if you want to indicate the constant for the single-quote character, as in

```
char singleQuote = '\'';
```

The Unicode Character Set

Most other programming languages use the ASCII character set, which is given in Appendix 3. The **ASCII** character set is simply a list of all the characters normally used on an English-language keyboard, together with a standard number assigned to each character. Java uses the Unicode character set instead. The **Unicode** character set includes the entire ASCII character set, plus many of the characters used in languages that have an alphabet different from English. As it turns out, this is not likely to be a big issue if you are using an English-language keyboard. Normally, you can just program as though Java were using

ASCII

Unicode

DISPLAY 2.9 Escape Characters

`\"` Double quote.
`\'` Single quote.
`\\` Backslash.
`\n` New line. Go to the beginning of the next line.
`\r` Carriage return. Go to the beginning of the current line.
`\t` Tab. Add whitespace up to the next tab stop.

the ASCII character set, because the ASCII character set is a subset of the Unicode character set. Thus, Appendix 3 can be thought of as listing the ASCII character set or as listing a subset of the Unicode character set. The advantage of the Unicode character set is that it makes it easy to handle languages other than English. The disadvantage is that it sometimes requires more computer memory to store each character than it would if Java used only the ASCII character set.

? Self-Test Questions

17. What is the output produced by the following?

```
String greeting = "How do you do";
System.out.println(greeting + "Seven of Nine.");
```

18. What is the output produced by the following?

```
String test = "abcdefg";
System.out.println(test.length( ));
System.out.println(test.charAt(1));
```

19. What is the output produced by the following?

```
String test = "abcdefg";
System.out.println(test.substring(3));
```

20. What is the output produced by the following?

```
System.out.println("abc\ndef");
```

21. What is the output produced by the following?

```
System.out.println("abc\\ndef");
```

22. What is the output produced by the following?

```
String test = "Hello John";
test = test.toUpperCase( );
System.out.println(test);
```

23. What is the output produced by the following?

```
String s1 = "Hello John";
String s2 = "hello john";
if (s1.equals(s2))
    System.out.println("Equal");
System.out.println("End");
```

If you do not understand the `if`, see Display 1.5 in Chapter 1.

24. What is the output produced by the following?

```
String s1 = "Hello John";
String s2 = "hello john";
s1 = s1.toUpperCase( );
```

```
s2 = s2.toUpperCase();
if (s1.equals(s2))
    System.out.println("Equal");
System.out.println("End");
```

If you do not understand the `if`, see Display 1.5 in Chapter 1.

2.3 KEYBOARD AND SCREEN I/O

Garbage in, garbage out. -Programmer's saying

Input and output of program data are usually referred to as **I/O.** There are many different ways that a Java program can perform I/O. In this section, we present some very simple ways to handle text input typed in at the keyboard and text output sent to the screen. In later chapters, we will discuss more elaborate ways to do I/O. I/O

In order to do I/O in Java, you almost always need to add some classes to the language. Sometimes these are classes that, although not part of the language proper, are nonetheless provided in all implementations of Java. Other times, these classes are not provided along with the language, and you must write the classes yourself (or obtain them from whoever wrote the class definitions). In this section, we will do output using a class provided automatically with the Java language. However, Java does not provide a class that handles simple keyboard input, so we will do input using the class `SavitchIn`, which is not provided with the Java language, but was written expressly for readers of this text.

Screen Output

We have been using simple output statements since the beginning of this book. This section will simply summarize and explain what we have already been doing. In Display 2.5, we used statements such as the following to send output to the display screen: `System.out.println`

```
System.out.println("Enter a whole number from 1 to 99.");
        . . .
System.out.println(quarters + " quarters");
```

`System.out` is an object that is part of the Java language. It may seem strange to spell an object name with a dot in it, but that need not concern you at this point.

The object `System.out` has `println` as one of its methods. So the preceding output statements are calls to the method `println` of the object `System.out`. Of course, you need not be aware of these details in order to use these output statements. You can simply consider `System.out.println` to be one rather peculiarly spelled statement. However, you may as well get used to this dot notation and the notion of methods and objects.

In order to use output statements of this form, simply follow the expression `System.out.println` with what you want to output, enclosed in parentheses, and then follow that with a semicolon. You can output strings of text in double quotes, like `"Enter a whole number from 1 to 99."` or `" quarters"`; variables, like `quarters`;

numbers, like 5 or `7.3`; and almost any other object or value. If you want to output more than one thing, simply place an addition sign between the things you want to output. For example,

```
System.out.println("Lucky number = " + 13
                      + "Secret number = " + number);
```

If the value of `number` is 7, the output will be

```
Lucky number = 13Secret number = 7
```

Notice that no spaces are added. If you want a space between the `13` and the word `Secret` in the preceding output (and you probably do), you should add a space at the beginning of the string

```
"Secret number = "
```

so that it becomes

```
" Secret number = "
```

Notice that you use double quotes, not single quotes, and that the left and right quotes are the same symbol. Finally, notice that it is OK to place the statement on two lines if it is too long. However, for readability, you should indent the second line, and you should break the line before or after a + sign. You cannot break a line in the middle of a quoted string or a variable name.

You can also use the `println` method to output the value of a `String` variable, as illustrated by the following:

```
String greeting = "Hello Programmers!";
System.out.println(greeting);
```

This will cause the following to be written on the screen:

```
Hello Programmers!
```

Every invocation of `println` ends a line of output. For example, consider the following statements:

```
System.out.println("One, two, buckle my shoe.");
System.out.println("Three, four, shut the door.");
```

These two statements will cause the following output to appear on the screen:

```
One, two, buckle my shoe.
Three, four, shut the door.
```

`print` versus `println`

If you want two or more output statements to place all of their output on a single line, use `print` instead of `println`. For example,

```
System.out.print("One, two,");
System.out.print(" buckle my shoe.");
System.out.println(" Three, four,");
System.out.println(" shut the door.");
```

will produce the following output:

```
One, two, buckle my shoe. Three, four,
 shut the door.
```

Notice that a new line is not started until you use a `println`, rather than a `print`. Notice also that the new line starts *after* the items specified in the `println` have been output. This is the only difference between `print` and `println`.

That is all you need to know in order to write programs with this sort of output, but we can still explain a bit more about what is happening. Consider the following statement:

```
System.out.println("The answer is " + 42);
```

The expression inside the parentheses should look familiar:

```
"The answer is " + 42
```

In the section on the class `String`, we said that you could use the + operator to concatenate a string, such as `"The answer is "`, and another item, such as the number constant `42`. The + operator inside these `System.out.println` statements is the same + operator that performs string concatenation. In the preceding `System.out.println` statement, Java converts the number constant `42` to the string `"42"` and then uses the + operator to obtain the string `"The answer is 42"`. The `System.out.println` statement then outputs the string `"The answer is 42"`. The `println` method always outputs strings. Technically speaking, it never outputs numbers, even though it looks as though it does.

Quick Reference: `println` Output

You can output one line with `System.out.println`. The items that are output can be quoted strings, variables, constants such as numbers, or almost any object you can define in Java.

Syntax:

```
System.out.println(Output_1 + Output_2 + ... + Output_Last);
```

Example:

```
System.out.println("Hello out there!");
System.out.println("Area = " + theArea + " square inches");
```

Quick Reference: `println` Versus `print`

`System.out.println` and `System.out.print` are almost the same method. The only difference is that with the `println` method, the *next* output goes on a *new line*, whereas with the `print` method, the next output will be placed on the *same line*.

Example:

```
System.out.print("one ");
System.out.print("two ");
System.out.println("three ");
System.out.print("four ");
```

will produce the following output

```
one two three
four
```

(The output would look the same whether the last line read `print` or `println`.)

Input Using SavitchIn

In order to do simple input in Java, you need to use some class that is defined for you (or that you define). In this section, we will handle input using the class SavitchIn, which is in the file SavitchIn.java provided with this text. SavitchIn is an extremely simple class, and once you learn a little more Java, you will have no problem understanding the code for this class definition. However, in the current section, we will not explain the definition of SavitchIn. We will explain only how to use the class SavitchIn.

It is very easy to obtain a copy of the class definition for SavitchIn. The definition is given in Appendix 4. However, there is no need to type it in. Simply copy the file SavitchIn.java, which is on the CD provided with this text, into the directory in which you keep your Java programs, and compile the class SavitchIn.java. At this point, you need not even read the definition of the class SavitchIn. Although it may seem strange at first to use a class definition without reading it, this is a common thing to do. A class definition is just another piece of software, and you use all kinds of software without reading their code. For example, you use an editor without ever seeing the code for the editor, you use the Java compiler without ever seeing the code for the Java compiler, and you use the Java classes String and System (as in System.out) without reading their definitions.

The class SavitchIn has methods that read a piece of data from the keyboard and return that data. When you place an invocation of one of these methods in an assignment statement, your program can read from the keyboard and place the data it reads into the variable on the left-hand side of the assignment operator. For example, the following statement from the program in Display 2.5 will read in one integer and make that integer the value of the variable amount:

```
amount = SavitchIn.readLineInt();
```

You may be wondering why there is nothing in the parentheses after the name readLineInt. This is because the method readLineInt does not use any arguments. You must still include the parentheses, however.

readLineInt

The method readLineInt expects the user to input one integer (of type int) on a line by itself, possibly with space before or after it. If the user inputs anything else, then an error message is output to the screen and the user is asked to reenter the input. Input is read only after the user starts a new line, so nothing happens until the user presses the Enter key.

readLine-Double

What if you want to read in a number of some type other than int? The methods readLineLong, readLineFloat, and readLineDouble work in exactly the same way as readLineInt, except that they read in values of type long, float, and double, respectively. For example, the following will read a single number of type double and store that number in the variable measurement:

```
double measurement;
measurement = SavitchIn.readLineDouble();
```

You can use the method readLineNonwhiteChar to read in a single nonwhitespace character, as in the following example:

```
char symbol;
symbol = SavitchIn.readLineNonwhiteChar();
```

Any whitespace characters at the start of the line will be ignored, and the first nonwhitespace character on the line will be read. If there is more than one nonwhitespace character on the line, `readLineNonwhiteChar` will read the first such character and discard the rest of the input line. **Whitespace** characters are all characters that print as whitespace if you output them to paper (or to the screen). The only whitespace character you are likely to be concerned with at first is the blank space character. (The start of a new line and the tab symbol are also whitespace characters, but those details are not likely to concern you yet.)

whitespace

There is a slight difference between `readLineNonwhiteChar` and the methods that read a single number. For the methods `readLineInt` and `readLineDouble`, the input number must be on a line with nothing before or after the number, except possibly whitespace. The method `readLineNonwhiteChar` allows anything to be on the line after the first nonwhitespace character, but it ignores the rest of the line. That way, when the user enters a word such as `yes`, `readLineNonwhiteChar` can read the first letter, like `'y'`, and ignore the rest of the word `yes`.

If you want to read in an entire line, you would use the method `readLine` (without any `Int` or `Double` or such at the end). For example,

```
String sentence;
sentence = SavitchIn.readLine();
```

reads in one line of input and places the string that is read into the variable `sentence`.

The class `SavitchIn` also has other methods, some of which are discussed in the next subsection.

The equal sign in a statement such as the second of the two that follow is the assignment operator:

```
int number;
number = SavitchIn.readLineInt();
```

As we pointed out earlier, you can combine a declaration of a variable and an assignment of a value to that variable into one longer statement. So the previous two lines of code can be expressed more compactly as

```
int number = SavitchIn.readLineInt();
```

Remember: `SavitchIn` Is Not Part of the Java Language

The class `SavitchIn` is not part of the Java language and does not come with the Java language. You must add the class yourself. This class was defined by the author for readers of this book. It is named `SavitchIn` to remind you that it was written by Savitch and is not part of the Java language. The class `SavitchIn` is given in Appendix 4, and a copy is provided on the CD that accompanies the book.

Why do we use the class `SavitchIn`? Why don't we simply use the classes provided with the Java language? Unfortunately, the Java language does not provide any classes for simple keyboard input. If you want to read simple input from the keyboard, you must add some class or classes that can do so.

Remember: Treat `SavitchIn.java` like Code That You Wrote

Since the class `SavitchIn` is not part of the Java language, you must treat it just like code that you yourself wrote. You must compile the class `SavitchIn.java`, and you (or some software that runs automatically) must link it with your program. If you obey the following rules, you should not have any problems with `SavitchIn`: Place a copy of `SavitchIn.java` in the same directory (the same folder) as your Java program, compile both `SavitchIn.java` and your program, and then run your program.

Quick Reference: Input Using `SavitchIn`

You use methods in the class `SavitchIn` to read values from the keyboard. When you invoke one of these methods, you use the class name `SavitchIn` as if it were the calling object. In other words, a typical method invocation has the form

Variable = `SavitchIn.`*Method_Name*`();`

Although there are other methods in `SavitchIn`, you should normally use the methods that include the word "`Line`." These methods each read a single value, such as a number, on a line by itself. The value may have whitespace before or after it, but other characters should not be on the line. (The method `readLineNonwhiteChar` is an exception and does allow nonwhitespace to follow the character that it reads.) There is a different method for each type of value you want to read from the keyboard. You need to use the method that matches the type of the value to be read, such as `int` for a whole number or `char` for a single character.

(The method invocation `SavitchIn.readLineInt()` returns an `int` value and can be used anyplace that an `int` value is allowed, such as in an arithmetic expression. The method invocation does not have to be used in a simple assignment statement as described shortly, but that is its most common usage. Similar remarks apply to the other methods, except that the type of the value returned is different for each method.)

Syntax:

Int_Variable = `SavitchIn.readLineInt();`
Long_Variable = `SavitchIn.readLineLong();`
Float_Variable = `SavitchIn.readLineFloat();`
Double_Variable = `SavitchIn.readLineDouble();`
Char_Variable = `SavitchIn.readLineNonwhiteChar();`
String_Variable = `SavitchIn.readLine();`

Example:

```
int count;
count = SavitchIn.readLineInt();
long bigOne;
bigOne = SavitchIn.readLineLong();
float increment;
increment = SavitchIn.readLineFloat();
double distance;
distance = SavitchIn.readLineDouble();
char letter;
letter = SavitchIn.readLineNonwhiteChar();
```

```
String wholeLine;
wholeLine = SavitchIn.readLine();
```

More Input Methods

All the methods in the class `SavitchIn` that begin with `readLine`, such as `readLine` and `readLineInt`, always read an entire line of text. That is why their names start with "read line." But sometimes you do not want to read a whole line. For example, let's say you are given the input

```
2 4 6
```

You might want to read these three numbers with three statements that put the numbers into three different variables. You can do this with the method `readInt`. For example, the following might appear in a program:

```
System.out.println("Enter 3 numbers on one line:");
int n1, n2, n3;
n1 = SavitchIn.readInt();
n2 = SavitchIn.readInt();
n3 = SavitchIn.readInt();
```

The user will be given the prompt

```
Enter 3 numbers on one line:
```

Suppose that, in response to the prompt, the user enters the following, all on one line, and then presses the Enter key:

```
2 4 6
```

The program will give `n1` the value 2, `n2` the value 4, and `n3` the value 6.

After an integer is read with `readInt`, the input continues on the same line (unless it happens to have reached the end of the line). For example, if the user enters

```
10 20 30
```

then the following code will set `n` equal to `10` and will set `theRest` equal to the string `"20 30"`:

```
int n;
n = SavitchIn.readInt();
String theRest;
theRest = SavitchIn.readLine();
```

Remember: Prompt for Input

Always prompt the user when your program needs the user to input some data, as in the following example:

```
System.out.println("Enter the number of trolls:");
int trolls = SavitchIn.readLineInt();
```

---

whitespace

Two other, similar methods in SavitchIn that read less than a whole line are readDouble and readNonwhiteChar. The only difference between these and readInt is that with readDouble, a value of type double is read, and with readNonwhiteChar, a nonwhitespace character is read. Recall that whitespace characters are blanks, tabs, and the new-line character. For the sort of simple things we will be doing, the only whitespace that will be relevant is the blank character.

The methods readInt, readDouble, and readNonwhiteChar each require that the input items be separated by one or more blank spaces. Moreover, these methods do not prompt the user if the input format is incorrect. When using these methods, you need to be certain that the input will be entered correctly the first time.

The last method from the class SavitchIn that we will consider here is readChar. The method readChar reads whatever single character is next in the input stream. For example, consider the following:

```
char c1, c2, c3;
c1 = SavitchIn.readChar();
c2 = SavitchIn.readChar();
c3 = SavitchIn.readChar();
```

If the user enters

```
a b c d e f g h i
```

where 'a' is the first thing on the line, then c1 will be set to the value 'a', c2 will have its value set to the blank character, and c3 will have its value set to 'b'. Any further reading would begin with the blank after the letter 'b'.

As indicated in the next Gotcha section, it is safer to use the methods that begin with readLine and that read a whole line, and to use the other methods sparingly and with caution.

▲ *Gotcha*
readInt and readDouble

The methods readLineInt and readLineDouble in the class SavitchIn will prompt the user to reenter the input if the user enters it in an incorrect format. The methods readInt and readDouble, on the other hand, have no such recovery mechanism. If the user enters the input in an incorrect format, the program will crash. For this reason, you should try to use the methods readLineInt and readLineDouble and avoid using the methods readInt and readDouble. The methods readInt and readDouble should be reserved for when you are certain the input will be in the correct format. For most of our applications, you cannot count on the user entering the input in the correct format.

The methods readChar and readNonwhiteChar also do no checking for the format of the input, but they are less dangerous, because they will process almost any kind of input the user enters. After all, any input consists of characters of some sort. Even the input 178, which might be considered an integer, can be processed as the three-character input '1', followed by '7', followed by '8'. △

FAQ: Why Aren't `readInt` and `readDouble` Better?

Why don't `readInt` and `readDouble` prompt the user to correctly reenter input that is incorrect? They could easily be written that way, but then they might confuse the user. The reason is that such prompts are likely to be in confusing places. The operating system always reads an entire line and then gives the entire line to Java. If the user enters four items, such as numbers, on a line, and there is a format mistake in the second item, the operating system will read the whole line before Java notices that something is wrong. So the prompt to reenter the input would come after the user entered the fourth item, not after the second one. It would be possible to design `readInt` and `readDouble` so that they prompted the user to reenter input correctly and in an understandable way, but it would be neither simple to write nor simple to understand. Moreover, many input methods in many languages behave like `readInt` and `readDouble`, so you should be made aware of such problems.

Programming Tip

Echo Input

echoing input

You should output all input, so that users can check whether they entered their input correctly. This practice is called **echoing the input.** For example, the following two statements from the program in Display 2.1 echo the two input values that were read into the variables `eggsPerBasket` and `numberOfBaskets`:

```
System.out.println(eggsPerBasket + " eggs per basket.");
System.out.println(numberOfBaskets + " baskets.");
```

It may seem that echoing input is not needed. After all, when the user enters input, it appears on the screen as it is entered. Why bother to write it to the screen a second time? There are several reasons for this. First, the input might be incorrect, even though it looks correct. For example, the user might type a comma instead of a decimal point or the letter "O" in place of a zero. Echoing the input will reveal such problems. Also, the echoed input gets the user's attention. Some users do not look at the screen as they type in input. In an ideal program, the user should even be given the opportunity to reenter the input if it is incorrect, but we don't have enough tools to do that yet. However, when something is wrong with the input, we do want the user to at least be aware that there is a problem.

? Self-Test Questions

25. Write Java statements that will cause the following to be written to the screen:

```
Once upon a time,
there were three little programmers.
```

26. What is the difference between `System.out.println` and `System.out.print`?

27. Write a Java statement that will set the value of the variable `number` equal to the number typed in at the keyboard. Assume that `number` is of type `int` and that the input is entered on a line by itself.

28. Write a Java statement that will set the value of the variable `amount` equal to the number typed in at the keyboard. Assume that `amount` is of type `double` and that the input is entered on a line by itself.

29. Write a Java statement that will set the value of the variable `answer` equal to the first nonwhitespace character typed in at the keyboard. The rest of the line of input is discarded. The variable `answer` is of type `char`.

30. What are the whitespace characters?

31. Is the class `SavitchIn` part of the Java language, or does the programmer have to define the class?

32. Write some Java code that will read a line of text and then output the line with all lowercase letters changed to uppercase.

2.4 DOCUMENTATION AND STYLE

"Don't stand there chattering to yourself like that," Humpty Dumpty said, looking at her for the first time, "but tell me your name and your business."
"My name is Alice, but—"
"It's a stupid name enough!" Humpty Dumpty interrupted impatiently. "What does it mean?"
"Must a name mean something?" Alice asked doubtfully.
"Of course it must," Humpty Dumpty said with a short laugh: "my name means the shape I am—and a good handsome shape it is too. With a name like yours, you might be any shape, almost."
-Lewis Carroll, *Through the Looking Glass*

A program that gives the correct output is not necessarily a good program. Obviously, you want your program to give the correct output, but that is not the whole story. Most programs are used many times and are changed at some point either to fix bugs or to accommodate new demands by the user. If the program is not easy to read and understand, it will not be easy to change, and it might even be impossible to change with any realistic effort. Even if the program is going to be used only once, you should pay some attention to readability. After all, you will have to read the program in order to debug it.

In this section, we discuss four techniques that can help make your program more readable: meaningful names, indenting, documentation, and defined constants.

Programming Tip

Use Meaningful Names for Variables

As we mentioned earlier, the names `x` and `y` are almost never good variable names. The name you give to a variable should be suggestive of what the variable is used for. If the variable holds a count of something, you might name it `count`. If the variable holds a tax rate, you might name it `taxRate`.

In addition to giving variables meaningful names and giving them names that the compiler will accept, you should choose names that follow the normal practice of programmers. That way, your code will be easier for others to read and to combine with their code, should you work on a project with more than one programmer. By convention, variable names are made up entirely of letters and digits. If the name consists of more than one word, "punctuate" it by using capital letters at the word boundaries, as in `taxRate`, `numberOfTries`, and `timeLeft`. Also, start each variable with a lowercase letter, as in the examples we just gave. The practice of starting with a lowercase letter may look strange at first, but it is a convention that is commonly used, and you quickly get used to it. We use names that start with an uppercase letter for something else, namely, for class names like `String` and `SavitchIn`. ○

Documentation and Comments

The documentation for a program tells what the program does and how it does it. The best programs are **self-documenting.** This means that, thanks to a very clean style and very well-chosen variable names (and other names), what the program does and how it does it will be obvious to any programmer who reads the program. You should strive for such self-documenting programs, but your programs may also need a bit of additional explanation to make them completely clear. This explanation can be given in the form of comments.

self-documenting

Remember: Write Self-Documenting Code

A **self-documenting** program (or other piece of code) is a program that uses well-chosen variable names (and other names) and has a style so clear that what the program does and how it does it will be obvious to any programmer who reads the program, even if the program has no comments. To the extent that it is possible, you should strive to make your programs self-documenting.

Comments are notes that you write into your program to help a person understand the program, but that are ignored by the compiler. In Java, there are two ways to insert comments. The first way is to use the two symbols // at the beginning of a comment. Everything after these symbols up to the end of the line is treated as a comment and is ignored by the compiler. This technique is handy for short comments, such as

// comments

```
String sentence; //Spanish version
```

If you want a comment of this form to span several lines, then each line must contain the symbols // at the beginning of the comment.

/* */ comments

The second kind of comment can more easily span multiple lines. Anything written between the matching symbol pairs /* and */ is a comment and is ignored by the compiler. For example,

```
/*
 This program should only
 be used on alternate Thursdays,
 except during leap years when it should
 only be used on alternate Tuesdays.
*/
```

This is not a very likely comment, but it does illustrate the use of /* and */.

Many text editors automatically highlight comments by showing them in a special color. In this book, we will also write comments in a different color, as illustrated by the following comment:

```
/**
 This program should only
 be used on alternate Thursdays,
 except during leap years when it should
 only be used on alternate Tuesdays.
*/
```

Notice that this comment uses two asterisks rather than one in the opening /**. This is not required to make it a comment, but it will be needed when we use a program named javadoc that automatically extracts documentation from Java software. We will discuss javadoc later in this book, but we will start using the double asterisks now.

It is difficult to explain just when you should and when you should not insert a comment. Too many comments can be as bad as too few comments. With too many comments, the really important information can be lost in a sea of comments that just state the obvious. As we show you more Java features, we will mention likely places for comments. For now, you should normally need only two kinds of comments.

First, every program file should have an explanatory comment at the beginning of the file. This comment should give all the important information about the file: what the program does, the name of the author, how to contact the author, the date the file was last changed, and, in a course, what the assignment is. This comment should be similar to the one shown at the top of Display 2.10.

The second kind of comment you need is one to explain any nonobvious details. For example, look at the program in Display 2.10. Note the two variables named `radius` and `area`. It is obvious that these two variables will hold the values for the radius and area of a circle, respectively. It would be a mistake to include comments like the following:

```
double radius; //holds the radius of a circle.
```

However, there is something that is not obvious. What units are used for the radius? Inches? Feet? Meters? Centimeters? You should add a comment that explains the units used, as follows:

```
double radius; //in inches
double area; //in square inches
```

These two comments are also shown in Display 2.10.

Indenting

A program has a lot of structure. There are smaller parts within larger parts. For example, there is the part that starts with

```
public static void main(String[] args)
{
```

indenting

This part ends with a closing brace, }. Within the part, there are statements, such as assignment statements and `System.out.println` statements. In a simple program of the kind we have seen thus far, there are basically three levels of nested structure, as indicated by the vertical lines in Display 2.10. Each level of nesting should be indented to show the nesting more clearly. The outermost structure is not indented at all. The next level of nested structure is indented. The nested structure within that is double indented.

DISPLAY 2.10 Comments and Indenting

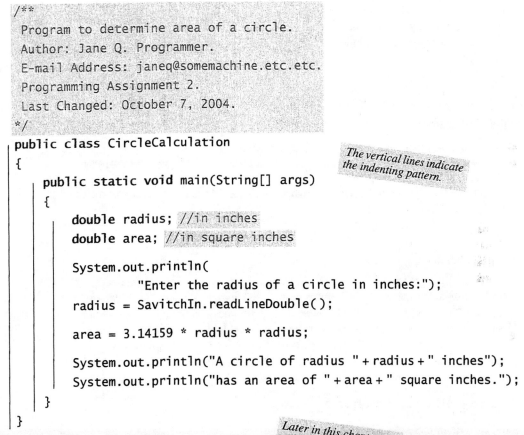

```
/**
 Program to determine area of a circle.
 Author: Jane Q. Programmer.
 E-mail Address: janeq@somemachine.etc.etc.
 Programming Assignment 2.
 Last Changed: October 7, 2004.
*/
public class CircleCalculation
{
    public static void main(String[] args)
    {
        double radius; //in inches
        double area; //in square inches

        System.out.println(
                 "Enter the radius of a circle in inches:");
        radius = SavitchIn.readLineDouble();

        area = 3.14159 * radius * radius;

        System.out.println("A circle of radius " + radius + " inches");
        System.out.println("has an area of " + area + " square inches.");
    }
}
```

The vertical lines indicate the indenting pattern.

Later in this chapter, we will give an improved version of this program.

Sample Screen Dialog

```
Enter the radius of a circle in inches:
2.5
A circle of radius 2.5 inches
has an area of 19.6349375 square inches.
```

These levels of nesting are frequently indicated by braces, { }, but regardless of whether there are any braces, you should still indent each level of nesting.

If a statement does not fit on one line, you can write it on two or more lines. However, when you write a single statement on more than one line, indent the second and all subsequent lines more than the first line.

We prefer to indent by four spaces for each level of indenting. Indenting more than that leaves too little room on the line for the statement itself, whereas a smaller indent just does not show up well. Indenting two or three spaces is not unreasonable, but we find four spaces to be the clearest. If you are in a course, follow the rules on indenting given by your instructor. On a programming project, there is likely to be a style sheet that dictates the number of spaces you should indent. In any event, you should indent consistently within any one program.

Quick Reference: **Java Comments**

There are two ways to add comments to a Java program (or piece of Java code):

1. **Everything after the two symbols // to the end of the line is a comment and is ignored by the compiler.**
2. **Anything written between the matching symbols pairs /* and */ is a comment and is ignored by the compiler.**

Named Constants

Look again at the program in Display 2.10. You probably recognize the number `3.14159` as the approximate value of pi, the number that is used in many calculations involving a circle and that is often written as π. However, you might not be sure that `3.14159` is pi and not some other number, and somebody other than you might have no idea as to where the number `3.14159` came from. To avoid such confusion, you should always give a name to constants such as `3.14159` and use the name instead of writing out the number. For example, you might give the number `3.14159` the name `PI`. Then the assignment statement

```
area = 3.14159 * radius * radius;
```

could be written more clearly as

```
area = PI * radius * radius;
```

How do you give a number, or other constant, a name like `PI`? You could use a variable named `PI` and initialize it to the desired value, like `3.14159`. But you might then inadvertently change the value of this variable. Java provides a mechanism that allows you to define and initialize a variable and moreover fix the variable's value so that it cannot be changed. The syntax is

`public static final` *Type Variable* = *Constant*;

For example, we can give the name `PI` to the constant `3.14159` as follows:

```
public static final double PI = 3.14159;
```

You can simply take this as a long, peculiarly worded way of giving a name (like PI) to a constant (like 3.14159), but we can explain most of what is on this line. The part

```
double PI = 3.14159;
```

simply declares PI as a variable and initializes it to 3.14159. The words that precede this modify the variable PI in various ways. The word public says that there are no restrictions on where you can use the name PI. The word static will have to wait until Chapter 5 for an explanation; for now, just be sure to include it. The word final means that the value 3.14159 is the final value assigned to PI or, to phrase it another way, that the program is not allowed to change the value of PI.

Quick Reference: **Naming Constants**

To define a name for a constant, such as a number, place the keywords public static final in front of a variable declaration that includes the constant as the initializing value. Place this declaration within the class definition, but outside of the main method and outside of any other method definitions. (See Display 2.11 for a complete example.)

Syntax:

public static final *Type Variable* = *Constant*;

Example:

```
public static final int MAX_STRIKES = 3;
public static final double MORTGAGE_INTEREST_RATE = 6.99;
public static final String MOTTO = "The customer is right!";
public static final char SCALE = 'K';
```

Although it is not required, it is the normal practice of programmers to spell named constants with all uppercase letters.

In Display 2.11, we have rewritten the program from Display 2.11 so that it uses the name PI as a defined name for the constant 3.14159. Note that the definition of PI is placed outside of the main part of the program. As indicated there, defined names for constants need not be near the beginning of a file, but it is a good practice to place them there. That way, they will be handy if you need to change the definition of a named constant. You are not likely to want to change the definition of the named constant PI, but you may want to change the definition of some other named constant in some other program. For example, suppose you have a banking program that contains the defined constant

```
public static final double MORTGAGE_INTEREST_RATE = 6.99;
```

and suppose the interest rate changes to 8.5 percent. You can simply change the defined constant to

```
public static final double MORTGAGE_INTEREST_RATE = 8.5;
```

You would then need to recompile your program, but you need not change anything else in it.

DISPLAY 2.11 Naming a Constant

```
/**
 Program to determine area of a circle.
 Author: Jane Q. Programmer.
 E-mail Address: janeq@somemachine.etc.etc.
 Assignment Number: 2.
 Last Changed: October 7, 2001.
*/
public class CircleCalculation2
{
    public static final double PI = 3.14159;

    public static void main(String[] args)
    {
        double radius; //in inches
        double area; //in square inches

        System.out.println(
                   "Enter the radius of a circle in inches:");
        radius = SavitchIn.readLineDouble();

        area = PI * radius * radius;

        System.out.println("A circle of radius "
                                   + radius + " inches");
        System.out.println("has an area of "
                                   + area + " square inches.");
    }

}
```

Although it would not be as clear, it is legal to place the definition of PI here instead.

Sample Screen Dialog

```
Enter the radius of a circle in inches:
2.5
A circle of radius 2.5 inches
has an area of 19.6349375 square inches.
```

Note that a defined constant, like MORTGAGE_INTEREST_RATE, can save you a lot of work if the constant ever needs to be changed. In order to change the mortgage interest rate from 6.99 percent to 8.5 percent, you need to change only one number. If the program did not use a defined constant, you would have to look for every occurrence of 6.99 and change it to 8.5. Moreover, even this might not be right. If some occurrences of 6.99 represented the mortgage interest rate and some of the numbers 6.99 represented another kind of interest, you would have to decide just what each 6.99 means. That would surely produce confusion and probably introduce errors.

Notice that we are spelling named constants using all uppercase letters (with the underscore symbol _ used for "punctuation"), as in the named constants PI and MORTGAGE_INTEREST_RATE. This is not required by the definition of the Java language. However, it is a custom that is almost universally followed and one that it would pay for you to adopt. Your programs will be easier to read if you can readily identify variables, constants, and so forth.

? Self-Test Questions

33. What are the two kinds of comments in Java?

34. What is the output produced by the following Java code:

```
/**
 Code for Exercise.
*/
System.out.println("One");
//System.out.println("Two");
System.out.println("And hit it!");
```

35. Although it is kind of silly, state legislatures have been known to pass laws that "change" the value of pi. Suppose you live in a state where, by law, the value of pi is exactly 3.14. How must you change the program in Display 2.11 to make it comply with the law?

36. What is the normal spelling convention for named constants?

CHAPTER SUMMARY

- A variable can be used to hold values, such as numbers. The type of the variable must match the type of the value stored in the variable.
- Variables (and all other items in a program) should be given names that indicate how the variable is used.
- All variables should be initialized before the program uses their values.
- Parentheses in arithmetic expressions indicate the order in which the operations are performed.

- The methods in the class `SavitchIn` can be used to read keyboard input. The class `SavitchIn` is not part of the Java language, so you must have a copy of `Savitch-In` in order to use it.
- Your program should output a prompt line when the user is expected to enter data from the keyboard.
- You can have variables and constants of type `String`. `String` is a class type that behaves very much like a primitive type.
- You can use the plus sign to concatenate two strings.
- There are methods in the class `String` that can be used for string processing.
- You should define names for number constants in a program and use these names rather than writing out the numbers within your program.
- Programs should be self-documenting to the extent possible. However, you should also insert comments to explain any unclear points.

✔ Answers to Self-Test Questions

1. The following are all legal variable names:

```
rate1, TimeLimit, numberOfWindows
```

   `TimeLimit` is a poor choice, however, since it violates the normal convention that variables should start with a lowercase letter. A better choice would be `timeLimit`.

   `1stPlayer` is illegal because it starts with a digit. `myprogram.java` is illegal because it contains an illegal character, the dot. Finally, `long` is illegal as a variable because it is a keyword.

2. Yes, a Java program can have two different variables with the names `aVariable` and `avariable`, since they use different capitalization and so are different identifiers in Java. However, it is not a good idea to use identifiers that differ only in the way they are capitalized.
3. `int count = 0;`
4. `double rate = 0.0, time = 0.0;`
   The following is also correct, because Java will automatically convert the `int` value `0` to the `double` value `0.0`:

```
double rate = 0, time = 0;
```

5.

```
int miles = 0;
double flowRate = 50.56;
```

6. `interest = 0.05 * balance;`

The following is also correct:

```
interest = balance * 0.05;
```

7. `interest = balance * rate;`
8. `count = count + 3;`
9.

```
b
c
c
```

The last output is `c`, because the last assignment, `a = b;`, has no quotes: This last assignment sets the variable `a` equal to the value of the variable `b`, which is `'c'`.

10.

```
(int)symbol - (int)'0'
```

To see that this works, note that it works for `'0'`, and then see that it works for `'1'`, and then `'2'`, and so forth. You can use an actual number in place of `(int)'0'`, but `(int)'0'` is a bit easier to understand.

11. `result is 30`
12.

```
quotient = 2
remainder = 1
```

13. `(1/2) * 2 is equal to 0.0`
This is because `1/2` is integer division, which discards the part after the decimal point and produces `0` instead of `0.5`.
14. The dialog would change to the following:

```
Enter a whole number from 1 to 99
I will output a combination of coins
that equals that amount of change.
87
2 cents in coins can be given as:
3 quarters
1 dimes
0 nickels and
2 pennies
```

15. `result is 5`
16.

```
n == 3
n == 2
```

17. `How do you doSeven of Nine.`
Note that there is no space in `doSeven`.

18.

```
7
b
```

19. `defg`

20.

```
abc
def
```

21. `abc\ndef`

22. `HELLO JOHN`

23. `End`

    Note that the strings are not equal.

24.

```
Equal
End
```

25.

```
System.out.println("Once upon a time,");
System.out.println("there were three little programmers.");
```

Since we did not specify where the next output goes, the following is also correct:

```
System.out.println("Once upon a time,");
System.out.print("there were three little programmers.");
```

26. With `System.out.println`, the next output goes on the next line. (By the next output, we mean the output that is produced by the first output statement after the `System.out.println` under discussion.) With `System.out.print`, the next output goes on the same line.

27. `number = SavitchIn.readLineInt();`

28. `amount = SavitchIn.readLineDouble();`

29. `answer = SavitchIn.readLineNonwhiteChar();`

30. The whitespace characters are the blank symbol, the tab symbol, and the new-line symbol, `'\n'`. At this point you are likely to be concerned mostly with the blank symbol when discussing whitespace characters.

31. The class `SavitchIn` is not part of the Java language. The programmer (like you) is supposed to define the class `SavitchIn`. To get you started, we have defined it for you, but think of it as a class that you have defined.

32.

```
String line;
System.out.println("Enter a line of input:");
line = SavitchIn.readLine();
line = line.toUpperCase();
System.out.println("With all uppercase, that is:");
System.out.println(line);
```

33. The two kinds of comments are // comments and /* */ comments. Everything following a // on the same line is a comment. Everything between a /* and a matching */ is a comment.

34.

```
One
And hit it!
```

35. Change the line

```
public static final double PI = 3.14159;
```

to

```
public static final double PI = 3.14;
```

Since values of type `double` are stored with only a limited amount of accuracy, you could argue that this is not "exactly" 3.14, but any legislator who is stupid enough to legislate the value of pi is unlikely to be aware of this subtlety.

36. The normal practice of programmers is to spell named constants with all uppercase letters, with the underscore symbol used to separate words.

Programming Projects

1. Write a program that reads in three whole numbers and outputs the average of the three numbers.
2. Write a program that reads in the amount of a monthly mortgage payment and the outstanding balance (i.e., the amount still owed) and then outputs the amount of the payment that goes to interest and the amount that goes to principal (i.e., the amount that goes to reducing the debt). Assume that the annual interest rate is 7.49 percent. Use a defined constant for the interest rate. Note that payments are made monthly, so the interest is only one-twelfth of the annual interest of 7.49 percent.
3. Write a program that reads in a four-digit number (such as `1998`) and outputs the number, one digit per line, like so:

```
1
9
9
8
```

Your prompt should tell the user to enter a four-digit number and can then assume that the user follows directions. Your program will not read the number as a value of type `int`, but as four characters of type `char`.

4. Write a program that reads in a line of text and then outputs the line with the first occurrence of `"hate"` changed to `"love"`. For example, a possible sample dialog might be

```
Enter a line of text.
I hate you.
I have rephrased that line to read:
I love you.
```

You can assume that the word `"hate"` occurs in the input. If the word `"hate"` occurs more than once in the line, your program will replace only the first occurrence of `"hate"`.

5. Write a program that will read a line of text as input and then output the line with the first word moved to the end of the line. For example, a possible sample dialog might be

```
Enter a line of text. No punctuation please.
Java is the language
I have rephrased that line to read:
Is the language Java
```

Assume that there is no space before the first word and that the end of the first word is indicated by a blank (not by a comma or other punctuation).

6. Write a program that will print out statistics for eight coin tosses. The user will input either an `'h'` for heads or a `'t'` for tails for the eight tosses. The program will then print out the total number and percentages of heads and tails. Use the increment operator to count each `'h'` and `'t'` that is input. For example, a possible sample dialog might be

```
For each coin toss enter either 'h' for heads
or 't' for tails.

First toss: h
Second toss: t
Third toss: t
Fourth toss: h
Fifth toss: t
Sixth toss: h
Seventh toss: t
Eighth toss: t

Number of heads: 3
Number of tails: 5
Percent heads: 37.5
Percent tails: 62.5
```

7. Write a program that asks the user to enter the first name of a friend or relative, a favorite color, a favorite food, and a favorite animal and then prints the following two lines, with the user's input replacing the items in italics:

`I had a dream that` *Name* `ate a` *Color Animal*
`and said it tasted like` *Food*`!`

For example, if the user entered `Jake` for the person's name, `blue` for the color, `hamburger` for the food, and `dog` for the animal, the output would be

```
I had a dream that Jake ate a blue dog
and said it tasted like hamburger!
```

Don't forget to put the exclamation mark at the end.

8. Write a program that converts degrees Celsius to Fahrenheit, using the formula

DegreesC = 5(*DegreesF* − 32)/9

Prompt the user to enter a temperature in degrees Fahrenheit (just a whole number of degrees, without a fractional part), and then let the program print out the equivalent Celsius temperature, including the fractional part to at least one decimal point. A possible dialog might be

```
Enter a temperature in degrees Fahrenheit: 72
72 degrees Fahrenheit = 22.2 degrees Celsius.
```

9. Write a program that determines the change to be dispensed from a vending machine. An item in the machine can cost between 25 cents and a dollar, in 5-cent increments (25, 30, 35, . . ., 90, 95, or 100), and the machine accepts only a single dollar bill to pay for the item. For example, a possible sample dialog might be

```
Enter price of item
(from 25 cents to a dollar, in 5-cent increments): 45

You bought an item for 45 cents and gave me a dollar,
so your change is
2 quarters,
0 dimes, and
1 nickel.
```

Chapter 3

Flow of Control

Flow of Control

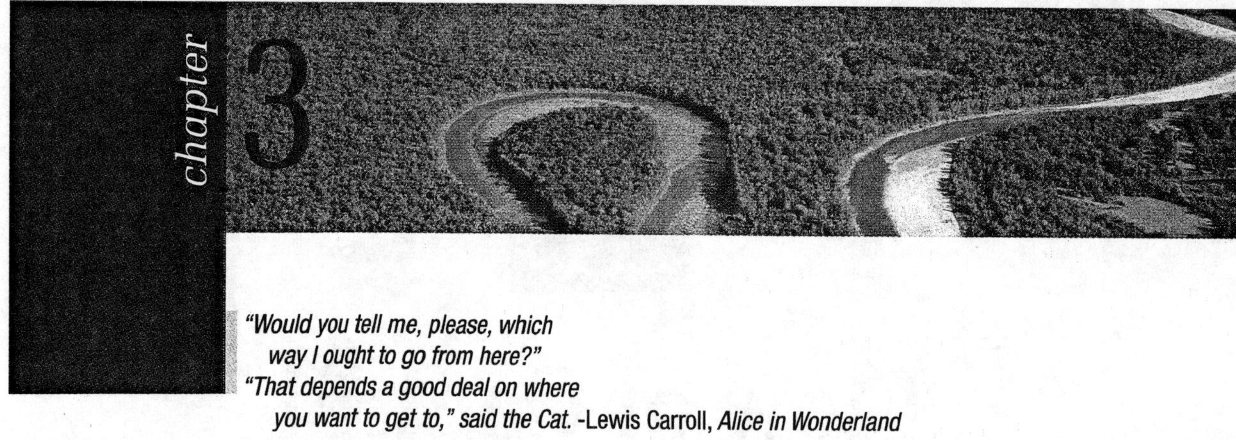

"Would you tell me, please, which way I ought to go from here?"
"That depends a good deal on where you want to get to," said the Cat. -Lewis Carroll, *Alice in Wonderland*

flow of control

Flow of control is the order in which a program performs actions. Until this chapter, that order has been simple. Actions were taken in the order in which they were written down. In this chapter, we show you how to write programs with a more complicated flow of control. Java, and most other programming languages, uses two kinds of statements to regulate flow of control: A **branching statement** chooses one action from a list of two or more possible actions. A **loop statement** repeats an action again and again until some stopping condition is met.

branching statement

loop statement

OBJECTIVES

Learn about Java branching statements.

Learn about loops.

Learn about the type `boolean`.

PREREQUISITES

You need to be familiar with all the material in Chapter 2 before reading this chapter.

3.1 BRANCHING STATEMENTS

When you come to a fork in the road, take it. -Attributed to Yogi Berra

We begin our discussion of branching with a kind of Java statement that chooses between two possible alternative actions.

The `if-else` Statement

In programs, as in everyday life, things can sometimes go in one of two different ways. With some checking accounts, if you have money in your checking account, the bank will pay you a little interest. On the other hand, if you have overdrawn your checking account so your account balance is negative, you will be charged a penalty that will make your balance more negative than it already is. This might be reflected in the bank's accounting program by the following Java statement, known as an `if-else` statement:

`if-else`

```
if (balance >= 0)
    balance = balance + (INTEREST_RATE * balance)/12;
else
    balance = balance - OVERDRAWN_PENALTY;
```

The pair of symbols >= is used to mean greater-than-or-equal-to in Java, because the symbol ≥ is not on the keyboard.

The meaning of an `if-else` Statement is really just the meaning it would have if read as an English sentence. When your program executes an `if-else` statement, it first checks the expression in parentheses after the `if`. This expression must be something that is either true or false. If it is true, the statement before the `else` is executed. If the expression is false, the statement after the `else` is executed. In the preceding example, if `balance` is positive (or zero), then the following action is taken (the division by 12 is because this is for only 1 of 12 months):

```
balance = balance + (INTEREST_RATE * balance)/12;
```

On the other hand, if the value of `balance` is negative, the following is done instead:

```
balance = balance – OVERDRAWN_PENALTY;
```

Display 3.1 shows this `if-else` statement in a complete program.

DISPLAY 3.1 A Program Using `if-else` *(Part 1 of 2)*

```
public class BankBalance
{
    public static final double OVERDRAWN_PENALTY = 8.00;
    public static final double INTEREST_RATE = 0.02;//2% annually

    public static void main(String[] args)
    {
        double balance;

        System.out.print("Enter your checking account balance: $");
        balance = SavitchIn.readLineDouble();
        System.out.println("Original balance $" + balance);

        if (balance >= 0)
            balance = balance + (INTEREST_RATE * balance)/12;
        else
            balance = balance - OVERDRAWN_PENALTY;

        System.out.println("After adjusting for one month");
        System.out.println("of interest and penalties,");
        System.out.println("your new balance is $" + balance);
    }
}
```

DISPLAY 3.1 A Program Using `if-else` *(Part 2 of 2)*

Sample Screen Dialog 1

```
Enter your checking account balance: $505.67
Original balance $505.67
After adjusting for one month
of interest and penalties,
your new balance is $506.51278
```

Sample Screen Dialog 2

```
Enter your checking account balance: $-15.53
Original balance $-15.53
After adjusting for one month
of interest and penalties,
your new balance is $-23.53
```

If you want to include more than one statement in each branch, simply enclose the statements in braces, as in the following example:

```
if (balance >= 0)
{
    System.out.println("Good for you. You earned interest.");
    balance = balance + (INTEREST_RATE * balance)/12;
}
else
{
    System.out.println("You will be charged a penalty.");
    balance = balance - OVERDRAWN_PENALTY;
}
```

`else` is optional

If you omit the `else` part, then nothing happens when the expression after the `if` is false. For example, if your bank does not charge any overdraft penalty, then the statement in its program would be like the following:

```
if (balance >= 0)
{
    System.out.println("Good for you. You earned interest.");
    balance = balance + (INTEREST_RATE * balance)/12;
}
```

To see how this statement works, let's give it a little more context by adding some additional statements, as shown on the next page:

Quick Reference: `if-else` Statements

The *Boolean_Expression* referred to in the following is an expression that is either true or false, such as `balance <= 0`.

Syntax: (Basic Form)

```
if (Boolean_Expression)
    Statement_1
else
    Statement_2
```

If the *Boolean_Expression* is true, then *Statement_1* is executed; otherwise, *Statement_2* is executed.

Example:

```
if (time < limit)
    System.out.println("You made it.");
else
    System.out.println("You missed the deadline.");
```

Syntax: (Omitting the `else` Part)

```
if (Boolean_Expression)
    Action_Statement
```

If the *Boolean_Expression* is true, then the *Action_Statement* is executed; otherwise, nothing happens and the program goes on to the next statement.

Example:

```
if (weight > ideal)
    calorieAllotment = calorieAllotment - 500;
```

Multiple Statement Alternatives:

If you want to include several statements as an alternative, group them using braces, as in the following example:

```
if (balance >= 0)
{
    System.out.println("Good for you. You earned interest.");
    balance = balance + (INTEREST_RATE * balance)/12;
}
else
{
    System.out.println("You will be charged a penalty.");
    balance = balance - OVERDRAWN_PENALTY;
}
```

```
System.out.print("Enter your balance $");
balance = SavitchIn.readLineDouble( );
if (balance >= 0)
{
    System.out.println("Good for you. You earned interest.");
    balance = balance + (INTEREST_RATE * balance)/12;
}
System.out.println("Your new balance is $" + balance);
```

Now suppose that your checking account balance is $100.00. The dialog would then be

```
Enter your balance $100.00
Good for you. You earned interest.
Your new balance is $100.16
```

The expression after the `if` is true, so you earn a little interest. (We are using an interest rate of 2 percent per year, as in Display 3.1, but all you need to note is that some interest was added. The exact amount is irrelevant to this example.)

Next, suppose that your balance is $–50.00 (that is, minus 50 dollars). The dialog would then be as follows:

```
Enter your balance $-50.00
Your new balance is $-50.00
```

In this case, the expression after the `if` is false and there is no `else` part, so nothing happens—the balance is not changed, and the program simply goes on to the next statement, which is an output statement.

Introduction to Boolean Expressions

boolean expression

A **boolean expression** is simply an expression that is either true or false. The name *boolean* is derived from George Boole, a 19th-century English logician and mathematician whose work was related to these kinds of expressions.

We have already been using simple boolean expressions in `if-else` statements. The simplest boolean expressions are comparisons of two expressions, such as

```
time < limit
```

and

```
balance <= 0
```

Note that a boolean expression need not be enclosed in parentheses to qualify as a boolean expression. However, a boolean expression does need to be enclosed in parentheses when it is used in an `if-else` statement,

Display 3.2 shows the various Java comparison operators you can use to compare two expressions.

&& for "and"

You can form more-complicated boolean expressions from simpler ones, by joining the expression with the Java version of "and." The Java version of "and" is spelled &&. For example, consider the following:

```
if ((pressure > min) && (pressure < max))
    System.out.println("Pressure is OK.");
else
    System.out.println("Warning: Pressure is out of range.");
```

DISPLAY 3.2 Java Comparison Operators

Math Notation	Name	Java Notation	Java Examples
$=$	Equal to	`==`	`balance == 0` `answer == 'y'`
$\neq$	Not equal to	`!=`	`income != tax` `answer != 'y'`
$>$	Greater than	`>`	`expenses > income`
$\geq$	Greater than or equal to	`>=`	`points >= 60`
$<$	Less than	`<`	`pressure < max`
$\leq$	Less than or equal to	`<=`	`expenses <= income`

If the value of `pressure` is greater than `min` *and* the value of `pressure` is less than `max`, then the output will be

```
Pressure is OK.
```

Otherwise, the output is

```
Warning: Pressure is out of range.
```

Note that you *cannot* use a string of inequalities in Java, like the following

```
min < pressure < max
```

Instead, you must express each inequality separately and connect them with &&, as follows:

```
(pressure > min) && (pressure < max)
```

When you form a larger boolean expression by connecting two smaller expressions with &&, the entire larger expression is true provided that both of the smaller expressions are true. If at least one of the smaller expressions is false, then the larger expression is false. For example,

```
(pressure > min) && (pressure < max)
```

is true provided that both `(pressure > min)` and `(pressure < max)` are true; otherwise, the expression is false.

Remember: Use && for "and"

The symbol pair && means "and" in Java. Using &&, you can form a larger boolean expression out of two smaller boolean expressions.

Syntax:

(*Sub_Expression_1*) && (*Sub_Expression_2*)

Example:

```
if ((pressure > min) && (pressure < max))
    System.out.println("Pressure is OK.");
else
    System.out.println("Warning: Pressure is out of range.");
```

|| for "or"

The Java way of expressing "or" is `||`, which you create by typing two vertical lines. (The symbol | prints with a break in the line on some systems.) You can form a larger boolean expression from smaller ones by using `||`. The meaning is essentially the same as the English word "or." For example, consider

```
if ((salary > expenses) || (savings > expenses))
    System.out.println("Solvent");
else
    System.out.println("Bankrupt");
```

If the value of `salary` is greater than the value of `expenses` *or* the value of `savings` is greater than the value of `expenses` (or both), then the output will be `Solvent`; otherwise, the output will be `Bankrupt`.

Remember: Use || for "or"

The symbol pair `||` means "or" in Java. Using `||`, you can form a larger boolean expression out of two smaller boolean expressions.

Syntax:

(*Sub_Expression_1*) `||` (*Sub_Expression_2*)

Example:

```
if ((salary > expenses) || (savings > expenses))
    System.out.println("Solvent");
else
    System.out.println("Bankrupt");
```

---

parentheses

As we noted earlier, the boolean expression in an `if-else` statement must be enclosed in parentheses. An `if-else` statement that uses the && operator is normally parenthesized as follows:

```
if ((pressure > min) && (pressure < max))
    System.out.println("Pressure is OK.");
else
    System.out.println("Warning: Pressure is out of range.");
```

The parentheses in `(pressure > min)` and the parentheses in `(pressure < max)` are not required, but we will normally include them to aid readability.

Parentheses are used in expressions containing `||` in the same way that they are used with &&.

In Java, you can negate a boolean expression with `!`. For example,

```
if (!(number >= min))
    System.out.println("Too small");
else
    System.out.println("OK");
```

This will output `Too Small` if `number` is not greater than or equal to `min`, and `OK` otherwise.

You normally can, and should, avoid using `!`. For example, the previous `if-else` statement is equivalent to

```
if (number < min)
    System.out.println("Too small");
else
    System.out.println("OK");
```

If you avoid using `!`, your programs will be easier to understand.

▲ *Gotcha*
Using == with Strings

Although == correctly tests two values of a primitive type, such as two numbers, to see if they are equal, it has a different meaning when applied to objects.[1] Recall that an object is something that is a member of a class, such as a string. All strings are in the class `String`, so == applied to two strings does not test to see whether the strings are equal. To test two strings (or any two objects) to see if they have equal values, you should use the method `equals` rather than ==.

The program in Display 3.3 illustrates the use of the method `equals` as well as the `String` method `equalsIgnoreCase`. The notation may seem a bit awkward at first, because it is not symmetric between the two things being tested for equality. The two expressions

```
s1.equals(s2)
s2.equals(s1)
```

are equivalent.

The method `equalsIgnoreCase` behaves similarly to `equals`, except that with `equalsIgnoreCase` the uppercase and lowercase versions of the same letter are considered the same. For example, `"Hello"` and `"hello"` are not equal because their first characters, `'H'` and `'h'`, are different characters. But they would be considered equal by the method `equalsIgnoreCase`. For example, the following will output `Equal`:

```
if ("Hello".equalsIgnoreCase("hello"))
    System.out.println("Equal");
```

Notice that it is perfectly valid to use a quoted string with a `String` method, as in the preceding use of `equalsIgnoreCase`. A quoted string is an object of type `String` and has all the methods that any other object of type `String` has.

For the kinds of applications we are looking at in this chapter, you could also use == to test for equality of objects of type `String`, and it would deliver the correct answer. However, there are situations in which == does not correctly test strings for equality, so you should get in the habit of using `equals` rather than == to test strings. △

---

1. When applied to two strings (or any two objects), == tests to see if they are stored in the same memory location, but we will not discuss that until Chapter 4. For now, we need only note that == does something other than test for the equality of two strings.

DISPLAY 3.3 Testing Strings for Equality

```
public class StringEqualityDemo
{
    public static void main(String[] args)
    {
        String s1, s2;

        System.out.println("Enter two lines of text:");
        s1 = SavitchIn.readLine();
        s2 = SavitchIn.readLine();

        if (s1.equals(s2))
            System.out.println("The two lines are equal.");
        else
            System.out.println("The two lines are not equal.");

        if (s2.equals(s1))
            System.out.println("The two lines are equal.");
        else
            System.out.println("The two lines are not equal.");

        if (s1.equalsIgnoreCase(s2))
            System.out.println(
                        "But the lines are equal, ignoring case.");
        else
            System.out.println(
                        "Lines are not equal, even ignoring case.");
    }
}
```

These two invocations of the method `equals` *are equivalent.*

Sample Screen Dialog

```
Enter two lines of text:
Java is not coffee.
Java is NOT COFFEE.
The two lines are not equal.
The two lines are not equal.
But the lines are equal, ignoring case.
```

Remember: The Methods equals and equalsIgnoreCase

When testing strings for equality, do not use ==. Instead, use either equals or equalsIgnoreCase.

Syntax:

String.equals(*Other_String*)
String.equalsIgnoreCase(*Other_String*)

Example:

```
String s1;
s1 = SavitchIn.readLine();
if ( s1.equals("Hello") )
    System.out.println("The string is Hello.");

else
    System.out.println("The string is not Hello.");
```

Programming Tip

Alphabetical Order

Programs frequently need to compare two strings to determine which is alphabetically before the other. There is no built-in Java comparison operator for alphabetic order, but it is easy to test for alphabetic order using the two String methods, compareTo and toUpperCase, which we described in Display 2.6.

lexicographic ordering

The method compareTo will test two strings to determine their lexicographic order. **Lexicographic ordering** is similar to alphabetic ordering and is sometimes, but not always, the same as alphabetic ordering. The easiest way to think about lexicographic ordering is to think of it as being the same as alphabetic ordering *but with the alphabet ordered differently*. Specifically, in lexicographic ordering, the letters and other characters are ordered as in the ASCII ordering, which is shown in Appendix 3. If you look at that appendix, you will see that *all* uppercase letters come before *all* lowercase letters. For example, 'Z' comes before 'a' in lexicographic order. So when comparing two strings consisting of a mix of lowercase and uppercase letters, lexicographic and alphabetic ordering are not the same. However, as shown in Appendix 3, all the lowercase letters are in alphabetic order. So for any two strings of all lowercase letters, lexicographic order is the same as ordinary alphabetic order. Similarly, in the ordering of Appendix 3, all the uppercase letters are in alphabetic order. So for any two strings of all uppercase letters, lexicographic order is the same as ordinary alphabetic order. Thus, to compare two strings of letters for (ordinary) alphabetic order, you need only convert the two strings to all uppercase letters (or to all lowercase letters) and then compare them for lexicographic ordering. Let's look at the Java details.

If s1 and s2 are two variables of type String that have been given String values, then

```
s1.compareTo(s2)
```

returns a negative number if s1 comes before s2 in lexicographic ordering, returns zero if the two strings are equal, and returns a positive number if s2 comes before s1. Thus,

```
s1.compareTo(s2) < 0
```

returns true if s1 comes before s2 in lexicographic order and returns false otherwise. For example, the following will produce correct output:

```
if (s1.compareTo(s2) < 0)
    System.out.println(
        s1 + " precedes " + s2 + " in lexicographic ordering");
else if (s1.compareTo(s2) > 0)
    System.out.println(
        s1 + " follows " + s2 + " in lexicographic ordering");
else //s1.compareTo(s2) == 0
    System.out.println(s1 + " equals " + s2);
```

As we mentioned previously, one way to test two strings for alphabetic ordering is to convert them each to all uppercase letters and then use compareTo to test the uppercase versions of s1 and s2 for lexicographic ordering. Thus, the following will produce correct output:

```
String upperS1 = s1.toUpperCase();
String upperS2 = s2.toUpperCase();
if (upperS1.compareTo(upperS2) < 0)
    System.out.println(
        s1 + " precedes " + s2 + " in ALPHABETIC ordering");
else if (upperS1.compareTo(upperS2) > 0)
    System.out.println(
        s1 + " follows " + s2 + " in ALPHABETIC ordering");
else //s1.compareTo(s2) == 0
    System.out.println(s1 + " equals " + s2 + " IGNORING CASE");
```

The preceding code will compile and produce results no matter what characters are in the strings s1 and s2. However, alphabetic order makes sense, and the output makes sense, only if the two strings consist entirely of letters. ○

? Self-Test Questions

1. Suppose goals is a variable of type int. Write an if-else statement that outputs the word Wow if the value of the variable goals is greater than 10 and outputs the words Oh Well if the value of goals is at most 10.
2. Suppose goals and errors are variables of type int. Write an if-else statement that outputs the word Wow if the value of the variable goals is greater than 10 and the value of errors is zero. Otherwise, the if-else statement outputs the words Oh Well.

3. Suppose salary and deductions are variables of type double that have been given values. Write an if-else statement that outputs OK and sets the variable net equal to salary minus deductions, provided that salary is at least as large as deductions. If, however, salary is less than deductions, the if-else statement simply outputs the word Crazy and does not change the value of any variables.

4. Suppose speed and visibility are variables of type int. Write an if statement that sets the variable speed equal to 25 and outputs the word Caution, provided the value of speed is greater than 25 and the value of visibility is under 20. There is no else part.

5. Suppose salary and bonus are variables of type double. Write an if-else statement that outputs the word OK provided that either salary is greater than or equal to MIN_SALARY or bonus is greater than or equal to MIN_BONUS. Otherwise, it outputs Too low. MIN_SALARY and MIN_BONUS are named constants.

6. Assume that nextWord is a String variable that has been given a String value consisting entirely of letters. Write some Java code that outputs the message "First half of the alphabet", provided nextWord precedes "N" in alphabetic ordering. If nextWord does not precede "N" in alphabetic ordering, it outputs "Second half of the alphabet". (Note that "N" uses double quotes to produce a String value, as opposed to using single quotes to produce a char value.)

7. Suppose x1 and x2 are two variables that have been given values. How do you test whether they are equal when the variables are of type int? How do you test whether they are equal when the variables are of type String?

Nested Statements and Compound Statements

Notice that an if-else statement contains two smaller statements within it. For example, consider the statement

```
if (balance >= 0)
    balance = balance + (INTEREST_RATE * balance)/12;
else
    balance = balance - OVERDRAWN_PENALTY;
```

This statement contains within it the following two smaller statements:

```
balance = balance + (INTEREST_RATE * balance)/12;
balance = balance - OVERDRAWN_PENALTY;
```

Note that these smaller statements are indented one more level than the if and the else. *indenting*

An if-else statement can contain any sort of statements within it. In particular, you can use one if-else statement within another if-else statement, as illustrated by the following:

```
if (balance >= 0)
    if (INTEREST_RATE >= 0)
        balance = balance + (INTEREST_RATE * balance)/12;
```

```
        else
            System.out.println("Cannot have a negative interest.");
    else
        balance = balance - OVERDRAWN_PENALTY;
```

If the value of balance is greater than or equal to zero, then the entire following if-else statement is executed:

```
    if (INTEREST_RATE >= 0)
        balance = balance + (INTEREST_RATE * balance)/12;
    else
        System.out.println("Cannot have a negative interest.");
```

Later in this chapter, we will discuss the most common way of using if-else statements nested within an if-else statement.

Another simple but useful way of nesting smaller statements within a larger statement is to place a list of statements in braces { }. When you enclose a list of statements within braces, they are considered to be one larger statement. So the following is one large statement that has two smaller statements inside of it:

```
    {
        System.out.println("Good for you. You earned interest.");
        balance = balance + (INTEREST_RATE * balance)/12;
    }
```

compound statement

These statements formed by enclosing a list of statements within braces are called **compound statements.** They are seldom used by themselves but are often used as substatements of larger statements such as if-else statements. The preceding compound statement might occur in an if-else statement such as the following:

```
    if (balance >= 0)
    {
        System.out.println("Good for you. You earned interest.");
        balance = balance + (INTEREST_RATE * balance)/12;
    }
    else
    {
        System.out.println("You will be charged a penalty.");
        balance = balance - OVERDRAWN_PENALTY;
    }
```

Notice that compound statements can simplify our description of an if-else statement. Once we know about compound statements, we can say that every if-else statement is of the form

if (*Boolean_Expression*)
    Statement_1
else
    Statement_2

If you want one branch to contain several statements instead of just one, use a compound statement. A compound statement is, technically speaking, just one statement, so each branch of the preceding if-else statement (the one that starts with if (balance >= 0)) is, technically speaking, a single statement.

Java Tip
Matching `else` and `if`

When writing nested `if-else` statements, you may sometimes become confused about which `if` goes with which `else`. To eliminate this confusion, you can use braces like parentheses to group statements.

For example, consider the following nested statement that we used earlier in this chapter:

```
if (balance >= 0)
    if (INTEREST_RATE >= 0)
        balance = balance + (INTEREST_RATE * balance)/12;
    else
        System.out.println("Cannot have a negative interest.");
else
    balance = balance - OVERDRAWN_PENALTY;
```

This statement can be made clearer with the addition of braces, as follows:

```
if (balance >= 0)
{
    if (INTEREST_RATE >= 0)
        balance = balance + (INTEREST_RATE * balance)/12;
    else
        System.out.println("Cannot have a negative interest.");
}
else
    balance = balance - OVERDRAWN_PENALTY;
```

In this case, the braces are an aid to clarity but are not, strictly speaking, needed. In other cases, they are needed. If we omit an `else`, things get a bit trickier. The following two statements differ only in that one has a pair of braces, but they do not have the same meaning:

```
//First Version
if (balance >= 0)
{
    if (INTEREST_RATE >= 0)
        balance = balance + (INTEREST_RATE * balance)/12;
}
else
    balance = balance - OVERDRAWN_PENALTY;

//Second Version
if (balance >= 0)
    if (INTEREST_RATE >= 0)
        balance = balance + (INTEREST_RATE * balance)/12;
else
    balance = balance - OVERDRAWN_PENALTY;
```

In an `if-else` statement, each `else` is paired with the nearest unmatched `if`. Thus, in the second version (the one without braces), the `else` is paired with the second `if`, so the meaning is

```
//Equivalent to Second Version
if (balance >= 0)
{
    if (INTEREST_RATE >= 0)
        balance = balance + (INTEREST_RATE * balance)/12;
    else
        balance = balance - OVERDRAWN_PENALTY;
}
```

To clarify the difference a bit more, consider what happens when `balance` is greater than or equal to zero. In the first version, this causes the following action:

```
if (INTEREST_RATE >= 0)
    balance = balance + (INTEREST_RATE * balance)/12;
```

If `balance` is not greater than or equal to zero in the first version, then the following action is taken instead:

```
balance = balance - OVERDRAWN_PENALTY;
```

In the second version, if `balance` is greater than or equal to zero, the following entire `if-else` statement is executed:

```
if (INTEREST_RATE >= 0)
    balance = balance + (INTEREST_RATE * balance)/12;
else
    balance = balance - OVERDRAWN_PENALTY;
```

If `balance` is not greater than or equal to zero in the second version, no action is taken. □

Multibranch `if-else` Statements

If you have the ability to branch two ways, then you have the ability to branch four ways. Just branch two ways and have each of those two outcomes branch two ways. Using this trick, you can use nested `if-else` statements to produce multiway branches that branch into any number of possibilities. There is a standard way of doing this. In fact, it has become so standard that it is treated as if it were a new kind of branching statement rather than just a nested statement made up of a lot of nested `if-else` statements. Let's start with an example.

Suppose `balance` is a variable that holds your checking account balance, and you want to know whether your balance is positive, negative (overdrawn), or zero. (To avoid any questions about accuracy, let's assume that `balance` is of type `int`. To be specific, let's say `balance` is the number of dollars in your account, with the cents ignored.) To find out if your balance is positive, negative, or zero, you could use the following nested `if-else` statement:

```
if (balance > 0)
   System.out.println("Positive balance");
else if (balance < 0)
   System.out.println("Negative balance");
else if (balance == 0)
   System.out.println("Zero balance");
```

First, note the way we have indented this statement. This is the preferred way of indenting a multibranch `if-else` statement. A multibranch `if-else` statement is really an ordinary nested `if-else` statement, but the way we have indented it reflects the way we think about multibranch `if-else` statements. indenting

When a multibranch `if-else` statement is executed, the computer tests the boolean expressions one after the other, starting from the top. When the first true boolean expression is found, the statement following that true boolean expression is executed. For example, if `balance` is greater than zero, the preceding code will output `"Positive balance"`. If `balance` is less than zero, then `"Negative balance"` will be output. If `balance` is equal to zero, then `"Zero balance"` will be output. Exactly one of the three possible outputs will be produced, depending on the value of the variable `balance`.

In this first example, we had three possibilities, but you can have any number of possibilities; just add more `else-if` parts.

In this first example, the possibilities were mutually exclusive. However, you can use any boolean expressions, even if they are not mutually exclusive. If more than one boolean expression is true, then only the action associated with the first true boolean expression is executed. A multibranch `if-else` statement never performs more than one action.

If none of the boolean expressions is true, nothing happens. However, it is a good practice to add an `else` clause (without any `if`) at the end, so that the `else` clause will be executed in case none of the boolean expressions is true. In fact, we can rewrite our original example (about a checking account balance) in this way. We know that, if `balance` is neither positive nor negative, it must be zero. So we do not need the test

```
if (balance == 0)
```

Our preceding multibranch `if-else` statement is equivalent to the following:

```
if (balance > 0)
   System.out.println("Positive balance");
else if (balance < 0)
   System.out.println("Negative balance");
else
   System.out.println("Zero balance");
```

Programming Example

Assigning Letter Grades

Display 3.4 contains a program that assigns letter grades according to the traditional rule that 90 or above is an A, 80 or above (up to 90) is a B, and so forth.

Quick Reference: Multibranch `if-else` Statement

Syntax:

```
if (Boolean_Expression_1)
    Action_1
else if (Boolean_Expression_2)
    Action_2
      .
      .
      .
else if (Boolean_Expression_n)
    Action_n
else
    Default_Action
```

Example:

```
if (number < 10)
    System.out.println("number < 10");
else if (number < 50)
    System.out.println("number >= 10 and number < 50");
else if (number < 100)
    System.out.println("number >= 50 and number < 100");
else
    System.out.println("number >= 100.");
```

The actions are Java statements. The boolean expressions are tested one after the other, starting from the top one. When the first true boolean expression is found, the action following that true boolean expression is executed. The *Default_Action* is executed if none of the boolean expressions is true.

DISPLAY 3.4 Multibranch `if-else` Statement *(Part 1 of 2)*

```
public class Grader
{
    public static void main(String[] args)
    {
        int score;
        char grade;

        System.out.println("Enter your score: ");
        score = SavitchIn.readLineInt();

        if (score >= 90)
            grade = 'A';
        else if (score >= 80)
            grade = 'B';
        else if (score >= 70)
            grade = 'C';
```

DISPLAY 3.4 Multibranch `if-else` Statement *(Part 2 of 2)*

```
            else if (score >= 60)
                grade = 'D';
            else
                grade = 'F';

            System.out.println("Score = " + score);
            System.out.println("Grade = " + grade);
        }
    }
```

Sample Screen Dialog

```
Enter your score:
85
Score = 85
Grade = B
```

Note that, as with any multibranch `if-else` statement, the boolean expressions are checked in order, so the second boolean expression is not checked unless the first boolean expression is found to be false. Thus, when and if the second boolean expression is checked, we know that the first boolean expression is false, and so we know that `score < 90`. Thus, the multibranch `if-else` statement would have the same meaning if we replaced

```
(score >= 80)
```

with

```
((score >= 80) && (score < 90))
```

Using the same sort of reasoning on each boolean expression, we see that the multibranch `if-else` statement in Display 3.4 is equivalent to the following:

```
if (score >= 90)
    grade = 'A';
else if ((score >= 80) && (score < 90))
    grade = 'B';
else if ((score >= 70) && (score < 80))
    grade = 'C';
else if ((score >= 60) && (score < 70))
    grade = 'D';
else
    grade = 'F';
```

Most programmers would use the version in Display 3.4, because it is a bit more efficient and is more elegant, but either version is acceptable. ■

? Self-Test Questions

8. What output is produced by the following code?

```
int time = 2, tide = 3;
if (time + tide > 6)
    System.out.println("Time and tide wait for no one.");
else
    System.out.println("Time and tide wait for me.");
```

9. What output is produced by the following code?

```
int time = 4, tide = 3;
if (time + tide > 6)
    System.out.println("Time and tide wait for no one.");
else
    System.out.println("Time and tide wait for me.");
```

10. What output is produced by the following code?

```
int time = 2, tide = 3;
if (time + tide > 6)
   System.out.println("Time and tide wait for no one.");
else if (time + tide > 5)
   System.out.println("Time and tide wait for some one.");
else if (time + tide > 4)
   System.out.println("Time and tide wait for every one.");
else
    System.out.println("Time and tide wait for me.");
```

11. Suppose `number` is a variable of type `int` that has been given a value. Write a multibranch `if-else` statement that outputs the word `High` if `number` is greater than 10, `Low` if `number` is less than 5, and `So-so` if `number` is anything else.

The `switch` Statement

`switch` statement

The `switch` **statement** is a multiway branch that makes its decision as to which way to branch based on the value of an integer or character expression. Display 3.5 shows a sample `switch` statement. The `switch` statement begins with the keyword `switch` followed by an expression in parentheses. In Display 3.5, the expression is the variable `numberOfBabies`. This expression is called the **controlling expression.**

controlling expression

Below this is a list of cases enclosed in braces, each case consisting of the keyword `case` followed by a constant, then a colon, and then a list of statements, which are the actions for that case. The constant that is placed after the word `case` is called a **case label.** When the `switch` statement is executed, the controlling expression—in this example `numberOfBabies`—is evaluated. The list of alternatives is searched until a case label that matches the controlling expression is found, and the action associated with that label is executed. You are not allowed to have repeated case labels. That would produce an ambiguous situation. If no match is found, the case labeled `default` is executed.

case label

`default` case

DISPLAY 3.5 A `switch` Statement *(Part 1 of 2)*

```
public class MultipleBirths
{
    public static void main(String[] args)
    {
        int numberOfBabies;
        System.out.print("Enter number of babies: ");
        numberOfBabies = SavitchIn.readLineInt();

        switch (numberOfBabies)
        {
            case 1:
                System.out.println("Congratulations.");
                break;
            case 2:
                System.out.println("Wow. Twins.");
                break;
            case 3:
                System.out.println("Wow. Triplets.");
                break;
            case 4:
            case 5:
                System.out.println("Unbelieveable.");
                System.out.println(numberOfBabies + " babies");
                break;
            default:
                System.out.println("I don't believe you.");
                break;
        }
    }
}
```

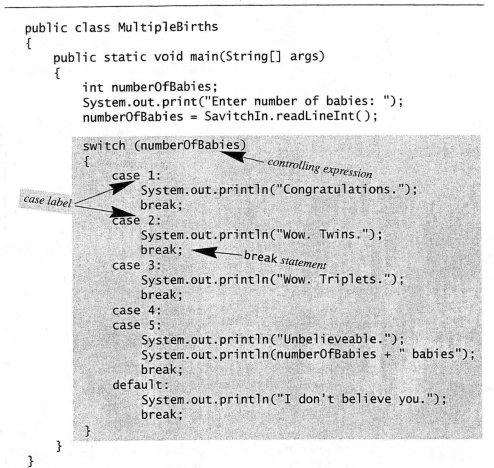

Sample Screen Dialog 1

```
Enter number of babies: 1
Congratulations.
```

Sample Screen Dialog 2

```
Enter number of babies: 3
Wow. Triplets.
```

■ DISPLAY 3.5 A `switch` Statement *(Part 2 of 2)*

Sample Screen Dialog 3

```
Enter number of babies: 4
Unbelievable.
4 babies
```

Sample Screen Dialog 4

```
Enter number of babies: 6
I don't believe you.
```

The `default` case is optional. If there is no `default` case and no match is found to any of the cases, then no action is taken. Although the `default` case is optional, you are encouraged to always use it. If you think your cases cover all the possibilities without a `default` case, you can insert an error message as the `default` case. You never know when you might have missed some obscure case.

break

Notice that the action for each case in Display 3.5 ends with the word `break`. This is a `break` **statement,** and it ends the `switch` statement. The `break` statement consists of the word `break` followed by a semicolon. If there is no `break` statement, then the action just continues on into the next case until either a `break` statement is encountered or the end of the `switch` statement is reached.

Sometimes you want a case without a `break` statement. You cannot have multiple labels in one case, but you can list cases one after the other so they all apply to the same action. For example, in Display 3.5, both case 4 and case 5 produce the same case action, because case 4 has no `break` statement (and, in fact, case 4 has no action statements at all).

As another example, consider the following `switch` statement:

```
switch (eggGrade)
{
    case 'A':
    case 'a':
        System.out.println("Grade A");
        break;
    case 'C':
    case 'c':
        System.out.println("Grade C");
        break;
    default:
        System.out.println("We only buy grade A and grade C.");
        break;
}
```

In this example, the variable `eggGrade` would be of type `char`.

Note that the cases need not form any sort of range; you can have `'A'` and `'C'` and no `'B'`, as in the preceding example. Similarly, in a `switch` statement with integer case labels, you could have integers `1` and `3`, but no `2`.

The controlling expression in a `switch` statement need not be a single variable. It can be a more complicated expression involving `+`, `*`, or other operators, but the expression must evaluate to something of an integer type, such as the type `int`, or to something of type `char`.

The Quick Reference box labeled "`switch` Statement" explains the `switch` statement syntax. Be sure to notice the colons after the case labels.

Quick Reference: `switch` Statement

Syntax:

```
switch (Controlling_Expression)
{
    case Case_Label:
        Statement;
        Statement;
          ...
        Statement;
        break;
    case Case_Label:
        Statement;
        Statement;
          ...
        Statement;
        break;
```

Each Case_Label is a constant of the same type as the Controlling_Expression. Each case must have a different Case_Label. The Controlling_Expression must be of type `char`, `int`, `short`, *or* `byte`.

A `break` *may be omitted. If there is no* `break`, *execution just continues to the next case.*

<There can be any number of cases like the above. The following default case is optional:>

```
    default:
        Statement;
        Statement;
          ...
        Statement;
        break;
}
```

Example:

```
int seatLocationCode;
 ...
switch (seatLocationCode)
{
    case 1:
        System.out.println("Orchestra.");
        price = 40.00;
        break;
```

```
        case 2:
            System.out.println("Mezzanine.");
            price = 30.00;
            break;
        case 3:
            System.out.println("Balcony.");
            price = 15.00;
            break;
        default:
            System.out.println("Unknown ticket code.");
            break;
    }
```

▲ *Gotcha*

Omitting a `break` Statement

If you test a program that contains a `switch` statement and it executes two cases when you expect it to execute only one case, you have probably forgotten to include a `break` statement where one is needed. △

The Conditional Operator *(Optional)*

To allow compatibility with older programming styles, Java included an operator that is a notational variant on certain forms of the `if-else` statement. For example, consider the statement

```
if (n1 > n2)
    max = n1;
else
    max = n2;
```

conditional operator

This can be expressed using the **conditional operator** as follows:

```
max = (n1 > n2) ? n1 : n2;
```

The expression on the right-hand side of the assignment statement is the conditional operator expression

```
(n1 > n2) ? n1 : n2
```

The ? and : together are known as the **conditional operator** (or **ternary operator**). A **conditional operator expression** starts with a boolean expression followed by a ? and then two expressions separated by a colon. If the boolean expression is true, then the first of the two expressions is returned; otherwise, the second of the two expressions is returned.

As illustrated here, the most common use of the conditional operator is to set a variable to one of two different values, depending on a boolean condition. Be sure to note that a conditional expression always returns a value and so is equivalent to only certain special kinds of `if-else` statements. Another example may help to illustrate the conditional operator.

Consider the following:

```
if (hoursWork <= 40)
    pay = hoursWorked*payRate;
else
    pay = hoursWorked*payRate + 1.5*(hoursWorked - 40)*payRate;
```

This says that an employee pay rate is the rate of pay multiplied by the hours worked, but if the employee works more than 40 hours, any time over 40 hours is paid at 1.5 times the usual pay rate. This can be expressed using the conditional operator, as follows:

```
pay =
    (hoursWorked <= 40) ?
       (hoursWorked*payRate) :
       (hoursWorked*payRate + 1.5*(hoursWorked - 40)*payRate);
```

? Self-Test Questions

12. What output is produced by the following code?

```
int code = 2;
switch (code)
{
    case 1:
        System.out.println("Hello.");
    case 3:
        System.out.println("Good-bye.");
        break;
    default:
        System.out.println("Till we meet again.");
        break;
}
```

13. Suppose you change the code in question 12 so that the first line is the following:

```
int code = 1;
```

What output would be produced?

14. What output is produced by the following code?

```
char letter = 'B';
switch (letter)
{
    case 'A':
    case 'a':
        System.out.println("Some kind of A.");
    case 'B':
    case 'b':
        System.out.println("Some kind of B.");
        break;
    default:
        System.out.println("Something else.");
        break;
}
```

15. What output is produced by the following code?

```
int key = 1;
switch (key + 1)
{
    case 1:
        System.out.println("Cake");
        break;
    case 2:
        System.out.println("Pie");
        break;
    case 3:
        System.out.println("Ice cream");
    case 4:
        System.out.println("Cookies");
        break;
    default:
        System.out.println("Diet time");
}
```

16. Suppose you change the code in question 15 so that the first line is the following:

```
int key = 3;
```

What output would be produced?

17. Suppose you change the code in question 15 so that the first line is the following:

```
int key = 5;
```

What output would be produced?

3.2 JAVA LOOP STATEMENTS

One more time. -Count Basie, Recording of "April in Paris"
Play it again, Sam. -Reputed (incorrectly) to be in the movie *Casablanca*, which does contain similar phrases, such as "Play it, Sam."

Programs often need to repeat some action. For example, a grading program would contain some code that assigns a letter grade to a student on the basts of the student's scores on assignments and exams. To assign grades to the entire class, the program would repeat this action for each student in the class. A portion of a program that repeats a statement or group of statements is called a **loop.** The statement (or group of statements) to be repeated in a loop is called the **body** of the loop. Each repetition of the loop body is called an **iteration** of the loop.

body

iteration

When you design a loop, you need to determine what action the body of the loop will take, and you need to determine a mechanism for deciding when the loop should stop repeating the loop body.

`while` Statements

One way to construct a loop in Java is with a `while` **statement**, which is also known as a `while` **loop.** A `while` statement repeats its action again and again until a controlling boolean expression becomes false. That is why it is called a `while` loop; the loop is repeated *while* the controlling boolean expression is true. For example, Display 3.6 contains a toy example of a `while` statement. The statement starts with the keyword `while` followed by a boolean expression in parentheses. That is the controlling boolean expression. The loop body (the repeated part) is repeated while that controlling boolean expression is true. The loop body is a statement, typically a compound statement enclosed in braces `{}`. The loop body normally contains some action that can change the controlling boolean expression from true to false and so end the loop. Let's step through the execution of the `while` loop in Display 3.6.

`while` loop

Consider the first sample dialog for the `while` statement in Display 3.6. The user enters a 2, and this 2 becomes the value of the variable `number`. The controlling boolean expression is

```
(count <= number)
```

DISPLAY 3.6 A `while` Loop *(Part 1 of 2)*

```
public class WhileDemo
{
    public static void main(String[] args)
    {
        int count, number;

        System.out.println("Enter a number");
        number = SavitchIn.readLineInt();

        count = 1;
        while (count <= number)
        {
            System.out.print(count + ", ");
            count++;
        }

        System.out.println();
        System.out.println("Buckle my shoe.");
    }
}
```

DISPLAY 3.6 A `while` Loop *(Part 2 of 2)*

Sample Screen Dialog 1

```
Enter a number:
2
1, 2,
Buckle my shoe.
```

Sample Screen Dialog 2

```
Enter a number:
3
1, 2, 3,
Buckle my shoe.
```

Sample Screen Dialog 3

```
Enter a number:
0

Buckle my shoe.
```

The loop body is iterated zero times.

Since `count` is `1` and `number` is 2, this boolean expression is true, so the loop body, shown here, is executed:

```
{
    System.out.println(count + ", ");
    count++;
}
```

The loop body writes out the value of `count` to the screen and then increases the value of `count` by 1, so `1` is written to the screen, and the value of `count` becomes `2`.

After one iteration of the loop body, the controlling boolean expression is checked again. Since `count` is 2 and `number` is 2, the boolean expression is still true. So the loop body executes one more time. It again writes out the value of `count` to the screen and again increases the value of `count` by 1, so 2 is written to the screen and the value of `count` becomes 3.

After the second iteration of the loop body, the controlling boolean expression is checked again. The value of `count` is now `3` and the value of `number` is still `2`, and so the controlling boolean expression, repeated in what follows, is now false:

```
(count <= number)
```

Because the controlling boolean expression is false, the `while` loop ends and the program goes on to execute the two `System.out.println` statements that follow the `while` statement. The first `System.out.println` statement ends the line of numbers output in the `while` loop, and the second outputs `"Buckle my shoe."`

All `while` statements are formed in a way similar to the sample shown in Display 3.6. The statement has the general form

```
while (Boolean_Expression)
    Body_Statement
```

The *Body_Statement* can be a simple statement, as in the following example:

```
while (next > 0)
    next = SavitchIn.readLineInt();
```

But it is much more likely that the *Body_Statement* is a compound statement, as in Display 3.6, and so the most common form of a `while` loop is

```
while (Boolean_Expression)
{
    First_Statement
    Second_Statement
      . . .
    Last_Statement
}
```

The semantics (meaning) of a `while` loop is described in Display 3.7.

Quick Reference: The `while` Statement

Syntax:

```
while (Boolean_Expression)
    Body
```

The *Body* may be either a simple statement or, more likely, a compound statement consisting of a list of statements enclosed in braces `{}`.

Example:

```
while (next > 0)
{
    next = SavitchIn.readLineInt();
    total = total + next;
}
```

DISPLAY 3.7 Semantics of the `while` Statement[2]

`while` (*Boolean_Expression*)
    Body

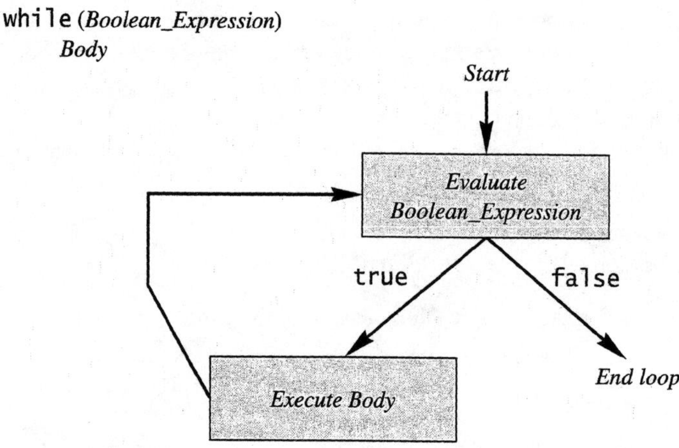

Example:

```
while (count <= number)
{
   System.out.print(count + ", ");
   count++;
}
```

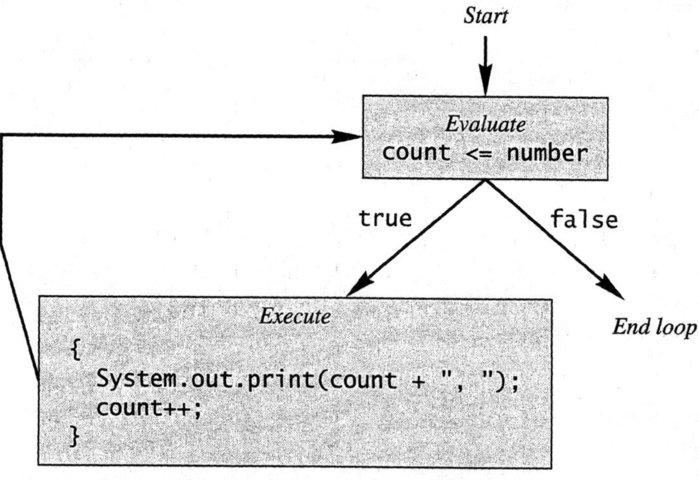

2. In a later subsection we discuss the use of the `break` statement within loops. This semantics assumes that there is no `break` statement in the body of the loop.

Java Tip
A `while` Loop Can Perform Zero Iterations

The body of a `while` loop can be executed zero times. The first thing that happens when a `while` loop is executed is that the controlling boolean expression is checked. If that boolean expression is false, then the loop body is not executed, not even one time. This may seem strange. After all, why write a loop if the body is never executed? The answer is that you may want a loop whose body is executed zero times or more than zero times, depending on input from the user. Perhaps the loop adds up the sum of all your bills for the day. If there are no bills, you do not want the loop body to be executed at all. Sample Screen Dialog 3 in Display 3.6 shows a toy example of a `while` loop that iterates its loop body zero times. □

zero loop iterations

The `do-while` Statement

The `do-while` **statement** (also called a `do-while` **loop**) is very similar to the `while`-statement. The main difference is that, with a `do-while` statement, the loop body is always executed at least once. As you will recall, the body of a `while` loop might be executed zero times. Display 3.8 contains a sample `do-while` loop that is similar (but not identical) to the `while` loop in Display 3.6. Note that with the `do-while` loop, the loop body is always executed at least once, even if the boolean expression starts out false, as in Sample Screen Dialog 3.

The syntax for a `do-while` statement is as follows:

`do-while` statement

```
do
    Body_Statement
while (Boolean_Expression);
```

The *Body_Statement* can be a simple statement, as in the following example:

```
do
    next = SavitchIn.readLineInt();
while (next > 0);
```

However, it is much more likely that the *Body_Statement* is a compound statement, as in Display 3.8, so the most common form of a `do-while` loop is

```
do
{
    First_Statement
    Second_Statement
      . . .
    Last_Statement
}while (Boolean_Expression);
```

Be sure to notice the semicolon after the *Boolean_Expression* in parentheses.

(Note that we place the ending brace } and the `while` on the same line. Some programmers prefer to place them on different lines. Either form is fine, but be consistent.)

DISPLAY 3.8 A do-while Loop

```
public class DoWhileDemo
{
    public static void main(String[] args)
    {
        int count, number;

        System.out.println("Enter a number");
        number = SavitchIn.readLineInt( );

        count = 1;
        do
        {
            System.out.print(count + ", ");
            count++;
        }while (count <= number);

        System.out.println( );
        System.out.println("Buckle my shoe.");
    }
}
```

Sample Screen Dialog 1

```
Enter a number:
2
1, 2,
Buckle my shoe.
```

Sample Screen Dialog 2

```
Enter a number:
3
1, 2, 3,
Buckle my shoe.
```

Sample Screen Dialog 3

```
Enter a number:
0
1,
Buckle my shoe.
```

The loop body is always executed at least one time.

When a `do-while` loop is executed, the first thing that happens is that the loop body is executed. *After that*, a `do-while` loop behaves in exactly the same way as a `while` loop. The boolean expression is checked. If the boolean expression is true, then the loop body is executed one more time. If the boolean expression is false, the loop ends. This is done again and again as long as the boolean expression is true.

Although we do not recommend rewriting your `do-while` loops in this way, it may help you to understand a `do-while` loop if you see the following rewriting done one time. The `do-while` loop in Display 3.8 can be written as the following equivalent code that includes a `while` loop:

```
{
    System.out.print(count + ", ");
    count++;
}
while (count <= number)
{
    System.out.print(count + ", ");
    count++;
}
```

When viewed in this way, it is obvious that a `do-while` loop differs from a `while` loop in only one detail. With a `do-while` loop, the loop body always executes at least once; with a `while` loop, the loop body may execute zero times.

The semantics (meaning) of a `do-while` loop is shown in Display 3.9.

Quick Reference: The `do-while` Statement

With a `do-while` statement, the loop body is always executed at least one time.

Syntax:

```
do
    Body
while (Boolean_Expression);
```

The *Body* may be either a simple statement or, more likely, a compound statement consisting of a list of statements enclosed in braces `{}`. Be sure to notice the semicolon after the *Boolean_Expression* in parentheses.

Example:

```
do
{
    next = SavitchIn.readLineInt();
    total = total + next;
}while (next > 0);
```

■ DISPLAY 3.9 Semantics of the do-while Statement[3]

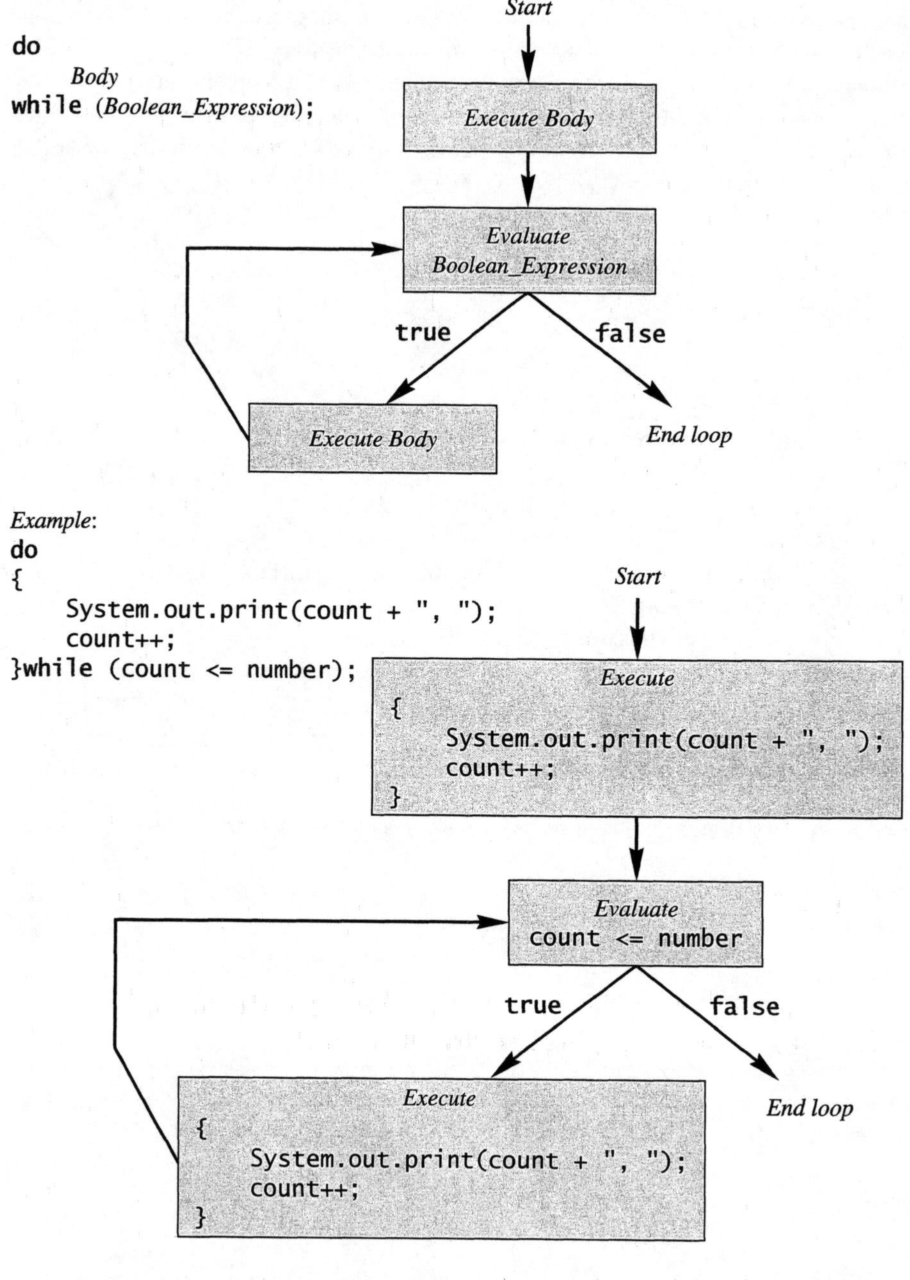

3. In a later subsection we discuss the break statement used within loops. This semantics assumes that there is no break statement in the body of the loop.

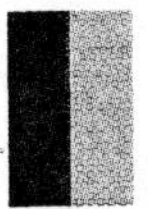

Programming Example

Bug Infestation

Your hometown has been hit with an infestation of roaches. This is not the most pleasant topic, but fortunately a local company called Debugging Experts Inc. has a treatment that can eliminate roaches from a house. As the saying goes, "It's a dirty job, but somebody has to do it." The only problem is that the town's citizens are too complacent and may not exterminate the roaches before they get out of hand. So the company has installed a computer at the local shopping mall to let people know how bad the problem could be at their particular house. The program that is run on this computer is shown in Display 3.10.

The defined constants give the basic facts about this species of roach. The population grows relatively slowly for roaches, but that is still pretty bad. Left unchecked, the population of roaches will almost double every week. If the population doubled every week, the growth rate would be 100 percent per week, but fortunately it is only 95 percent per week. These roaches are also pretty big. Expressed in cubic feet, their average size is 0.002 cubic feet (which is just a bit smaller than 0.3 cubic inches). The program does make some simplifying assumptions. It assumes that there is no furniture in the house, and it assumes that the roaches would fill the house with no space between them. The real situation would be even worse than that portrayed by this program with its simplifying assumptions.

Let's look at the `while` loop from the program in Display 3.10:

```
while (totalBugVolume < houseVolume)
{
    population = population + (GROWTH_RATE*population);
    totalBugVolume = population*ONE_BUG_VOLUME;
    countWeeks++;
}
```

This loop simply updates the population of the roaches and the volume of roaches, using the following statements, which show how the population and volume will change in one week:

```
population = population + (GROWTH_RATE*population);
totalBugVolume = population*ONE_BUG_VOLUME;
```

Because the growth rate and the volume of one bug are both positive, we know that the value of `population`, and hence the value of `totalBugVolume`, will increase with each loop iteration. So eventually, the value of `totalBugVolume` will exceed the value of `houseVolume` and the controlling boolean expression, reproduced here, will become false and end the `while` loop:

```
(totalBugVolume < houseVolume)
```

The variable `countWeeks` starts out as zero and is increased by 1 on each loop iteration, so when the loop ends, the value of `countWeeks` is the total number of weeks it takes for the volume of roaches to exceed the volume of the house. ■

■ DISPLAY 3.10 Roach Population Program *(Part 1 of 2)*

```
/**
 Program to calculate how long it will take a population of
 roaches to completely fill a house from floor to ceiling.
*/
public class BugTrouble
{
    public static final double GROWTH_RATE = 0.95;//95% per week
    public static final double ONE_BUG_VOLUME = 0.002;//cubic feet

    public static void main(String[] args)
    {
        System.out.println("Enter the total volume of your house");
        System.out.print("in cubic feet: ");
        double houseVolume = SavitchIn.readLineDouble();

        System.out.println("Enter the estimated number of");
        System.out.print("roaches in your house:");
        int startPopulation = SavitchIn.readLineInt();
        int countWeeks = 0;
        double population = startPopulation;
        double totalBugVolume = population*ONE_BUG_VOLUME;

        while (totalBugVolume < houseVolume)
        {
            population = population + (GROWTH_RATE*population);
            totalBugVolume = population*ONE_BUG_VOLUME;
            countWeeks++;
        }

        System.out.println("Starting with a roach population of "
                                                + startPopulation);
        System.out.println("and a house with a volume of "
                                + houseVolume + " cubic feet,");
        System.out.println("after " + countWeeks + " weeks,");
        System.out.println("the house will be filled");
        System.out.println("floor to ceiling with roaches.");
        System.out.println("There will be " + (int)population
                                            + " roaches.");
        System.out.println("They will fill a volume of "
                            + (int)totalBugVolume + " cubic feet.");
        System.out.println("Better call Debugging Experts Inc.");
    }
}
```

(int) *is a type cast as discussed in Chapter 2.*

DISPLAY 3.10 Roach Population Program *(Part 2 of 2)*

Sample Screen Dialog

```
Enter the total volume of your house
in cubic feet: 20000
Enter the estimated number of
roaches in your house: 100
Starting with a roach population of 100
and a house with a volume of 20000.0 cubic feet,
after 18 weeks,
the house will be filled
floor to ceiling with roaches.
There will be 16619693 roaches.
They will fill a volume of 33239 cubic feet.
Better call Debugging Experts Inc.
```

▲ ***Gotcha***

Infinite Loops

A common program bug is a loop that does not end, but simply repeats its loop body again and again forever. (Well, conceptually forever.) A loop that iterates its body repeatedly without ever ending is called an **infinite loop.** Normally, some statement in the body of a `while` loop or `do-while` loop will change some variables so that the controlling boolean expression becomes false. However, if the variable does not change in the right way, you could get an infinite loop. In order to provide an example of an infinite loop, we need only make a slight change to a loop you have already seen.

infinite loop

Let's consider a slight variation of the program in Display 3.10. Suppose your town is hit by an infestation of roach-eating frogs. These frogs eat roaches so quickly that the roach population actually decreases, so that the roaches have a negative growth rate. To reflect this fact, you could change the definition of one defined constant to the following and recompile the program:

```
public static final double GROWTH_RATE = -0.05;//-5% per week
```

If you make this change and run the program, the `while` loop will be an infinite loop (provided the house starts out with a relatively small number of roaches). This is because the total number of roaches, and so the volume of roaches, continually *decreases*, and hence the controlling boolean expression, shown again in what follows, is always true:

```
(totalBugVolume < houseVolume)
```

Therefore, the loop never ends.

Some infinite loops will not really run forever but will instead end your program in an abnormal state when some system resource is exhausted. However, some infinite loops will run forever if left alone. To be able to end a program with an infinite loop, you should learn how to force a program to stop running. The way to do this is different for different operating systems. On many systems (but not all), you can stop a program by typing Control-C, which you do by holding down the Control key while pressing the C key.

Sometimes a programmer might intentionally write an infinite loop. For example, an ATM machine would typically be controlled by a program with an infinite loop that handles deposits and withdrawals indefinitely. However, at this point in your programming, an infinite loop is likely to be an error. △

? Self-Test Questions

18. What output will be produced by the following code?

```
int count = 0;
while (count < 5)
{
    System.out.println(count);
    count++;
}
System.out.println("count after loop = " + count);
```

19. Can the body of a `while` loop execute zero times? Can the body of a `do-while` loop execute zero times?

20. What output will be produced by the following code?

```
int count = 0;
do
{
    System.out.println(count);
    count++;
}while (count < 0);
System.out.println("count after loop = " + count);
```

21. Rewrite the following `do-while` loop to obtain some equivalent code that does not contain a `do-while` loop:

```
int number;
do
{
    System.out.println("Enter a whole number:");
    number = SavitchIn.readLineInt( );
    System.out.println("You entered " + number);
}while (number > 0);
System.out.println("number after loop = " + number);
```

22. What output is produced by the following code?

```
int count = 0;
while (count < 5)
```

```
{
    System.out.println(count);
    count--;
}
System.out.println("count after loop = " + count);
```

The `for` Statement

The `for` statement is a specialized loop statement that allows you to easily convert pseudocode such as the following into a Java loop:

`for` loop

```
Do the following for each value of count from 1 to 3:
    System.out.println(count);
System.out.println("Go");
```

This particular pseudocode can be expressed in Java as the following `for` statement (followed by an output statement):

```
for (count = 1; count <= 3; count++)
    System.out.println(count);
System.out.println("Go");
```

The first two of the preceding lines are a `for` statement that causes the output

```
1
2
3
```

After the `for` statement ends, the last line outputs the word `"Go"`.

In this first example of a `for` statement, the loop body is the statement

```
System.out.println(count);
```

The iteration of the loop body is controlled by the line

```
for (count = 1; count <= 3; count++)
```

The first of the three expressions in parentheses, `count = 1`, tells what happens before the loop body is executed for the first time. The third expression, `count++`, is executed after each iteration of the loop body. The middle expression, `count <= 3`, is a boolean expression that determines when the loop will end, and it does so in the same way as the controlling boolean expression in a `while` loop. Thus, the loop body is executed while `count` <= 3 is true. To rephrase what we just said, the `for` statement

```
for (count = 1; count <= 3; count++)
    for-loop body
```

is equivalent to

```
count = 1;
while (count <= 3)
{
    for-loop body
    count++;
}
```

The syntax for a `for` statement is as follows:

```
for (Initializing_Action; Boolean_Expression; Update_Action)
        Body_Statement
```

The *Body_Statement* can be a simple statement, as in the following example:

```
for (count = 1; count <= 3; count++)
    System.out.println(count);
```

However, it is more likely that the *Body_Statement* is a compound statement, as in Display 3.11, so the more common form of a `for` loop can be described as follows:

```
for (Initializing_Action; Boolean_Expression; Update_Action)
{
    First_Statement
    Second_Statement
        .
        .
        .
    Last_Statement
}
```

When it is executed, a `for` statement of the preceding form is equivalent to the following:

```
Initializing_Action;
while (Boolean_Expression)
{
    First_Statement
    Second_Statement
        .
        .
        .
    Last_Statement
    Update_Action;
}
```

DISPLAY 3.11 A `for` Statement *(Part 1 of 2)*

```
public class ForDemo
{
    public static void main(String[] args)
    {
        int countDown;

        for (countDown = 3; countDown >= 0; countDown--)
        {
            System.out.println(countDown);
            System.out.println("and counting.");
        }

        System.out.println("Blast off!");
    }
}
```

■ DISPLAY 3.11 A `for` Statement *(Part 2 of 2)*

Screen Output

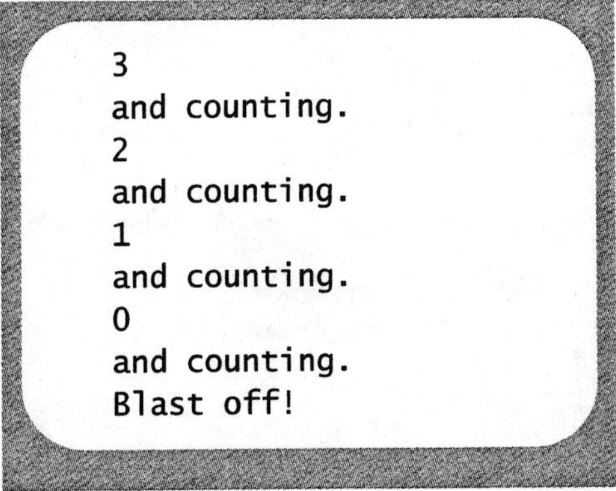

Notice that a `for` statement is basically another notation for a kind of `while` loop. Thus, just like a `while` loop, a `for` statement might repeat its loop body zero times.

The semantics (meaning) of the `for` loop is described in Display 3.12.

■ DISPLAY 3.12 Semantics of the `for` Statement *(Part 1 of 2)*

`for` (*Initializing_Action*; *Boolean_Expression*; *Update_Action*)
    Body

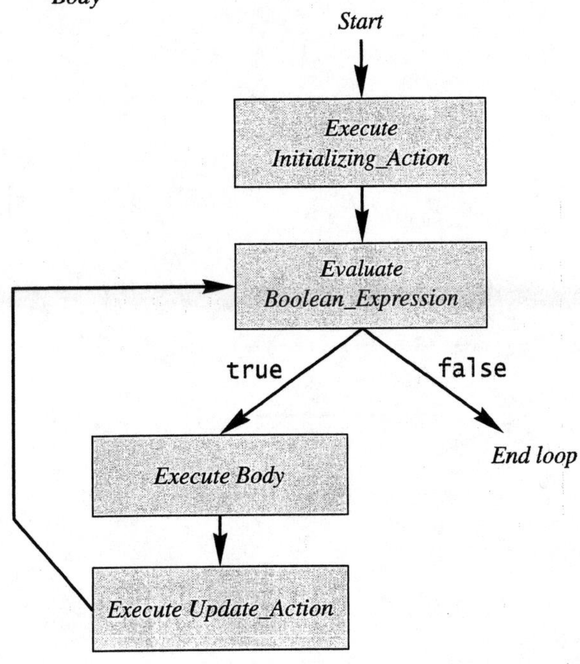

Example:

```
for (countDown = 3; countDown >= 0; countDown--)
{
    System.out.println(countDown);
    System.out.println("and counting.");
}
```

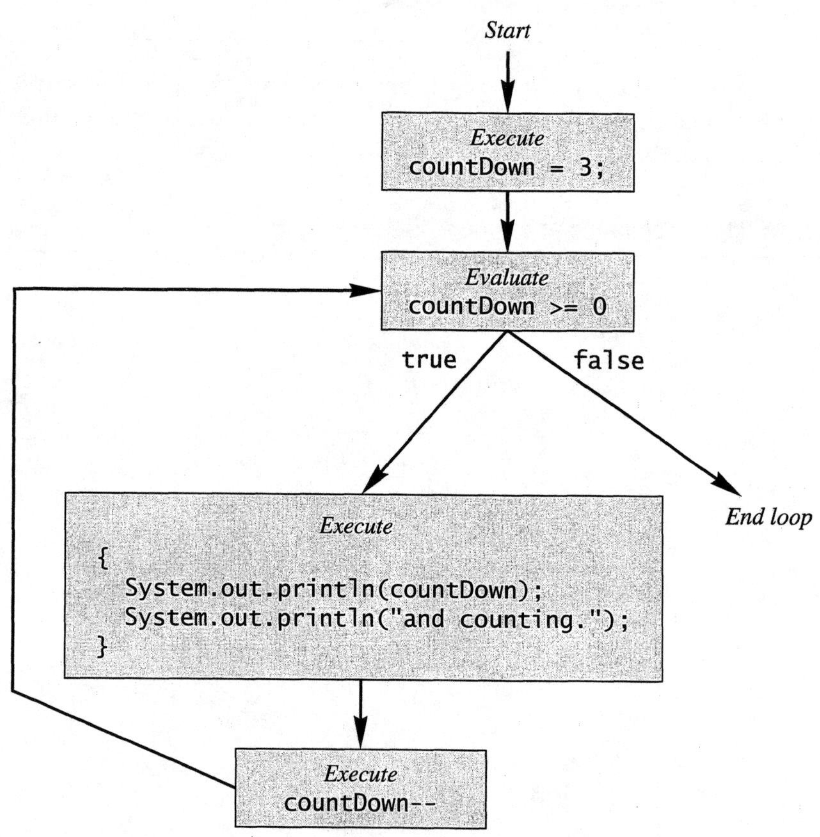

The Comma in `for` Statements *(Optional)*

A `for` loop can perform more than one initialization. To use a list of initialization actions, simply separate the actions with commas, as in the following example:

```
for (n = 1, product = 1; n <= 10; n++)
    product = product*n;
```

This `for` loop initializes `n` to `1` and also initializes `product` to `1`. Note that we use a comma, not a semicolon, to separate the initialization actions.

You cannot have multiple boolean expressions to test for ending a `for` loop. However, you can string together multiple tests using the && operator to form one larger boolean expression.

You can have multiple update actions by stringing them together with commas. This can sometimes lead to a situation in which the `for` statement has an empty body and still does something useful. For example, the previous `for` statement can be rewritten as follows:

```
for (n = 1, product = 1; n <= 10; product = product*n, n++);
```

In effect, we have made the loop body part of the update action. However, your code will be more readable if you use the update action only for the variables that control the loop, as in the previous version of this `for` loop. We do not advocate using `for` loops with no body, but many programmers consider them "clever." As indicated in the Gotcha section "Extra Semicolon in a Loop Statement," `for` loops with no body can also often occur as the result of a programmer error.

(If you have programmed in other programming languages that have a general-purpose comma operator, you need to be warned that, in Java, the comma operator can be used only in `for` statements.)

Quick Reference: The `for` Statement

Syntax:

for (*Initializing_Action*; *Boolean_Expression*; *Update_Action*)
        Body

The *Body* may be either a simple statement or, more likely, a compound statement consisting of a list of statements enclosed in braces `{}`. Notice that the three items in parentheses are separated by two, not three, semicolons.

Our `for` loops *Update_Action* will always change only one variable. However, you are allowed to use any Java expression, and so you can use more, or fewer, than one variable in this expression, and moreover, the variables can be of any types. The *Initializing_Action* and *Boolean_Expression* also may include multiple variables.

Example:

```
for (next = 0; next <= 10; next = next + 2)
{
    sum = sum + next;
    System.out.println("sum now is " + sum);
}
```

▲ *Gotcha*

Extra Semicolon in a Loop Statement

The following code looks quite ordinary. Moreover, it will compile and run with no error messages. It does, however, contain a mistake. See if you can find the mistake before reading on.

```
int product = 1, number;
for (number = 1; number <= 10; number++);
    product = product * number;
System.out.println(
          "Product of the numbers 1 through 10 is " + product);
```

If you include this code in a program and run the program, the output will be

```
Product of the numbers 1 through 10 is 11
```

Now can you see what is wrong? Try to explain the problem before reading on.

If you were testing the program that produced this puzzling output, it could leave you bewildered. Clearly, something is wrong with the `for` loop, but what? The `for` loop is supposed to set the value of `product` equal to

```
1 * 2 * 3 * 4 * 5 * 6 * 7 * 8 * 9 * 10
```

but instead, it sets the value of `product` equal to 11. How could that happen?

The problem is typographically very small. The `for` statement has an extra semicolon at the end of the first line:

```
for (number = 1; number <= 10; number++);
    product = product * number;
```

What does this `for` statement do? The semicolon at the end means that the body of the `for` statement is empty. A semicolon by itself is considered a statement that does nothing. (This statement that does nothing is called the **empty statement** or the **null statement.**) This `for` statement with the extra semicolon is equivalent to

empty statement

```
for (number = 1; number <= 10; number++)
{
    //Do nothing.
}
```

Thus, the body of the `for` statement is in fact executed 10 times; however, each time it executes, the loop does nothing but increment the variable `number` by 1. That leaves `number` equal to 11 when the program reaches the statement

```
    product = product * number;
```

(Remember, `number` starts out equal to 1 and is increased by one 10 times, which adds 10 more to the initial 1, so the value becomes 11.)

Let's look again at the entire piece of troublesome code:

```
int product = 1, number;
for (number = 1; number <= 10; number++);
    product = product * number;
System.out.println(
        "Product of the numbers 1 through 10 is " + product);
```

After the line that starts with `for` has executed, the value of `product` is `1` and, as we have just seen, the value of `number` is `11`. Then the following assignment statement is executed:

```
product = product * number;
```

This sets the value of `product` to `1 * 11`, and so `product` ends up with the value `11`, as the output says. To fix the problem, simply remove the extra semicolon at the end of the line that begins with `for`.

The same sort of problem can occur with a `while` loop. The following `while` loop has the same problem as our troublesome `for` loop, but the results are even worse:

```
int product = 1, number = 1;
while (number <= 10);
{
    product = product * number;
    number++;
}
System.out.println(
          "Product of the numbers 1 through 10 is " + product);
```

The extra semicolon ends the `while` loop, so the body of the `while` loop is the empty statement. Because the body of the loop is the empty statement, nothing happens on each loop iteration. Therefore, the value of `number` never changes, and the condition

```
number <= 10
```

is always `true`. So the loop is an infinite loop that does nothing and does it forever! △

? Self-Test Questions

23. What output is produced by the following code?

```
int n;
for (n = 1; n <= 4; n++)
    System.out.println(n);
```

24. What output is produced by the following code?

```
int n;
for (n = 1; n > 4; n++)
    System.out.println(n);
```

25. What output is produced by the following code?

```
int n;
for (n = 4; n > 0; n--)
    System.out.println(n);
```

26. What output is produced by the following code?

```
int n;
for (n = 4; n > 0; n--);
    System.out.println(n);
```

(This is not the same as the previous question. Look carefully.)

27. What output is produced by the following code?

```
double test;
for (test = 0; test < 3; test = test + 0.5)
   System.out.println(test);
```

28. Write a `for` statement that writes out the even numbers 2, 4, 6, 8, and 10. The output should put each number on a separate line. Declare all the variables you use.

■ Java Tip
Choosing a Loop Statement

Suppose you decide that your program needs a loop. How do you decide whether to use a `while` statement, a `do-while` statement, or a `for` statement? There are some general guidelines we can give you: You *cannot* use a `do-while` statement unless you are certain that, for all possible inputs to your program, the loop should be iterated at least one time. If you know that your loop will always be iterated at least one time, a `do-while` statement is likely to be a good choice. However, more often than you might think, a loop requires the possibility of iterating the body zero times. In those cases, you must use either a `while` statement or a `for` statement. If it is a computation that changes some numeric quantity by some equal amount on each iteration, consider a `for` statement. If the `for` statement does not work well, use a `while` statement. The `while` statement is always the safest choice. You can easily realize any sort of loop as a `while` statement, but sometimes one of the other alternatives is nicer. □

The `break` Statement in Loops

`break`

As we have presented them so far, the `while`, `do-while`, and `for` statements always complete their entire loop body on each iteration. Sometimes, however, you may want to end a loop in the middle of the loop body. You can do this by using the `break` statement. For example, the program in Display 3.13 reads a list of purchase amounts and totals them to see how much the user has spent. However, the user has a limit of $100, so as soon as the total reaches (or exceeds) $100, the program uses a `break` statement to end the loop immediately. When a `break` statement is executed, the immediately enclosing loop ends, and the remainder of the loop body is not executed. The break statement can be used with a while loop, a do-while loop, or a for loop.

This is the same break statement that we used earlier in switch statements. If the loop is contained within a larger loop (or if the loop is inside a switch statement), then the break statement ends only the innermost loop. Similarly, if the break statement is within a switch statement that is inside a loop, then the break statement ends the switch statement but not the loop. The break statement ends only the *innermost* loop or switch statement that contains the break statement.

DISPLAY 3.13 Ending a Loop with a break Statement *(Part 1 of 2)*

```
public class BreakDemo
{
    public static void main(String[] args)
    {
        int itemNumber;
        double amount, total;

        System.out.println("You may buy ten items, but");
        System.out.println("the total price must not exceed $100.");

        total = 0;
        for (itemNumber = 1; itemNumber <= 10; itemNumber++)
        {
            System.out.print("Enter cost of item #"
                                       + itemNumber + ": $");
            amount = SavitchIn.readLineDouble();
            total = total + amount;
            if (total >= 100)
            {
                System.out.println("You spent all your money.");
                break;
            }
            System.out.println("Your total so far is $" + total);
            System.out.println("You may purchase up to "
                           + (10 - itemNumber) + " more items.");
        }
        System.out.println("You spent $" + total);
    }
}
```

■ DISPLAY 3.13 Ending a Loop with a `break` Statement *(Part 2 of 2)*

Sample Screen Dialog

```
You may buy ten items, but
the total price must not exceed $100.
Enter cost of item #1: $90.93
Your total so far is $90.93
You may purchase up to 9 more items.
Enter cost of item #2: $10.50
You spent all your money.
You spent $101.43
```

▲ *Gotcha*

Misuse of `break` Statements

A loop *without* a `break` statement has a simple, easy-to-understand structure. There is a test for ending the loop at the top (or bottom) of the loop, and every iteration will go to the end of the loop body. When you add a `break` statement, this can make it more difficult to understand the loop. The loop might end because of the condition given at the start (or bottom) of the loop or because of the `break` statement. Some loop iterations may go to the end of the loop body, but one loop iteration may end prematurely. Because of the complications they introduce, `break` statements in loops should be avoided. Some authorities contend that a `break` statement should never be used to end a loop, but virtually all programming authorities agree that they should be used at most sparingly. △

Quick Reference: The `break` Statement in Loops

The `break` statement can be used in a `switch` statement or in any kind of loop statement. When the `break`- statement is executed, the immediately enclosing loop (or `switch` statement) ends, and the remainder of the loop body is not executed.

The `exit` Method

Sometimes your program can encounter a situation that makes continuing with the program pointless. In such cases, you can end your program with a call to the `exit` method, as follows:

```
System.exit(0);
```

The preceding statement will end a Java program as soon as it is executed.

For example,

```
if (numberOfWinners == 0)
{
    System.out.println("Error: Dividing by zero.");
    System.exit(0);
}
else
{
    oneShare = payoff/numberOfWinners;
    System.out.println("Each winner will receive $" + oneShare);
}
```

This statement will normally output the share that each winner should receive. However, if the number of winners is zero, that would produce a division by zero, which is an invalid operation. To avoid this division by zero, the program checks to see whether the number of winners is zero, and if it is zero, it ends the program with a call to the `exit` method.

The number `0` given as the argument to `System.exit` is returned to the operating system. In many situations, you can use any number and the program will behave in the same way. But most operating systems use `0` to indicate a normal termination of the program and `1` to indicate an abnormal termination of the program (just the opposite of what most people would guess). Thus, if your `System.exit` statement ends your program normally, the argument should be `0`. In this case, *normal* means the program did not violate any system or other important constraints. It does not mean that the program did what you wanted it to do. So you would almost always use `0` as the argument.

Quick Reference: The `exit` Method

An invocation of the `exit` method ends the program. The normal form for an `exit` method invocation is

```
System.exit(0);
```

? Self-Test Questions

29. What output is produced by the following code?

```
int n;
for (n = 1; n <= 5; n++)
{
    if (n == 3)
        break;
    System.out.println("Hello");
}
System.out.println("After the Loop.");
```

30. What output is produced by the following code?

```
int n;
for (n = 1; n <= 5; n++)
{
    if (n == 3)
        System.exit(0);
    System.out.println("Hello");
}
System.out.println("After the Loop.");
```

31. What output is produced by the following code?

```
int n;
for (n = 1; n <= 3; n++)
{
    switch (n)
    {
        case 1:
            System.out.println("One.");
            break;
        case 2:
            System.out.println("Two.");
            break;
        case 3:
            System.out.println("Three.");
            break;
        default:
            System.out.println("Default case.");
            break;
    }
}
System.out.println("After the Loop.");
```

3.3 PROGRAMMING WITH LOOPS

The cautious seldom err. -Confucius

A loop is often broken into three parts: the initializing statements that must precede the loop, the loop body, and the mechanism for ending the loop. In this section we give you techniques for designing each of these loop components. Although the initializing statements come before the loop body, the loop body is naturally designed first, and so we will start our discussion with the loop body.

The Loop Body

One way to design a loop body is to write out the sequence of actions that you want your code to accomplish. For example, you might want your loop to perform the following actions:

Output instructions to the user.
Initialize variables.

```
Read a number into the variable next.
 sum = sum + next;
Output the number and the sum so far.
Read another number into the variable next.
 sum = sum + next;
Output the number and the sum so far.
Read another number into the variable next.
 sum = sum + next;
Output the number and the sum so far.
Read another number into the variable next.
      and so forth.
```

Then look for a repeated pattern in the list of actions. In this case, we have the repeated pattern is

```
Read another number into the variable next.
 sum = sum + next;
Output the number and the sum so far.
```

So the body of the loop, expressed in pseudocode, can be the preceding three actions. The entire pseudocode can be

```
Output instructions to the user.
Initialize variables.
Do the following for the appropriate number of times:
{
   Read a number into the variable next.
        sum = sum + next;
   Output the number and the sum so far.
}
```

Note that the pattern need not start with the first action. There may be some actions that need to be done before or after the loop is executed.

Quick Reference: **Pseudocode**

In Chapter 1, we said that algorithms are usually written in pseudocode. **Pseudocode** is a mixture of English and Java. When using pseudocode, you simply write each part the algorithm in whatever language is easiest for you. If a part is easier to express in English, you use English. If another part is easier to express in Java, you use Java. The following simple algorithm is an example of pseudocode:

```
Read another number into the variable next.
sum = sum + next;
Output the number and the sum so far.
```

Initializing Statements

Consider the pseudocode we designed in the previous subsection. Notice that the variable sum is expected to have a value every time the following loop body statement is executed:

```
sum = sum + next;
```

In particular, this is true the first time the loop is iterated. So sum must be initialized to some value before the loop starts. When trying to decide on the correct initializing value for sum, it helps to consider what you want to happen after one loop iteration. In the loop we are currently designing, after one loop iteration, the value of sum should be set to the first value of next. The only way that sum + next can evaluate to next is if sum is 0. This means that the value of sum must be initialized to 0. Thus, one of the variable initializations must be

```
sum = 0;
```

The only other variable used in the loop is next. The first statement performed with next is

Read a number into the variable next.

This statement gives next a value, so next does not need to have a value before the loop is started. Thus, the only variable that needs to be initialized is sum, and we can rewrite the pseudocode as follows:

```
Output instructions to the user.
sum = 0;
Do the following the appropriate number of times:
{
     Read a number into the variable next.
     sum = sum + next;
     Output the number and the sum so far.
}
```

Variables are not always initialized to zero. To see this, consider another example. Suppose your loop was computing the product of n numbers as follows:

```
for (count = 1; count <= n; count++)
{
    Read a number into the variable next.
    product = product * next;
}
```

In this case, let's say that all variables are of type int.

If you initialize the variable product to 0, then no matter how many numbers are read in and multiplied, the value of product will still be 0. So 0 clearly is not the correct initialization value for product. The correct initializing value for product is 1. To see that 1 is the correct initial value, notice that the first time through the loop, you want product to be set equal to the first number read in. Initializing product to 1 will make this happen. Thus, the loop, with a correct initialization statement, is

```
product = 1;
for (count = 1; count <= n; count++)
```

```
{
    Read a number into the variable next.
    product = product * next;
}
```

Ending a Loop

In this subsection, we discuss some standard techniques you can use to end a loop.

If you are lucky, your program will know exactly how many times the loop body must be repeated before the loop starts. In this simple case, you can use a `for` loop to count the number of loop body iterations. For example, suppose that `numberOfStudents` contains the number of students in a class, and you want to know the average score on an exam in the course. The following will do nicely:

```
double next, average, sum = 0;
int count;
for (count = 1; count <= numberOfStudents; count++)
{
    next = SavitchIn.readLineDouble();
    sum = sum + next;
}
if (numberOfStudents > 0)
    average = sum/numberOfStudents;
else
    System.out.println("No scores to average.");
```

Notice that the variable `count` is not used in the loop body. The `for` loop mechanism is simply being used to count from `1` to `numberOfStudents` and repeat the loop body that many times. Loops such as this one, that know the number of loop iterations before the loop starts, are called **count-controlled loops.** Count-controlled loops do not need to be implemented as `for` loops, but that is the easiest way to implement them. (Also note that we have allowed for the possibility of no students being in the class. In that case, the loop body is iterated zero times and the `if-else` statement prevents division by zero.)

count-controlled loops

The most straightforward way of ending a loop is simply to ask the user if it is time to end the loop. This technique is called **ask-before-iterating**. It works very well in situations in which the total number of loop body iterations is expected to be fairly small. For example, the following would work nicely if each customer makes only a few purchases:

ask before iterating

```
do
{
    System.out.println("Enter price $");
    price = SavitchIn.readLineDouble();
    System.out.print("Enter number purchased: ");
    number = SavitchIn.readLineInt();
    System.out.println(number + " items at $" + price);
    System.out.println("Total cost $" + price*number);
    System.out.println("Want to make another purchase?");
    System.out.println("Enter y for yes or n for no.");
    answer = SavitchIn.readLineNonwhiteChar();
}while ((answer == 'y') || (answer == 'Y'));
```

In some situations, this is best done with a `while` loop. But if you know that each user will want at least one loop iteration, a `do-while` loop will work fine.

sentinel value

For long input lists, you can sometimes use a **sentinel value.** A sentinel value is used to signal the end of the input. It must be a value that is different from all possible real input values. For example, suppose you want some code to compute the highest and lowest scores on an exam, and suppose you know that there will be at least one exam score. If you know that nobody is ever given a negative score on the exam, then you can ask the user to mark the end of the list of scores with a negative number. The negative number is the sentinel value. It is not one of the exam scores. It is just an end marker. The code for computing the highest and lowest scores could be as follows:

```
System.out.println("Enter scores for all students.");
System.out.println("Enter a negative number after");
System.out.println("you have entered all the scores.");
double max = SavitchIn.readLineDouble();
double min = max;//The max and min so far are the first score.
double next = SavitchIn.readLineDouble();
while (next >= 0)
{
    if (next > max)
        max = next;
    if (next < min)
        min = next;
    next = SavitchIn.readLineDouble();
}
System.out.println("The highest score is " + max);
System.out.println("The lowest score is " + min);
```

Be sure to notice that the last number (the sentinel value) is not used to determine the lowest score (or to determine the highest score). Suppose the user enters the scores as follows:

```
100
90
10
-1
```

The output will be

```
The highest score is 100
The lowest score is 10
```

Be sure to note that the lowest score is `10`, not `–1`. The `–1` is just an end marker.

In Section 3.4 we will discuss another method for ending a loop, but the three methods discussed here cover most situations you are likely to encounter.

Programming Example

Nested Loops

The body of a loop can contain any sort of statements. In particular, you can have a loop statement within the body of a larger loop statement. For example, the program in Display 3.14

computes the average of a list of scores, using a `while` loop. The program asks the user to enter a list of nonnegative scores, with a negative sentinel value to mark the end of the list. This `while` loop is then placed inside a `do-while` loop, so that the user can repeat the entire process for another exam, and another, until the user wishes to end the program. ■

Programming Tip
Avoid Declaring Variables in a Loop Body

Note that in Display 3.14, we have placed the declaration of all the variables at the beginning of the program so that they are outside of the body of the outer `do-while` loop. If we had left some of the declarations inside the `do-while` loop, those declarations would be repeated on each execution of the body of the `do-while` loop. Depending on how the compiler is written, this can be inefficient, because it may be re-creating the variables on each loop iteration. There are times when it makes sense to declare a variable in a loop body, but if the variable declaration can easily be moved outside the loop, it is usually a good idea to do so. ○

? Self-Test Questions

32. Write a Java loop statement that will output the phrase `"One more time."` to the screen four times. Also, give any declarations or initializing statements that are needed.
33. Give a Java loop statement that will set the variable `result` equal to 2^5. Do this with a loop that starts out with the value of `result` equal to `1` and multiplies the value of `result` by `2` for each of 5 loop iterations. Also, give any declarations or initializing statements that are needed.
34. What output is produced by the following code:

```
int count, innerCount;
for (count = 0; count <= 3; count++)
    for (innerCount = 0; innerCount < count; innerCount++)
        System.out.println(innerCount);
```

35. Give a Java loop statement that will read in a list of numbers of type `double` and then output their average. The numbers are all greater than or equal to `1.0`. The list is ended with a sentinel value. You must specify the sentinel value. Also, give any declarations or initializing statements that are needed.

Loop Bugs

Programs with loops are more likely to contain mistakes than the simpler programs you saw before you started using loops. Fortunately, there is a pattern to the kinds of mistakes you are most likely to make in designing a loop, so we can tell you what to look for. Moreover, there are some standard techniques you can use to locate and fix bugs in your loops.

■ DISPLAY 3.14 **Nested Loops** *(Part 1 of 2)*

```
/**
 Determines the average of a list of (nonnegative) exam scores.
 Repeats for more exams until the user says she/he is finished.
*/
public class ExamAverager
{
    public static void main(String[] args)
    {
        System.out.println("This program computes the average of");
        System.out.println("a list of (nonnegative) exam scores.");

        double sum;
        int numberOfStudents;
        double next;
        char answer;

        do
        {
            System.out.println();
            System.out.println("Enter all the scores to be averaged.");
            System.out.println("Enter a negative number after");
            System.out.println("you have entered all the scores.");
            sum = 0;
            numberOfStudents = 0;
            next = SavitchIn.readLineDouble();
            while (next >= 0)
            {
                sum = sum + next;
                numberOfStudents++;
                next = SavitchIn.readLineDouble();
            }
            if (numberOfStudents > 0)
                System.out.println("The average is "
                                    + (sum/numberOfStudents));
           else
                System.out.println("No scores to average.");

            System.out.println("Want to average another exam?");
            System.out.println("Enter y for yes or n for no.");
            answer = SavitchIn.readLineNonwhiteChar();
        }while ((answer == 'y') || (answer == 'Y'));
    }
}
```

DISPLAY 3.14 Nested Loops *(Part 2 of 2)*

Sample Screen Dialog

```
This program computes the average of
a list of (nonnegative) exam scores.

Enter all the scores to be averaged.
Enter a negative number after
you have entered all the scores.
100
90
100
90
-1
The average is 95.0
Want to average another exam?
Enter y for yes or n for no.
y

Enter all the scores to be averaged.
Enter a negative number after
you have entered all the scores.
90
70
80
-1
The average is 80.0
Want to average another exam?
Enter y for yes or n for no.
n
```

The two most common kinds of loop errors are unintended infinite loops and off-by-one errors. Let's consider them in order.

infinite loops

We have already discussed infinite loops. There is, however, one subtlety about infinite loops that we need to emphasize. A loop might terminate for some input values but be an infinite loop for other values. Just because you tested your loop for some program input values and found that the loop ended, that does not mean that it will not be an infinite loop for some other input values. Let's consider an example.

You have a friend whose checking account balance is overdrawn. The bank charges a penalty each month that the balance is negative. Your friend wants a program that will tell him how long it will take to get a nonnegative account balance if he deposits a fixed amount each month. You design the following code:

```
count = 0;
while (balance < 0)
{
    balance = balance - penalty;
    balance = balance + deposit;
    count++;
}
System.out.println("You will have a nonnegative balance in "
                                        + count + " months.");
```

You place this code in a complete program and test the code with some reasonable values, like $15 for the penalty and $50 for the size of the deposit. The program runs fine. So you give it to your friend, who runs it and finds that it goes into an infinite loop. What happened? Your friend obviously does not have a head for numbers and has decided to make small deposits of only $10 per month. But, the bank charges a penalty of $15 per month when an account goes negative. So the account simply gets a larger negative balance every month, even though your friend makes deposits.

It may seem as though this could not happen. Your friend would not make such a stupid mistake. Don't count on it! It can happen even if your friend is not stupid. People are sometimes careless. One way to fix this bug is to add code that will test to see whether the loop is infinite or not. For example, you might change the code to the following:

```
if (payment <= penalty)
    System.out.println("payment is too small.");
else
{
    count = 0;
    while (balance < 0)
    {
        balance = balance - penalty;
        balance = balance + payment;
        count++;
    }
    System.out.println("You will have a nonnegative balance in "
                                        + count + " months.");
}
```

off-by-one error

The other common kind of loop bug is an **off-by-one error.** This means that your loop repeats the loop body one too many times or one too few times. These sorts of errors can result from carelessness in designing a controlling boolean expression. For example, if you use less-than when you should use less-than-or-equal, your loop could easily iterate the body the wrong number of times.

Another common problem with the controlling boolean expression of a loop has to do with the use of == to test for equality. This sort of equality testing works satisfactorily for integers and characters but is not reliable for floating-point numbers. This is because the floating-point numbers are approximate quantities, and == tests for exact equality. The result of such a test is unpredictable. When comparing floating-point numbers, always use something involving less-than or greater-than, such as <=; do not use == or !=. Using ==

or != to test floating-point numbers can produce an off-by-one error, an unintended infinite loop, or even some other type of error.

One big danger with off-by-one errors is that they can easily go unnoticed. If a loop is iterated one too many times, or one too few times, the results might still look reasonable but be off by enough to cause trouble later on. Always make a specific check for off-by-one errors by comparing your loop results to results you know to be true by some other means, such as a pencil-and-paper calculation of a simple case.

Remember: Always Retest

Whenever you find a bug in a program and "fix" it, always retest the program. There may be yet another bug, or your "fix" may have introduced a new bug.

Tracing Variables

If your program misbehaves but you cannot see what is wrong, your best bet is to trace some key variables. **Tracing variables** means watching the variables change value while the program is running. A program typically does not output the value of a variable every time it changes, but seeing how the variables change can help you to debug your program.

tracing variables

Many systems have a built-in utility that lets you easily trace variables without making any changes to your program. These debugging systems vary from one installation to another. If you have such a debugging facility, it is worth learning how to use it. If you do not have such a debugging facility, you can trace variables simply by inserting some extra, temporary output statements in your program. For example, suppose you want to trace the variables in the following code (which contains an error):

```
count = 0;
while (balance < 0)
{
    balance = balance + penalty;
    balance = balance - deposit;
    count++;
}
System.out.println("Nonnegative balance in "
                                + count + " months.");
```

You can trace the variables by adding the following output statements:

```
count = 0;
System.out.println("count == " + count);//trace
System.out.println("balance == " + balance);//trace
System.out.println("penalty == " + penalty);//trace
System.out.println("deposit == " + deposit);//trace
while (balance < 0)
{
    balance = balance + penalty;
    System.out.println(
             "balance + penalty == " + balance);//trace
    balance = balance - deposit;
```

```
        System.out.println(
                 "balance - deposit == " + balance);//trace
        count++;
        System.out.println("count == " + count);//trace
    }
    System.out.println("Nonnegative balance in "
                                     + count + " months.");
```

After you have discovered the error and fixed the bugs in the code, you can remove the trace statements.

It may seem like a lot of bother to insert all the trace statements in the preceding example, but it is not so very much work. If you wish, you can first try tracing only some of the variables to see if that gives you enough information to find the problem. However, it is usually fastest to just trace all, or almost all, of the variables right from the start.

? Self-Test Questions

36. What is the bug in the code in the subsection "Tracing Variables"?

37. Add some suitable output statements to the following code, so that all variables are traced:

```
int n, sum = 0;
for (n = 1; n < 10; n++)
    sum = sum + n;
System.out.println("1 + 2 + ...+ 9 + 10 == " + sum);
```

38. What is the bug in the following code? What do you call this kind of loop bug?

```
int n, sum = 0;
for (n = 1; n < 10; n++)
    sum = sum + n;
System.out.println("1 + 2 + ...+ 9 + 10 == " + sum);
```

3.4 THE TYPE `boolean`

The truth is out there. -Included in the credits for the television program *The X Files.*
He who would distinguish the true from the false must have an adequate idea of what is true and false. -Benedict Spinoza, *Ethics*

The type boolean is a primitive type, just like the types `int`, `double`, and `char`. As with these other types, you can have expressions of type `boolean`, values of type `boolean`, constants of type `boolean`, and variables of type `boolean`. However, there are only two values of type `boolean`: `true` and `false`. You can use the two values `true` and `false` in a program, just as you use numeric constants, such as 2 and `3.45`, and character constants, such as `'A'`.

Boolean variables can be used, among other things, to make your program easier to read. For example, a program might contain the following statement, where `systemsAreOK` is a boolean variable that is `true` if, in fact, the launch systems are ready to go:

```
if (systemsAreOK)
    System.out.println("Initiate launch sequence.");
else
    System.out.println("Abort launching sequence.");
```

If you do not use a boolean variable, the preceding code is likely to read something like the following:

```
if ((temperature <= 100) && (thrust >= 12000)
                         && (cabinPressure > 30))
    System.out.println("Initiate launch sequence.");
else
    System.out.println("Abort launching sequence.");
```

Clearly, the first version with the boolean variable is easier for a human being to understand.

Of course, your program needs to set the value of the boolean variable `systemsAreOK` in some way. As you will see, that is easy to do.

Boolean Expressions and Boolean Variables

A boolean expression evaluates to one of the two values `true` or `false`. For example, the expression `number > 0` in the following is a boolean expression:

```
if (number > 0)
    System.out.println("The number is positive.");
else
    System.out.println("The number is negative or zero.");
```

If `number > 0` evaluates to `true`, the output is `"The number is positive."` If, on the other hand, `number > 0` evaluates to `false`, then the output is `"The number is negative or zero."` The meaning of a boolean expression like `number > 0` is a bit easier to understand within a context, such as an `if-else` statement. However, when programming with boolean variables, you need to think about a boolean expression more or less without a context. A boolean expression can be evaluated and can produce a value of `true` or `false` without reference to any `if-else` statement, `while` loop, or other context that you have seen before this section.

boolean variables in assignments

A boolean variable can be given the value of a boolean expression by using an assignment statement, in the same way that you use an assignment statement to set the value of an `int` variable or any other type of variable. For example, the following sets the value of the boolean variable `isPositive` to `false`.:

```
int number = -5;
boolean isPositive;
isPositive = (number > 0);
```

If you prefer, you can combine the last two lines as follows:

```
boolean isPositive = (number > 0);
```

The parentheses are not needed, but they do make it a bit easier to read.

Once a boolean variable has a value, you can use the boolean variable just as you would use any other boolean expression. For example,

```
boolean isPositive = (number > 0);
if (isPositive)
    System.out.println("The number is positive.");
else
    System.out.println("The number is negative or zero.");
```

is equivalent to

```
if (number > 0)
    System.out.println("The number is positive.");
else
    System.out.println("The number is negative or zero.");
```

Of course, this is just a toy example. It is unlikely that anybody would use the first of the preceding two examples, but you might use something like it if the value of `number`, and therefore the value of the boolean expression, might change, as in the following code, which could (by some stretch of the imagination) be part of a program to evaluate lottery tickets:

```
System.out.println("Enter your number:");
number = SavitchIn.readLineInt();
boolean isPositive = (number > 0);
while (number > 0);
{
    System.out.println("Wow!");
    number= number - 1000;
}
if (isPositive)
    System.out.println("Your number is positive.");
else
    System.out.println("Sorry, your number is not positive.");
System.out.println("Only positive numbers can win.");
```

More complicated boolean expressions can be used in the same way. For example, if `systemsAreOK` is a variable of type `boolean`, it can be given a value as follows:

```
systemsAreOK = (temperature <= 100) && (thrust >= 12000)
                                    && (cabinPressure > 30);
```

Programming Tip
Naming Boolean Variables

When naming a boolean variable, choose a statement that will be true when the value of the boolean expression is `true`, such as `isPositive`, `systemsAreOK`, and so forth. That way you can easily understand the meaning of the boolean variable when it is used in a `while` loop, `if-else` statement, or other control statement. Avoid names that do not unambiguously describe the meaning of the value of the variable. Do not use names like `numberSign`, `systemStatus`, and so forth.

Precedence Rules

Java evaluates boolean expressions using the same strategy that it uses to evaluate arithmetic expressions. Let's consider an example:

```
(score >= 80) && (score < 90)
```

Suppose the value of `score` is 95. The first subexpression `(score >= 80)` evaluates to `true`. The second subexpression `(score < 90)` evaluates to `false`. So the entire expression is reduced to

```
true && false
```

The computer combines the values of `true` and `false` according to rules called **truth tables** that are given in Display 3.15. So, the preceding expression evaluates to `false`.

truth tables

DISPLAY 3.15 Truth Tables for Boolean Operators *(Part 1 of 2)*

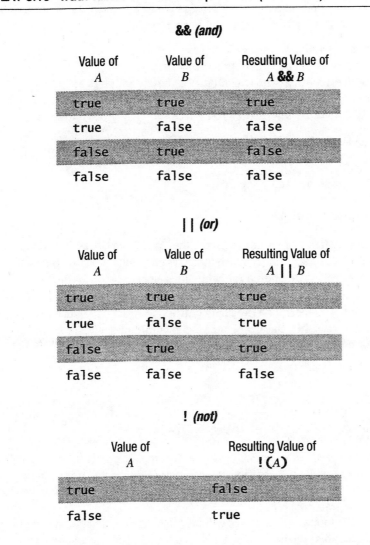

&& (and)

Value of *A*	Value of *B*	Resulting Value of *A* **&&** *B*
`true`	`true`	`true`
`true`	`false`	`false`
`false`	`true`	`false`
`false`	`false`	`false`

|| (or)

Value of *A*	Value of *B*	Resulting Value of *A* **||** *B*
`true`	`true`	`true`
`true`	`false`	`true`
`false`	`true`	`true`
`false`	`false`	`false`

! (not)

Value of *A*	Resulting Value of **!**(*A*)
`true`	`false`
`false`	`true`

complete evaluation

Java also allows you to ask for **complete evaluation.** In complete evaluation, when two expressions are joined by an "and" or an "or," *both* subexpressions are *always evaluated*, and then the truth tables are used to obtain the value of the final expression. To obtain complete evaluation in Java, you use & rather than && for "and" and use | in place of || for "or."

In most situations, short-circuit evaluation and complete evaluation give the same result, but as you have just seen, there are times when short-circuit evaluation can avoid a run-time error. There are also some situations in which complete evaluation is preferred, but we will not use those techniques in this book, and so we will always use && and || to obtain short-circuit evaluation.

Input and Output of Boolean Values

The values `true` and `false` of the type `boolean` can be input and output in the same way that values of the other primitive types, such as `int` and `double`, can. For example, consider the following fragment from a Java program:

```
boolean booleanVar = false;
System.out.println(booleanVar);
System.out.println("Enter a boolean value:");
booleanVar = SavitchIn.readLineBoolean();
System.out.println("You entered " + booleanVar);
```

This code could produce the following dialog:

```
false
Enter a boolean value:
true
You entered true
```

As you can see from this example, the class `SavitchIn` has a method named `readLineBoolean` that will read a single `boolean` value on a line by itself. For this method, you may spell `true` and `false` with either uppercase or lowercase letters; you also may use the single letter `t` or `f` (uppercase or lowercase) for `true` and `false`. These spelling variations of `true` and `false` apply only to input and only when using the method `readLineBoolean`. In a Java program, the spelling must always be either `true` or `false`, spelled out and in all lowercase.

T and F

Case Study
Using a Boolean Variable to End a Loop

In this case study, you will not solve a complete problem, but you will design a loop for a commonly occurring subtask and place it in a demonstration program. This will allow you to become familiar with one of the most common uses of boolean variables.

task specification

The loop you will design will read in a list of numbers and compute the sum of all the numbers on the list. You know that the numbers are all nonnegative. For example, the numbers might be a list of the number of hours worked for each person on a programming team. Because nobody works a negative number of hours, you know the numbers are all nonnegative, and so you can use a negative number as a sentinel value to mark the end of the list. For this task, you know the numbers will all be integers, but the same technique would work for other kinds of numbers and even for reading in nonnumeric data.

You will get a better grasp of the problem and possible solutions if you first design the loop in pseudocode. So, you design the following pseudocode:

```
int sum = 0;
Do the following for each number on the list:
    if (the number is negative)
        Make this the last loop iteration.
    else
        sum = sum + the number;
```

Because you know that there is a negative number marking the end of the list, you refine the pseudocode to the following:

```
int next, sum = 0;
while (There are numbers left to read.)
{
    next = SavitchIn.readLineInt();
    if (next < 0)
        Make this the last loop iteration.
    else
        sum = sum + next;
}
```

There are a number of different ways to finish converting this pseudocode to Java code. You have just learned about boolean variables, so let's say you decide to try them (and that will turn out to be a good decision). One nice thing about a boolean variable is that it can read just like an English sentence. So you decide to try a boolean variable named `thereAreNumbersLeftToRead`. Simply declaring this boolean variable and substituting it for the phrase "There are numbers left to read." yields the following:

```
int next, sum = 0;
boolean thereAreNumbersLeftToRead;
Initialize the variable thereAreNumbersLeftToRead.
while (thereAreNumbersLeftToRead)
{
    next = SavitchIn.readLineInt();
    if (next < 0)
        Make this the last loop iteration.
    else
        sum = sum + next;
}
```

Now it is straightforward to complete this loop to produce working Java code. The phrase "Make this the last loop iteration." can be translated in one obvious way. The loop ends when the boolean variable `thereAreNumbersLeftToRead` has a value of `false`. So the way to end the loop is to set `thereAreNumbersLeftToRead` equal to `false`. Thus, "Make this the last loop iteration." will translate into

```
thereAreNumbersLeftToRead = false;
```

All that is left to do is to determine the initial value for the boolean variable `thereAreNumbersLeftToRead`. You know that even if the list of numbers is empty, there will at least be the sentinel value to read, so you know the loop body must be iterated at least once. Thus, in order for the loop to get started, `thereAreNumbersLeftToRead` must be `true`, meaning that it must be initialized to `true`. Thus, you come up with the following code:

```
int next, sum = 0;
boolean thereAreNumbersLeftToRead = true;
while (thereAreNumbersLeftToRead)
{
    next = SavitchIn.readLineInt();
    if (next < 0)
        thereAreNumbersLeftToRead = false;
    else
        sum = sum + next;
}
```

When the loop ends, the variable `sum` contains the sum of the numbers on the input list (not including the sentinel value).

All that is left is to put the loop into a program. You decide that the variable name `thereAreNumbersLeftToRead` is a bit too long, and so you shorten it to `numbersLeft` and produce the program shown in Display 3.17. ■

? Self-Test Questions

39. What output is produced by the following statements?

```
int number = 7;
boolean isPositive = (number > 0);
if (number > 0);
    number = -100;
if (isPositive)
    System.out.println("Positive.");
else
    System.out.println("Not positive.");
```

40. What output is produced by the following statements?

```
System.out.println(false);
System.out.println(7 < 0);
System.out.println(7 > 0);
int n = 7;
System.out.println(n > 0);
```

DISPLAY 3.17 Use of a Boolean Variable to End a Loop

```
/**
 Illustrates the use of a boolean variable to control loop ending.
*/
public class BooleanDemo
{
    public static void main(String[] args)
    {
        System.out.println(
                   "Enter nonnegative numbers, one per line.");
        System.out.println("Place a negative number at the end");
        System.out.println("to serve as an end marker.");

        int next, sum = 0;
        boolean numbersLeft = true;
        while (numbersLeft)
        {
            next = SavitchIn.readLineInt();
            if (next < 0)
                 numbersLeft = false;
            else
                 sum = sum + next;
        }

        System.out.println("The sum of the numbers is " + sum);
    }
}
```

Sample Screen Dialog

```
Enter nonnegative numbers, one per line.
Place a negative number at the end
to serve as an end marker.
1
2
3
-1
The sum of the numbers is 6
```

41. What output is produced by the following statements?

```
System.out.println(true && false);
System.out.println(true || false);
System.out.println(true || (x > 0));
```

CHAPTER SUMMARY

- A statement that chooses one of a number of actions to perform is called a branch. The `if-else` and `switch` statements are branch statements.
- Java has two forms of multiway branches: the `switch` statement and the multibranch `if-else` statement.
- A loop is a programming construct that repeats an action some number of times. The part that is repeated is called the body of the loop. Every repetition of the loop body is called a loop iteration.
- Java has three kinds of loop statements: the `while` statement, the `do-while` statement, and the `for` statement.
- One way to end an input loop is to place a sentinel value at the end of the input list and have your loop check for the sentinel value.
- The most common kinds of loop bugs are unintended infinite loops and off-by-one errors.
- Tracing a variable means that the value of the variable is output every time the variable is changed. This can be done with special debugging utilities or by inserting temporary output statements. (Sometimes you do not output every change but just selected changes.)
- The value of a boolean expression can be stored in a variable of type `boolean`. This variable of type `boolean` can then be used to control an `if-else` statement or a `while` statement and can also be used anyplace else that a boolean expression is allowed.

✔ Answers to Self-Test Questions

1.

```
if (goals > 10)
    System.out.println("Wow");
else
    System.out.println("Oh Well");
```

2.

```
if ((goals > 10) && (errors == 0))
    System.out.println("Wow");
else
    System.out.println("Oh Well");
```

3.

```
if (salary >= deductions)
{
    System.out.println("OK");
    net = salary - deductions;
}
else
{
    System.out.println("Crazy");
}
```

It is also acceptable to omit the braces in the `else` part.

4.

```
if ((speed > 25) && (visibility < 20))
{
    speed = 25;
    System.out.println("Caution");
}
```

5.

```
if ((salary >= MIN_SALARY) || (bonus >= MIN_BONUS))
    System.out.println("OK");
else
    System.out.println("Too low");
```

6.

```
String upperWord = nextWord.toUpperCase( );
if (upperWord.compareTo("N") < 0)
    System.out.println("First half of the alphabet");
else
    System.out.println("Second half of the alphabet");
```

7. If they are of type `int`, you use `x1 == x2`. If they are of type `String`, you use `x1.equals(x2)`.

8. `Time and tide wait for me.`

9. `Time and tide wait for no one.`

10. `Time and tide wait for every one.`

11.

```
if (number > 10)
    System.out.println("High");
else if (number < 5)
    System.out.println("Low");
else
    System.out.println("So-so");
```

12. `Till we meet again.`

13.

```
Hello
Good-bye
```

14. Some kind of B.

15. Pie

16. Cookies

17. Diet time

18.

```
0
1
2
3
4
count after loop = 5
```

19. Yes, the body of a `while` loop can execute zero times. No, the body of a `do-while` loop must execute at least once.

20.

```
0
count after loop = 1
```

21.

```
int number;
{
    System.out.println("Enter a whole number:");
    number = SavitchIn.readLineInt();
    System.out.println("You entered " + number);
}
while (number > 0)
{
    System.out.println("Enter a whole number:");
    number = SavitchIn.readLineInt();
    System.out.println("You entered " + number);
}
System.out.println("number after loop = " + number);
```

22. This is an infinite loop. The `println` statement after the loop will never be executed. The output begins

```
0
-1
-2
-3
.
.
.
```

23.

```
1
2
3
4
```

24. This loop causes no output. The boolean expression `n > 4` is not satisfied the first time through the loop, so the loop ends without iterating its body.

25.

```
4
3
2
1
```

26. The only output is

```
0
```

Be sure to notice the semicolon that was added at the end of the first line of the `for` loop.

27.

```
0.0
0.5
1.0
1.5
2.0
2.5
```

28.

```
int n;
for (n = 1; n <= 5; n++)
    System.out.println(2*n);
```

29.

```
Hello
Hello
After the Loop.
```

30.

```
Hello
Hello
```

Note that it does not output `"After the Loop."` because the program ends.

31.

```
One
Two
Three
After the Loop.
```

Note that the `break` statement ends the `switch` statement, but does not end the `for` loop.

32.

```
int time;
for (time = 1; time <= 4; time++)
    System.out.println("One more time.");
```

33.

```
int result = 1;
int count;
for (count = 1; count <= 5; count++)
    result = 2*result;
```

34.

```
0
0
1
0
1
2
```

35. You can use any number less than 1.0 as a sentinel value, but to avoid any problems with the approximate nature of double values, the number you choose should be significantly less than 1.0.

```
double sum = 0, next;
System.out.println("Enter a list of numbers. All the");
System.out.println("numbers must be 1.0 or larger");
System.out.println("Place a zero at the end");
System.out.println("to mark the end of the list.");
next = SavitchIn.readLineDouble();
int count = 0;
while (next > 0.9)
            //next >=1.0 runs a risk of being inaccurate.
{
    sum = sum + next;
    count++;
    next = SavitchIn.readLineDouble();
}
if (count > 0)
    System.out.println("Average is " + (sum/count));
else
    System.out.println("No numbers to average.");
```

36. The code contains

```
balance = balance + penalty;
balance = balance - deposit;
```

but it should contain

```
balance = balance - penalty;
balance = balance + deposit;
```

Even after it is fixed in this way, it still has the following problem: If penalty is greater than deposit, it is an infinite loop. This is discussed in the subsection "Loop Bugs."

37.
```
int n, sum = 0;
System.out.println("sum == " + sum);
for (n = 1; n < 10; n++)
{
    sum = sum + n;
    System.out.println("n == " + n);
    System.out.println("sum == " + sum);
}
System.out.println("1 + 2 + ... + 9 + 10 == " + sum);
```

38. The boolean expression should be `n <= 10`, not `n < 10`. This is an off-by-one error.

39. `Positive`

40. The output produced is

```
false
false
true
true
```

41. The output produced is

```
false
true
true
```

Because of short-circuit evaluation, you do not need to know the value of `x`.

Programming Projects

1. Write a program that takes a one-line sentence as input and then outputs the following response: If the sentence ends with a question mark `'?'` and the input contains an even number of characters, then output the word `"Yes"`. If the sentence ends with a question mark `'?'` and the input contains an odd number of characters, output the word `"No"`. If the sentence ends with an exclamation mark `'!'`, output the word `"Wow"`. In all other cases, your program will output the string `"You always say "` followed by the input string enclosed in quotes. Your output should all be on one line. Be sure to note that in the last case, your output must include quotation marks around the echoed input string. In all other cases, there are no quotes in the output. Your program should have a loop that allows the user to repeat this until the user indicates that she/he wants to end the program. Your program does not have to check the input to see that the user has entered a legitimate sentence.

2. Write a program that allows the user to convert either from degrees Celsius to Fahrenheit or from degrees Fahrenheit to Celsius. Use the following formulas:

$$degreesC = 5(degreesF - 32)/9$$
$$degreesF = (9(degreesC)/5) + 32$$

Prompt the user to enter a temperature and either a `'C'` (or `'c'`) for Celsius or an `'F'` (or `'f'`) for Fahrenheit; allow either uppercase or lower case, but if anything other than `'C'`, `'c'`, `'F'`, or `'f'` is entered, print an error message and ask the user to reenter a valid selection (uppercase or lowercase `'C'` or `'F'`). Convert the temperature to Fahrenheit if Celsius is entered, or to Celsius if Fahrenheit is entered, and then ask the user to press `'Q'` or `'q'` to quit or to press any other key to repeat the loop and perform another conversion.

3. Write a program to read in a list of nonnegative integers and to output the largest integer, the smallest integer, and the average of all the integers. The end of the input is indicated by the user entering a negative sentinel value. Note that the sentinel value is not used in finding the largest, smallest, or average. It is only an end marker. The average should be a value of type `double` so that the average is computed with a fractional part.

4. Write a program to read a list of exam scores (integer percentages in the range 0 to 100) and to output the total number of grades and the number of grades in each letter-grade category (90 to 100 = A, 80 to 89 = B, 70 to 79 = C, 60 to 69 = D, and 0 to 59 = F). The end of the input is indicated by a negative score as a sentinel value. (The negative value is used only to end the loop, so do not use it in the calculations). For example, if the input is

```
98
87
86
85
85
78
73
72
72
72
70
66
63
50
-1
```

   the output would be

```
Total number of grades = 14
Number of A's = 1
Number of B's = 4
Number of C's = 6
Number of D's = 2
Number of F's = 1
```

5. Combine the programs from Programming Projects 3 and 4 to read in test scores (whole-number percentages from 0 to 100) and print out the following statistics:

   Total number of scores
   Total number of each letter grade
   Percentage of total for each letter grade
   Range of scores: lowest and highest
   Average score

As before, enter a negative score as a sentinel value to end the data input and print out the statistics.

6. Write a program that takes as input a bank account balance and an interest rate and outputs the value of the account in 10 years. The output should show the value of the account for three different methods of compounding interest: annually, monthly, and daily. When compounded annually, the interest is added once per year at the end of the year. When compounded monthly, the interest is added 12 times per year. When computed daily, the interest is added 365 times per year. You do not have to worry about leap years. Assume all years have 365 days. For annual interest, you can assume that the interest is posted exactly one year from the date of deposit. In other words, you do not have to worry about interest being posted on a specific day of the year, like December 31. Similarly, you can assume that monthly interest is posted exactly one month after it is deposited. Since the account earns interest on the interest, the account should have a higher balance when interest is posted more frequently. Be sure to adjust the interest rate for the time period of the interest. If the rate is 5 percent, then when posting monthly interest, you use (5/12) percent. When posting daily interest, you use (5/365) percent. Do your calculation using a loop that adds in the interest for each time period. (In other words, do not use some sort of algebraic formula.) Your program should have an outer loop that allows the user to repeat this calculation for a new balance and interest rate. The calculation is repeated until the user indicates that she/he wants to end the program.

7. Modify Programming Project 9 from Chapter 2 to include input checking. Print the change only if a valid price is entered (no less than 25 cents, no more than 100 cents, and an integer multiple of 5 cents). Otherwise, print separate error messages for any of the following invalid inputs: a cost under 25 cents, a cost that is not an integer multiple of 5, and a cost that is more than a dollar.

8. Write a program that asks the user to enter the size of triangle to print out (an integer from 1 to 50), then print the triangle by printing a series of lines consisting of asterisks. The first line will have one asterisk, the next two, and so on, with each line having one more asterisk than the previous line, up to the number entered by the user. On the next line print one less asterisk and continue by decreasing the number of asterisks by 1 for each successive line until only one asterisk is printed. Hint: Use nested `for` loops; the outside loop controls the number of lines to print, and the inside loop controls the number of asterisks to print on a line. For example, if the user enters 5, the output would be

```
*
**
***
****
*****
****
***
**
*
```

Chapter 4

Defining Classes and Methods

Chapter

4

Defining Classes and Methods

class n. 1. a. A set, collection, group, or configuration containing members having or thought to have at least one attribute in common; kind; sort. . . . -The American Heritage Dictionary of the English Language, Third Edition

Recall that an object is named by a variable of a class type. Objects have data, but they also can take actions. The actions they can take are called methods. You have already been using some objects. The type `String` is a class, and values of type `String` are objects. For example, if `name` is an object of type `String`, then the method `length` can be used to determine the length of the string. The length of the string is the value returned by the expression `name.length( )`. In this chapter, we will show you how to define your own simple classes and how to use objects and methods of those classes.

OBJECTIVES

Become familiar with the concepts of a class and of an object that instantiates the class.

Learn how to define classes in Java.

Learn to define and use methods (object actions) in Java.

Learn to create objects in Java.

Find out how parameters work in Java.

Learn about information hiding and encapsulation.

Become familiar with the notion of reference so that you can understand class variables and class parameters.

PREREQUISITES

You need to be familiar with the material in Chapters 2 and 3 before reading this chapter.

4.1 CLASS AND METHOD DEFINITIONS

A Java program consists of objects, from various classes, interacting with one another. Before we go into the details of how you define and use classes and objects in Java, it will help to have a general idea of what classes and objects are all about.

Objects can represent objects in the real word, like automobiles, houses, employee records—almost anything you want. A **class** is the definition of a kind of object. It is like an outline or a plan for constructing specific objects. For example, Display 4.1 describes a class called `Automobile`. The class is a general description of what an automobile is and what it can do. Objects are particular automobiles. The figure shows three `Automobile` objects. An object that satisfies the class definition of an `Automobile` is said to **instantiate** the `Automobile` class. Thus, objects are the individual automobiles, while the `Automobile` class is a description of what an automobile is and does. This is, of course, a very simplified `Automobile` class, but it illustrates the basic idea of what a class is. Let's look at some details. instantiate

A class specifies the kind of data the objects of that class have. The `Automobile` class definition says that an `Automobile` object has three pieces of data: a number telling how many gallons of fuel are in the fuel tank, another number telling how fast the automobile is moving, and a string that shows what is written on the license plate. The class definition has no data (that is, no numbers and no string). The individual objects have the data, but the class specifies what kind of data they have.

■ DISPLAY 4.1 A Class as an Outline

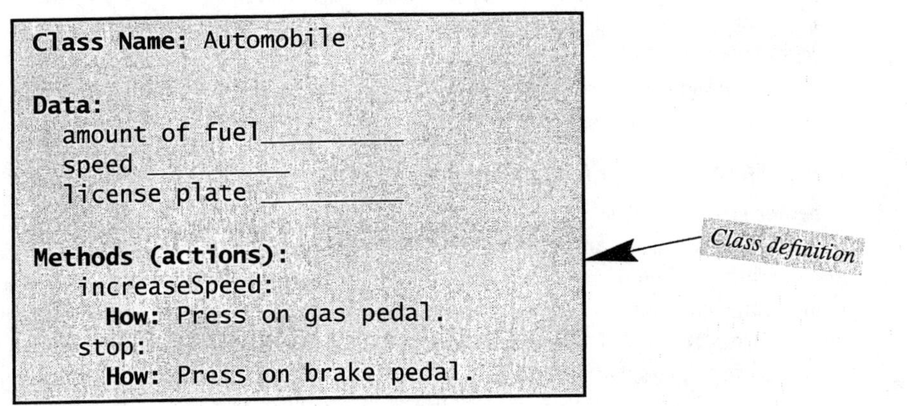

Class Name: Automobile
Data:
amount of fuel________
speed ________
license plate ________
Methods (actions):
increaseSpeed:
How: Press on gas pedal.
stop:
How: Press on brake pedal.
Class definition

Instantiations of the Class Automobile :

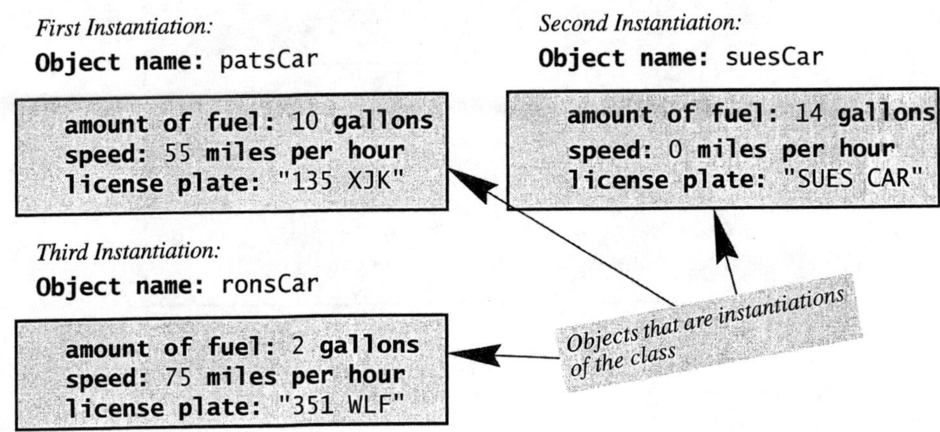

The class also specifies what actions the objects can take and how they accomplish those actions. The `Automobile` class specifies two actions: `increaseSpeed` and `stop`. Thus, in a program that uses the class `Automobile`, the only actions an `Automobile` object can take are `increaseSpeed` and `stop`. These actions are called **methods.** All objects of the class `Automobile` have identical methods. All objects of any one class have the same methods. As you can see in our sample `Automobile` class, the definitions of the methods (how the actions are performed) are given in the class definition. However, the methods' actions are performed by the objects.

method

The notation in Display 4.1 is a bit cumbersome, so programmers often use a simpler graphical notation to summarize some of the main properties of a class. This notation, illustrated in Display 4.2, is called a **UML class diagram,** or simply a **class diagram.** (UML is an acronym for Universal Modeling Language.) The class described in Display 4.2 is the same as the one described in Display 4.1. Any annotations in Display 4.2 that are new will be explained later in the chapter.

class diagram

UML

Notice a few more things about a class and the objects that instantiate the class. Each object has a name. In Display 4.1, the names are `patsCar`, `suesCar`, and `ronsCar`. Among other things, a class is a data type. In a Java program, these object names (`patsCar`, `suesCar`, and `ronsCar`) would be variables of type `Automobile`.

Before we get further into the nitty gritty of Java code by defining a simple class, we should tell you how to store classes in files and how to compile them.

Class Files and Separate Compilation

Whether you use a class taken from this book or a class that you write yourself, you need to know a few basic details about how a Java class definition is stored in a file. Each Java class definition should be in a file by itself,[1] the name of the file should be the same as the name of the class, and the file name should end in `.java`. So if you write a definition for a class called `Automobile`, it should be in a file named `Automobile.java`. If you write a definition for a class called `MyClass`, it should be in a file named `MyClass.java`.

DISPLAY 4.2 A Class Outline as a UML Class Diagram

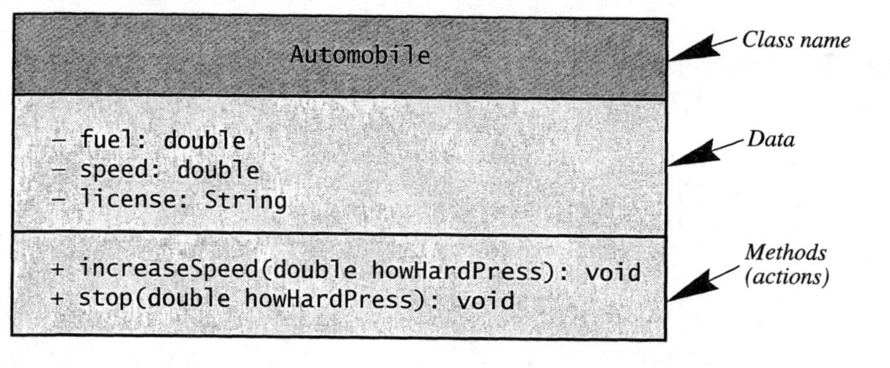

1. There are exceptions to this rule, but we will seldom encounter them, and we need not be concerned about them yet.

You can compile a Java class before you have a program in which to use it. The compiled byte-code for the class will be stored in a file of the same name, but ending in `.class` rather than `.java`. So compiling the file `Automobile.java` will create a file called `Automobile.class`. Later, you can compile a program file with a `main` part that uses the class `Automobile`, and you will not need to recompile the class definition for `Automobile`. This naming requirement applies to full programs as well as to classes. Notice that every program with a `main` part has a class name at the start of the file; this is the name you need to use for the file that holds the program. For example, the program in Display 4.4 should be in a file named `SpeciesFirstTryDemo.java`. As long as all the classes you use in a program are in the same directory as the program file, you need not worry about directories. In Chapter 5, we will discuss how you can place files in more than one directory.

Instance Variables

Display 4.3 contains a simple class definition. We have simplified this class to make this first example easier to explain. Later in the chapter, we will give the same example in a better style. But this example has all the essentials of a class definition.

DISPLAY 4.3 A Class Definition *(Part 1 of 2)*

We will give a better version of this class later in this chapter.

```
public class SpeciesFirstTry
{
    public String name;
    public int population;
    public double growthRate;

    public void readInput()
    {
        System.out.println("What is the species' name?");
        name = SavitchIn.readLine();
        System.out.println("What is the population of the species?");
        population = SavitchIn.readLineInt();
        while (population < 0)
        {
            System.out.println("Population cannot be negative.");
            System.out.println("Reenter population:");
            population = SavitchIn.readLineInt();
        }
        System.out.println(
                      "Enter growth rate (percent increase per year):");
        growthRate = SavitchIn.readLineDouble();
    }

    public void writeOutput()
    {
         System.out.println("Name = " + name);
         System.out.println("Population = " + population);
         System.out.println("Growth rate = " + growthRate + "%");
    }
```

Later in this chapter you will see that the modifier `public` *should be replaced with* `private`.

DISPLAY 4.3 A Class Definition (Part 2 of 2)

```
    public int populationIn10( )
    {
        double populationAmount = population;
        int count = 10;
        while ((count > 0) && (populationAmount > 0))
        {
            populationAmount = (populationAmount +
                                (growthRate/100) * populationAmount);
            count--;
        }
        if (populationAmount > 0)
            return (int)populationAmount;
        else
            return 0;
    }
}
```

(int) *is a type cast, as discussed in Chapter 2.*

The class name is SpeciesFirstTry, and the class is designed to hold records of endangered species. (It's called FirstTry because we will later give an improved version of this class.) Each object of this class has three pieces of data: a name, a population size, and a growth rate. The objects have three methods: readInput, writeOutput, and populationIn10. Both the data items and the methods are sometimes called **members** of the object because they belong to the object; they are also sometimes called **fields.** However, we will call the data items **instance variables** and we will call the methods **methods.** Let's discuss the data items (that is, the instance variables) first.

member

field

instance variable

The following three lines from the start of the class definition define three instance variables (three data members):

```
public String name;
public int population;
public double growthRate;
```

The word public simply means that there are no restrictions on how these instance variables are used. Each of these lines declares one instance variable name. You can think of an object of the class as a complex item with instance variables inside of it. So you can think of an instance variable as a smaller variable inside each object of the class. In this case, the instance variables are called name, population, and growthRate. Each object of the class will have these three instance variables. Display 4.4 contains a program that demonstrates the use of this class definition. Let's see how it handles these instance variables.

The following line from Display 4.4 creates an object of type SpeciesFirstTry and attaches the name speciesOfTheMonth to this object:

```
SpeciesFirstTry speciesOfTheMonth = new SpeciesFirstTry();
```

DISPLAY 4.4 Using Classes and Methods

```
public class SpeciesFirstTryDemo
{
    public static void main(String[] args)
    {
        SpeciesFirstTry speciesOfTheMonth = new SpeciesFirstTry( );
        int futurePopulation;

        System.out.println("Enter data on the Species of the Month:");
        speciesOfTheMonth.readInput( );
        speciesOfTheMonth.writeOutput( );

        futurePopulation = speciesOfTheMonth.populationIn10( );
        System.out.println("In ten years the population will be "
                                          + futurePopulation);

        speciesOfTheMonth.name = "Klingon ox";
        speciesOfTheMonth.population = 10;
        speciesOfTheMonth.growthRate = 15;
        System.out.println("The new Species of the Month:");
        speciesOfTheMonth.writeOutput( );
        System.out.println("In ten years the population will be "
                              + speciesOfTheMonth.populationIn10( ));
    }
}
```

Sample Screen Dialog

```
Enter data on the Species of the Month:
What is the species' name?
Ferengie fur ball
What is the population of the species?
1000
Enter growth rate (percent increase per year):
-20.5
Name = Ferengie fur ball
Population = 1000
Growth rate = -20.5%
In ten years the population will be 100
The new Species of the Month:
Name = Klingon ox
Population = 10
Growth rate = 15.0%
In ten years the population will be 40
```

Like all objects of type SpeciesFirstTry, the object speciesOfTheMonth has three instance variables called name, population, and growthRate. You can refer to one of these instance variables by writing the object name followed by a dot and then the instance variable's name. For example,

```
speciesOfTheMonth.name
```

denotes the name instance variable for the object speciesOfTheMonth. Look again at the three lines that define the instance variables (repeated here):

```
public String name;
public int population;
public double growthRate;
```

Notice that each instance variable has a type. For example, the instance variable name is of type String, and so the instance variable speciesOfTheMonth.name is a variable of type String and can be used anyplace that you can use a variable of type String. For example, all of the following are valid Java expressions:

```
speciesOfTheMonth.name = "Klingon ox.";
System.out.println("Save the " + speciesOfTheMonth.name);
String niceName = speciesOfTheMonth.name;
```

Each object of type SpeciesFirstTry has its own three instance variables. For example, suppose that your program also contained the statement

```
SpeciesFirstTry speciesOfLastMonth = new SpeciesFirstTry();
```

Then speciesOfTheMonth.name and speciesOfLastMonth.name would be two different instance variables that might have different string values.

FAQ: Why Do We Need new?

When new is used in an expression such as the following, you can think of it as creating the instance variables of the object.

```
SpeciesFirstTry speciesOfLastMonth = new SpeciesFirstTry();
```

An object of a class type, such as speciesOfLastMonth, can have smaller variables inside of it, namely, the instance variables of the object. The new places these instance variables inside of the object. We will explain this use of new more completely in Section 4.3.

Using Methods

invoke
call

When you use a method, you are said to **invoke** or **call** it. You have already invoked methods. For example, your programs have invoked the method readLineInt( ) of the class SavitchIn. You have also invoked the method println with the object System.out, as in the following statement:

```
System.out.println("Enter data on the Species of the Month:");
```

There are two kinds of methods: (1) those that return a single value and (2) those that perform some action other than returning a single value. The method readLineInt is an example of a method that returns a single value. It returns a value of type `int`. The method `println` is an example of a method that performs some action other than returning a single value. These two different kinds of methods are used in slightly different ways.

Remember: Two Kinds of Methods

There are two kinds of methods: (1) those that return a single value and (2) those that perform some action other than return a value. Methods that perform some action other than returning a value are called **`void` methods.**

Let's first discuss how you invoke a method that returns a value, using the method `readLineInt` as an example. Suppose you have the following declaration in a program:

```
int next;
```

The following is an example of an invocation of the method `readLineInt` for the class `SavitchIn`:

```
next = SavitchIn.readLineInt();
```

(If you want to see this invocation in the context of a full program, refer back to Display 3.17 in Chapter 3.) Let's look at this method invocation in more detail.

A method defined in a class is usually invoked using an object of that class. This object is known as the **calling object,** and it is the first item that you give when writing a method invocation. For certain special methods, you can use the name of the class instead of using an object of the class, and our first example will use the class name `SavitchIn` rather than an object of that class. You invoke a method by writing the calling object name or the class name (such as `SavitchIn`), followed by a dot, and then the name of the method (such as `readLineInt`), and finally a set of parentheses that may (or may not) have information for the method. If the method is one that returns a single value, such as the method `readLineInt`, you can use this method invocation anyplace that it is valid to use a value of the type returned by the method. The method `readLineInt` returns a value of type `int`, and so you can use the method invocation

calling object

value returned

```
SavitchIn.readLineInt()
```

anyplace that it is valid to use a value of type `int`. For example, a value of type `int`, such as 6, can be used in an assignment statement, like this:

```
next = 6;
```

So, the method invocation `SavitchIn.readLineInt()` can be used in the same way, like so:

```
next = SavitchIn.readLineInt();
```

When a method that returns a single value is invoked, it is as if the method invocation were replaced by the value returned. So, if `SavitchIn.readLineInt()` returns the value 3, then the assignment statement

```
next = SavitchIn.readLineInt();
```

produces the same effect as

```
next = 3;
```

not returning a value

Methods that perform some action other than returning a single value are similar, except that they are used to produce Java statements rather than Java values. For example, the following statement from the program in Display 4.4 includes an invocation of the method `println` with the calling object `System.out`:

```
System.out.println("Enter data on the Species of the Month:");
```

This method call causes the string `"Enter data on the Species of the Month:"` to be written to the screen. The method `writeOutput` for the class `SpeciesFirstTry` (used in Display 4.4) is similar, except that you do not have to tell `writeOutput` what to output by including something inside the parentheses. The method `writeOutput` gets the information to send to the screen from its calling object.

For example, the program in Display 4.4 (after doing some other things) sets the values of the instance variables of the object `speciesOfTheMonth` with the following three assignment statements:

```
speciesOfTheMonth.name = "Klingon ox";
speciesOfTheMonth.population = 10;
speciesOfTheMonth.growthRate = 15;
```

The program then uses the following statements to output these values:

```
System.out.println("The new Species of the Month:");
speciesOfTheMonth.writeOutput();
```

The second of the previous two lines of code contains an invocation of the method `writeOutput` with the calling object `speciesOfTheMonth`. This invocation produces the output

```
Name = Klingon ox
Population = 10
Growth rate = 15.0%
```

Recall that, to invoke a method for an object, you write the calling object name (such as `speciesOfTheMonth`), followed by a dot, the name of the method (such as `writeOutput`), and finally a set of parentheses that may have information for the method. If, as is true in this case, the method invocation is one that produces some action other than returning a single value, then you make it into a Java statement by placing a semicolon after the method invocation. For example, the following is an invocation of the method `writeOutput` for the object `speciesOfTheMonth`:

```
speciesOfTheMonth.writeOutput();
```

This causes the method to perform whatever action is specified in the method definition.

Quick Reference: Method Invocation (Calling a Method)

You **invoke** a method by writing the calling object followed by a dot, then the name of the method, and finally a set of parentheses that may (or may not) have information to pass to the method.

If the method invocation returns a value, then you can use the method invocation anyplace that you are allowed to write a value of the type returned by the method. For example, the following includes an invocation of the method `populationIn10` by the calling object `speciesOfTheMonth`:

```
futurePopulation = speciesOfTheMonth.populationIn10();
```

If the method invocation is one that performs some action other than returning a single value, then you place a semicolon after the method invocation, and that produces a Java statement. (These methods that perform actions are called `void` methods.) For example, the following is an invocation of the `void` method `readInput` with the calling object `speciesOfTheMonth`:

```
speciesOfTheMonth.readInput();
```

This method invocation causes the method to perform whatever action is specified in the method definition.

For certain special methods (like the methods in the class `SavitchIn`), you can use the class name rather than a calling object. These kinds of methods are discussed more fully in Chapter 5.

`void` Method Definitions

The following method invocation is from Display 4.4:

```
speciesOfTheMonth.writeOutput();
```

Let's look at the definition of the method `writeOutput` to see how method definitions are written. The definition is given in Display 4.3 and is repeated here:

```
public void writeOutput()   <-- Heading
{
    System.out.println("Name = " + name);
    System.out.println("Population = " + population);
    System.out.println("Growth rate = " + growthRate + "%");
}
```

All method definitions belong to some class, and all method definitions are given inside the definition of the class to which they belong. If you look at Display 4.3, you will see that this method definition is inside the definition of the class `SpeciesFirstTry`. This means that the method can be used only with objects of the class `SpeciesFirstTry`.

`void` method

The definition of a method that does not return a value starts with the keywords `public void`, followed by the name of the method and a pair of parentheses. The word `public` indicates that there are no special restrictions on the use of the method. Later in this chapter, you will see that the word `public` can sometimes be replaced with other modifiers to restrict the use of the method. The word `void` is a rather poor choice, but it is what is used in Java and in other languages. The word `void` indicates that the method does not return a value. The parentheses enclose any extra information that the method will need. In this case, no extra information is needed, and so there is nothing inside the parentheses. Later in the chapter, you will see examples of the sorts of things that might appear inside these parentheses (for other method definitions). This first part of the method definition is called the **heading** for the method. The heading is normally written on a single line; but, if it is too long for one line, it can be broken into two (or more) lines. Because of the

method heading

method body

use of the word `void` in the method heading, these methods (that do not return a value) are called `void` **methods**.

After the heading comes the **body** of the method definition, and that completes the method definition. The body of the method definition is enclosed between braces { }. Between the braces, you can place any statement or declaration that you can place in the `main` part of a program. Any variable used in a method definition (other than an instance variable) should be declared within that method definition.

When a `void` method is invoked, it is as if the method invocation were replaced by the body of the method definition, and the statements (and declarations) within the body are executed. There are some subtleties about this replacement process, but for the simple examples we will look at now, it is like a literal replacement of the method invocation by the body of the method definition. Eventually, you'll want to learn to think of the method definition as defining an action to be taken, rather than as a list of statements to substitute for the method invocation, but this substitution idea is correct and is a good way to start understanding method invocations.

For example, the following method invocation occurs in the program in Display 4.4:

```
speciesOfTheMonth.writeOutput();
```

When this method invocation is executed, it is as if the line with the method invocation were replaced by the body of the method definition for the method `writeOutput`. In this case, it is as if the preceding method invocation were replaced with the following:

```
{
    System.out.println("Name = " + name);
    System.out.println("Population = " + population);
    System.out.println("Growth rate = " + growthRate + "%");
}
```

The instance variable names (`name`, `population`, and `growthRate`) refer to the instance variables of the calling object; in this example, they refer to the instance variables of the object `speciesOfTheMonth`. To be more precise, the invocation is equivalent to the following:

```
{
    System.out.println("Name = " + speciesOfTheMonth.name);
    System.out.println("Population = "
                        + speciesOfTheMonth.population);
    System.out.println("Growth rate = "
                            + speciesOfTheMonth.growthRate + "%");
}
```

To be very concrete, if `speciesOfTheMonth.name` has the value `"Klingon ox"`, `speciesOfTheMonth.population` has the value `10`, and `speciesOfTheMonth.growthRate` has the value `15`, then the method invocation

```
speciesOfTheMonth.writeOutput();
```

will cause the following to be written to the computer screen:

```
Name = Klingon ox
Population = 10
Growth rate = 15.0%
```

If you look at the program in Display 4.4, you will see that it looks like a class definition that has no instance variables and only a single method that is named `main`. It is in fact true that `main` is a method. A program is simply a class that has a method named `main`. All the programs that we have written so far have no instance variables and no methods other than the method `main`, but a program can have other methods and can have instance variables. When you run a program, you are simply invoking the `void` method that is named `main`. Of course, this is a special kind of method invocation, but it is a method invocation nonetheless. For now, those extra words like `static` and `String[] args` will remain a bit of a mystery. Just put them in, and eventually we will explain them all.

`main` method

Methods That Return a Value

methods that return a value

You define a method that returns a single value in basically the same way that you define a `void` method, with one added complication—namely, specifying the value returned. Let's consider the method `populationIn10` from the class `SpeciesFirstTry`. The method is used in the following line of the program in Display 4.4:

```
futurePopulation = speciesOfTheMonth.populationIn10( );
```

This sets the value of the variable `futurePopulation` equal to the value returned by the method invocation

```
speciesOfTheMonth.populationIn10( )
```

The definition of the method `populationIn10` tells the computer how to compute the value returned. Let's look at that method definition, reproduced here from Display 4.3:

```
public int populationIn10( )
{
    double populationAmount = population;
    int count = 10;
    while ((count > 0) && (populationAmount > 0))
    {
        populationAmount = (populationAmount +
                      (growthRate/100) * populationAmount);
        count--;
    }
    if (populationAmount > 0)
        return (int)populationAmount;
    else
        return 0;
}
```

As was true of a `void` method definition, the definition of a method that returns a value can be divided into two parts: the method heading and the method body. The following is the method heading for the method `populationIn10`:

```
public int populationIn10( )
```

The description of a method heading for a method that returns a value is almost the same as that for the heading of a `void` method. The only difference is that a method that returns a value uses a type name instead of the keyword `void`. The heading begins with the keyword `public`, followed by a type name (rather than the word `void`), followed by the name of the method and a pair of parentheses. The parentheses enclose a description of any extra information that the method will need. In this case, no extra information is needed, and so there is nothing inside the parentheses. The keyword `public` indicates that there are no special restrictions on the use of the method. Later in this chapter, you will see that the word `public` can be replaced with other modifiers to restrict the use of the method. The important new element is the use of a type name—`int` in this example—in the method heading. Let's consider that type name.

type returned

The heading of a method that returns a value includes a type name. The type name is the type of the value returned. Each method can return values of only one type. In different situations, a method may return different values, but they must all be values of the type specified in the method heading.

`return` statement

The body of a method definition that returns a value is just like the body of a `void` method definition, except that it must contain the following in one or more places:

```
return Expression;
```

This is called a `return` **statement.** The *Expression* can be any expression that produces a value of the type specified in the heading of the method definition. This statement says that the value returned by the method is the value of this expression. For example, the definition of the method `populationIn10` contains two `return` statements:

```
return (int)populationAmount;
```

and

```
return 0;
```

When a method that returns a value is invoked, the statements in the body of the method definition are executed. For example, consider the following method invocation from Display 4.4:

```
futurePopulation = speciesOfTheMonth.populationIn10( );
```

When this assignment statement is executed, the body of the method definition for `populationIn10` is executed. That body follows:

```
{
    double populationAmount = population;
    int count = 10;
    while ((count > 0) && (populationAmount > 0))
    {
        populationAmount = (populationAmount +
                        (growthRate/100) * populationAmount);
        count--;
    }
    if (populationAmount > 0)
        return (int)populationAmount;
    else
        return 0;
}
```

`(int)` *is a type cast, as discussed in Chapter 2.*

The instance variable `population` refers to the instance variable of the calling object, which in this case is `speciesOfTheMonth`. The value of `population` is copied into the variable `populationAmount`, and then the `while` loop is executed. Each iteration of the loop increases the value of populationAmount by the amount that the population will change in one year, and the loop is iterated 10 times. So when the while loop ends, the value of populationAmount is the projected size of the population in 10 years. At that point, populationAmount has the value that we want the method to return. For now, let's assume that that number is positive (that is, that the species is not extinct). In that case, the following return statement is executed, and it says that the value (int)populationAmount is the value computed by (returned by) the method invocation:

```
return (int)populationAmount;
```

The (int) is a type cast that changes the double value to an int value so that you do not have a fraction of an animal. (Ugh!) It is as if the method invocation were replaced by (int)populationAmount. In this case, the method invocation is in the following assignment statement:

```
futurePopulation = speciesOfTheMonth.populationIn10( );
```

Therefore, the variable futurePopulation is set to the value of (int)populationAmount.

If populationAmount happens to be zero or negative, the following return statement is executed instead:

```
return 0;
```

This is a minor detail that ensures that the projected population will not be negative. After all, in the real world, once a population reaches zero individuals, the population just stays at zero; it does not go negative.

When a return statement is executed, that statement determines the value returned by the method. When a return statement is executed, that also ends the method invocation. If there are more statements after the return statement, they are not executed.

A method that returns a value may perform some other action as well, such as reading a value from the keyboard, but it definitely must return a value.

Remember: Naming Methods

Java will let you use any valid (nonkeyword) identifier as the name for a method. But if you choose clear, meaningful names, your code will be easier to read. A good rule to follow when naming methods is to (usually) use verbs to name void methods and to (usually) use nouns to name methods that return a value. This is because, like a verb, a void method names an action. On the other hand, a method that returns a value can be used like a value, and a value is a thing, and nouns are used to denote things.

The normal convention when naming classes and methods is to start all method names with a lowercase letter and to start all class names with an uppercase letter.

FAQ: What Is a Function?

Methods that return a value are called functions in some other programming languages, and a method that returns a value does correspond to the mathematical notion of a function. However, in Java they are called methods (that return a value). They are not called functions.

■ Java Tip
Use of `return` in `void` Methods

A `void` method returns no value and so is not required to have any `return` statement. However, there is a kind of `return` statement that you may sometimes want to use in a `void` method. A `return` statement within a `void` method has the form

```
return;
```

It is just like the other `return` statements you have seen, except that you do not include any expression for the value returned (because no value is returned). When this `return` statement is executed, the invocation of the `void` method ends. This can be used to end a method invocation early, such as when the method discovers some sort of problem. For example, you might add the following method to the definition of the class `SpeciesFirstTry`:

```
public void showLandPortion()
{
    if (population == 0)
    {
        System.out.println("Population is zero.");
        return;//Ends here to avoid division by zero.
    }
    double fraction;
    fraction = 6.0/population;
    System.out.println("If the population were spread");
    System.out.println("over 6 continents, then each");
    System.out.println("individual would have a fraction of");
    System.out.println("its continent equal to " + fraction);
}
```

The method ends with a `return` if the rest of the method would involve a division by zero. (It's not a very likely method, but it does illustrate the point.) □

Quick Reference: Method Definitions

Every method belongs to some class. The definition of a method is given in the definition of the class to which it belongs. The two most common forms for a method definition follow.

`void` Method Definition:

```
public void Method_Name(Parameters)
{
    Statement_1
    Statement_2
       ...
```

```
        Statement_Last
    }
```

(So far, we have not discussed *Parameters*, but we will do so shortly. If there are no *Parameters*, the parentheses are empty.)

Example:

```
public void writeOutput()
{
    System.out.println("Name = " + name);
    System.out.println("Population = " + population);
    System.out.println("Growth rate = " + growthRate + "%");
}
```

Definition of a Method That Returns a Value:

```
public Type_Returned Method_Name(Parameters)
{
    <List of statements, at least one of which
          must contain a return statement.>
}
```

(So far, we have not discussed *Parameters*, but we will do so shortly. If there are no *Parameters*, the parentheses are empty.)

Example: (this could be added to the class in Display 4.3):

```
public int halfThePopulation()
{
    return (population/2);
}
```

Quick Reference: `return` Statements

Every method definition for a method that returns a value must have one or more `return` statements. A `return` statement specifies the value returned by the method and ends the method invocation.

Syntax:

```
return Expression;
```

Example:

```
public int halfThePopulation()
{
    return (population/2);
}
```

A `void` method is not required to have a `return` statement, but it can have one if you want to end the method invocation before the end of the code. The form for a `return` statement in a `void` method is

```
return;
```

The `this` Parameter

Look back at the class definition of the class `SpeciesFirstTry` in Display 4.3, and then look at the program in Display 4.4 that uses this class. Notice that instance variables are written differently depending on whether they are within the class definition or someplace outside the class definition, such as in a program that uses the class. Outside of the class definition, you name an instance variable by giving the name of an object of the class, followed by a dot and the name of the instance variable, as in the following reference to the instance variable `name` that appears in Display 4.4:

```
speciesOfTheMonth.name = "Klingon ox";
```

However, inside the definition of a method of that same class, you can simply use the instance variable name without any object name or dot. For example, the following line occurs inside the definition of the method `readInput` of the class `SpeciesFirstTry` in Display 4.3:

```
name = SavitchIn.readLine();
```

As you know, every instance variable, including this instance variable `name`, is an instance variable of some object. In cases like this, the object is understood to be there, but its name usually is omitted. This understood object has the somewhat unusual name of

`this` `this`. Although `this` is usually omitted (but understood to be there), you can include it if you want. For example, the preceding assignment of the instance variable `name`, which we copied from the definition of the method `readInput` in Display 4.3, is equivalent to the following:

```
this.name = SavitchIn.readLine();
```

As another example, the following is a rewrite of the method definition for the method `writeOutput`. It is equivalent to the version used in Display 4.3.

```
public void writeOutput()
{
    System.out.println("Name = " + this.name);
    System.out.println("Population = " + this.population);
    System.out.println("Growth rate = " + this.growthRate + "%");
}
```

The keyword `this` stands for the calling object. For example, consider the following method invocation from Display 4.4:

```
speciesOfTheMonth.writeOutput();
```

The calling object is `speciesOfTheMonth`. So this invocation of the method `writeOutput` is equivalent to

```
{
    System.out.println("Name = " + speciesOfTheMonth.name);
    System.out.println("Population = "
                              + speciesOfTheMonth.population);
    System.out.println("Growth rate = " +
                                  speciesOfTheMonth.growthRate + "%");
}
```

which we got by replacing `this` with `speciesOfTheMonth`.

The keyword `this` is like a blank waiting to be filled in by the object that invokes the method. Because you would be using `this` so often if it were required, Java lets you omit it and the dot that follows it, but the `this` and the dot are understood to be there implicitly. This is an abbreviation that is almost always used. Programmers seldom use the `this` parameter, but there are some situations in which it is needed.

Quick Reference: The `this` Parameter

When giving a method definition, you can use the keyword `this` as a name for the calling object.

? Self-Test Questions

1. Consider the program in Display 4.4. Suppose you wanted to add another species object called `speciesOfTheYear`, and suppose you wanted the user to give it data, specifically a name, population, and growth rate. What code do you need to add to the program? (*Hint:* It requires only three or four lines of code.)
2. Suppose `Employee` is a class with a `void` method named `readInput` and `dilbert` is an object of the class `Employee`. So `dilbert` was named and created by the following:

   ```
   Employee dilbert = new Employee();
   ```

   Write an invocation of the method `readInput` with `dilbert` as the calling object. The method `readInput` needs no information in parentheses.
3. Let's say you want to assign a number as well as a name to each species in the world, perhaps to make it easier to catalog them. Modify the definition of the class `SpeciesFirstTry` in Display 4.3 so that it allows for a number. The number is to be of type `int`. (*Hint:* You mostly have to just add stuff. Note that part of what you need to do is to change some methods by adding stuff.)
4. Suppose you live in an idealized world where every species has exactly the same number of male and female members in its population. Give the definition of a method, called `femalePopulation`, that you could add to the definition of the class `SpeciesFirstTry` in Display 4.3. The method `femalePopulation` returns the number of females in the population. If the population is an odd number, you have one species member left over after pairing; assume that member is a female. For example, if the population is 6, there are 3 males and 3 females. If the population is 7, there are 3 males and 4 females. Also give the definition of a method called `malePopulation` that similarly returns the number of males in the population. (*Hint:* The definitions are very short. The bodies of the two definitions are a little bit different.)
5. Rewrite the definition of the method `writeOutput` in Display 4.3, using the `this` parameter. Note that the meaning of the definition will not change at all. You

will just write it slightly differently. (*Hint:* All you need to do is add `this` and dots in certain places.)

6. Rewrite the definition of the method `readInput` in Display 4.3, using the `this` parameter.
7. Rewrite the definition of the method `PopulationIn10` in Display 4.3, using the `this` parameter.
8. What is the meaning of `(int)` that appears in the definition of the method `PopulationIn10` in Display 4.3, and why is it needed?

Local Variables

local variable

Notice the definition of the method `populationIn10` given in Display 4.3. That method definition includes the declaration of variables called `populationAmount` and `count`. A variable declared within a method is called a **local variable.** It is called local because its meaning is local to—that is, confined to—the method definition. If you have two methods and each of them declares a variable of the same name—for example, if both were named `populationAmount`—they would be two different variables that just happened to have the same name. Any change that was made to the variable named `populationAmount` within one method would have no effect upon the variable named `populationAmount` in the other method. It would be as if the two methods were executed on different computers, or as if the computer changed the name of the variable named `populationAmount` in one of the two methods to `populationAmount2`.

Since the `main` part of a program is itself a method, all variables declared in `main` are local variables for the method `main`. If one happens to have the same name as a variable declared in some other method, then they are two different variables that just happen to have the same name. For example, look at the program and class definition in Display 4.5. First consider the program, which is shown in the lower half of the display. The method `main` in the program includes the declaration of a variable named `newAmount`. Now look at the class definition in the upper half of the display. The method `showNewBalance` in the class also declares a variable named `newAmount`. These are two different variables, both of which are named `newAmount`. The variable named `newAmount` in `main` is set equal to `800.00`. After that, there is the following method invocation:

```
myAccount.showNewBalance( );
```

If you look at the definition of the method `showNewBalance` and do a little arithmetic, you will see that, within this method, another variable named `newAmount` is set equal to `105.00`. Yet this variable has no effect on the other variable named `newAmount` that is in `main`. After that method invocation, the variable named `newAmount` in `main` is written out, and its value is still `800.00`. Changing the value of `newAmount` in the method `showNewBalance` had no effect on the variable named `newAmount` in `main`. In this case, the two variables with the same name are in different definitions in two different files. However, the situation would be the same if the two methods were in the same class definition and thus in the same file.

DISPLAY 4.5 Local Variables

```
/**
 This class is used in the program LocalVariablesDemoProgram.
*/
public class BankAccount
{
    public double amount;
    public double rate;

    public void showNewBalance( )
    {
        double newAmount = amount + (rate/100.0)*amount;
        System.out.println("With interest added the new amount is $"
                                        + newAmount);
    }
}
```

This class definition goes in a file named BankAccount.java.

Two different variables named newAmount.

This program goes in a file named LocalVariableDemoProgram.java.

```
/**
 A toy program to illustrate how local variables behave.
*/
public class LocalVariablesDemoProgram
{
    public static void main(String[] args)
    {
        BankAccount myAccount = new BankAccount( );
        myAccount.amount = 100.00;
        myAccount.rate = 5;

        double newAmount = 800.00;
        myAccount.showNewBalance( );
        System.out.println("I wish my new amount were $"+newAmount);
    }
}
```

This does not change the value of the variable newAmount *in* main.

Screen Output

```
With interest added the new amount is $105.0
I wish my new amount were $800.0
```

Quick Reference: **Local Variable**

A variable declared within a method definition is called a **local variable.** If two methods each have a local variable of the same name, they are two different variables, even though they have the same name.

Quick Reference: **Global Variables**

Thus far, we have discussed two kinds of variables: instance variables, whose meaning is confined to an object of a class, and local variables, whose meaning is confined to a method definition. Some programming languages have another kind of variable, called a **global variable,** whose meaning is confined only to the program, which means that it's not confined at all. Java does not have these global variables.

Blocks

compound statement

block

The terms **block** and **compound statement** really mean the same thing, namely, a set of Java statements enclosed in braces `{}`. However, the two terms tend to be used in different contexts. When you declare a variable within a compound statement, the compound statement is usually called a block.

If you declare a variable within a block (that is, within a compound statement), that variable is local to the block. This means that when the block ends, all variables declared within the block disappear. In many programming languages, you can even use that variable's name to name some other variable outside of the block. However, *in Java, you cannot have two variables with the same name inside of a single method definition.*

Local variables within blocks can sometimes be a little troublesome in Java. In Java, you cannot reuse the local variable name outside the block for another variable. Thus, it is sometimes easier to declare the variable outside the block. If you declare a variable outside of a block, you can use it both inside and outside the block, and it will have the same meaning whether it is in the block or outside the block.

Quick Reference: **Blocks**

A **block** is another name for a compound statement, that is, a list of statements enclosed in braces. Although a block and a compound statement are the same thing, we tend to use the term *block* when there is a variable declaration contained within the braces. The variables declared in a block are local to the block, and so these variables disappear when the execution of the block is completed. However, even though the variables are local to the block, their names cannot be used for anything else within the same method definition.

▲ *Gotcha*

Variables Declared in a Block

When you declare a variable within a block, that variable becomes a local variable for the block. This means that you cannot use the variable outside of the block. If you want to use a variable outside of a block, you must declare it outside of the block. Declaring the variable outside of the block will let you use the variable both outside and inside the block. △

Java Tip
Declaring Variables in a `for` Statement

You can declare a variable within the initialization part of a `for` statement, as in the following example:

```
int sum = 0;
for (int n = 1; n <= 10; n++)
    sum = sum + n*n;
```

If you do this, the variable, in this case `n`, will be **local to the `for` loop,** and cannot be used outside of the `for` loop. For example, the following use of `n` in the `System.out.println` statement is not allowed:

```
for (int n = 1; n <= 10; n++)
    sum = sum + n*n;
System.out.println(n);//Invalid
```

This can sometimes be more of a nuisance than a helpful feature. Moreover, variables declared in the initialization part of a `for` loop are treated differently in different programming languages and even in different versions of Java. For these reasons, we prefer not to use this feature and to instead declare our variables outside of the `for` loop. However, you should be aware of this feature, since you will see it in other programmers' code. □

Parameters of a Primitive Type

Consider the method `populationIn10` for the class `SpeciesFirstTry` defined in Display 4.3. It returns the projected population of a species 10 years in the future. But what if you want the projection for 5 years in the future or 50 years in the future? It would be much more useful to have a method that starts with an integer for some number of years and returns the projected population for that many years into the future. In order to do this, we need some way of leaving a blank in a method, so that each call of the method can have the blank filled in with a different value for the number of years. The things that serve as blanks in methods are called formal parameters, or simply **parameters**. They are a bit more complicated than simple blanks, but you will not go too far wrong if you think of them as blanks or placeholders to be filled in with some value when the method is invoked.

parameter

The class `SpeciesSecondTry` defined in Display 4.6 includes a method called `projectedPopulation` that has one formal parameter called `years`. When you call the method, you give the value that you want to have substituted for the parameter `years`. For example, if `speciesOfTheMonth` is declared to be of type `SpeciesSecondTry`, you can use the method `projectedPopulation` to calculate the population in 12 years as follows:

```
futurePopulation = speciesOfTheMonth.projectedPopulation(12);
```

DISPLAY 4.6 A Method with a Parameter

```
public class SpeciesSecondTry
{
    public String name;
    public int population;
    public double growthRate;

    public void readInput( )
    {
        <The definition of the method readInput is the same as in Display 4.3.>
    }

    public void writeOutput( )
    {
        <The definition of the method writeOutput is the same as in Display 4.3.>
    }

    /**
     Returns the projected population of the calling object
     after the specified number of years.
    */
    public int projectedPopulation(int years)
    {
        double populationAmount = population;
        int count = years;
        while ((count > 0) && (populationAmount > 0))
        {
            populationAmount = (populationAmount +
                          (growthRate/100) * populationAmount);
            count--;
        }
        if (populationAmount > 0)
            return (int)populationAmount;
        else
            return 0;
    }
}
```

Later in the chapter, you will see that the modifier `public` *should be replaced with* `private`.

We will give an even better version of the class later in the chapter.

In Display 4.7, we have rewritten the program from Display 4.4 so that it uses the class `SpeciesSecondTry` and its method `projectedPopulation`. With this version of the class, we could project a population any number of years into the future. We could even use a variable for the number of years, as follows:

```
int projectedYears, futurePopulation;
System.out.println("Enter the projected number of years:");
```

```
projectedYears = SavitchIn.readLineInt();
futurePopulation =
      speciesOfTheMonth.projectedPopulation(projectedYears);
System.out.println("In " + projectedYears + " years, the");
System.out.println("population will be " + futurePopulation);
```

Let's look at the definition of the method `projectedPopulation` in more detail. The heading, shown below, has something new:

```
public int projectedPopulation(int years)
```

DISPLAY 4.7 Using a Method with a Parameter

```
/**
 Demonstrates the use of a parameter
 with the method projectedPopulation.
*/
public class SpeciesSecondTryDemo
{
    public static void main(String[] args)
    {
        SpeciesSecondTry speciesOfTheMonth = new SpeciesSecondTry();
        int futurePopulation;

        System.out.println("Enter data on the Species of the Month:");
        speciesOfTheMonth.readInput();
        speciesOfTheMonth.writeOutput();

        futurePopulation = speciesOfTheMonth.projectedPopulation(10);
        System.out.println("In ten years the population will be " +
                                                  futurePopulation);

        speciesOfTheMonth.name = "Klingon ox";
        speciesOfTheMonth.population = 10;
        speciesOfTheMonth.growthRate = 15;
        System.out.println("The new Species of the Month:");
        speciesOfTheMonth.writeOutput();
        System.out.println("In ten years the population will be " +
                           speciesOfTheMonth.projectedPopulation(10));
    }
}
```

Sample Screen Dialog

The dialog is exactly the same as in Display 4.4.

formal parameter

argument

The word `years` is called a **formal parameter** or simply a **parameter.** A formal parameter is used in the method definition as a stand-in for a value that will be plugged in when the method is called. The item that is plugged in is called an **argument.** (In some other books arguments are called **actual parameters.**) For example, in the following call, the value `10` is an argument:

```
futurePopulation = speciesOfTheMonth.projectedPopulation(10);
```

When you have a method invocation like the preceding, the argument (in this case `10`) is plugged in for the formal parameter *everywhere that the parameter occurs in the method definition.* In this case, the argument `10` would be plugged in for the formal parameter `years` in the definition of the method `projectedPopulation` in Display 4.6. After that, the method invocation proceeds as in all previous method invocations you have seen. The statements in the body of the method definition are executed until they reach a `return` statement. At that point, the value specified by the expression in the `return` statement is returned as the value returned by the method call.

It is important to note that only the value of the argument is used in this substitution process. If the argument in a method invocation is a variable, it is the value of the variable that is plugged in, not the variable name. For example, consider the following, which might occur in some program that uses the class `SpeciesSecondTry` defined in Display 4.6:

```
SpeciesSecondTry mySpecies = new SpeciesSecondTry( );
int yearCount = 12;
int futurePopulation;
futurePopulation =
      mySpecies.projectedPopulation(yearCount);
```

In this case, it is the value `12` that is plugged in for the formal parameter `years` in the definition of the method `projectedPopulation` (in Display 4.6). It is *not* the variable `yearCount` that is plugged in for `years`. Because only the value of the argument is used, this method of plugging in arguments for formal parameters is known as the **call-by-value** mechanism. In Java, this is the only method of substitution that is used with parameters of a primitive type, such as `int`, `double`, and `char`. As you will eventually see, parameters of a class type use a somewhat different substitution mechanism, but for now, we are concerned only with parameters and arguments of primitive types, such as `int`, `double`, and `char`.

call-by-value

parameters as local variables

The exact details of this method of parameter substitution are a bit more complicated than what we have said so far. Usually, you need not be concerned with this extra detail, but occasionally, you will need to know how the substitution mechanism actually works. So here are the exact technical details: *The formal parameter that occurs in the method definition is a local variable that is initialized to the value of the argument.* The argument is given in parentheses in the method invocation. For example, consider the following method call:

```
futurePopulation =
   mySpecies.projectedPopulation(yearCount);
```

The parameter `years` of the method `projectedPopulation` in Display 4.6 is a local variable of the method `projectedPopulation`, and in this method invocation, the local variable years is set equal to the value of the argument yearCount. The effect is the same as if the body of the method definition were changed to the following:

```
{
    years = yearCount;
    double populationAmount = population;
    int count = years;
    while ((count > 0) && (populationAmount > 0))
    {
        populationAmount = (populationAmount +
                         (growthRate/100) * populationAmount);
        count--;
    }
    if (populationAmount > 0)
        return (int)populationAmount;
    else
        return 0;
}
```

This is the effect of plugging in the argument yearCount.

parameters have a type

Finally, notice that the formal parameter in a method heading has a type, such as the type int before the parameter years, as shown here:

```
public int projectedPopulation(int years)
```

Every formal parameter has a type, and the argument that is plugged in for the parameter in a method invocation must match the type of the parameter. Thus, for the method projectedPopulation, the argument given in parentheses in a method invocation must be of type int. This rule is not as strict in practice as what we have just said. In many cases, Java will perform an automatic type conversion (type cast) if you use an argument in a method call that does not match the type of the formal parameter. For example, if the type of the argument in a method call is int and the type of the parameter is double, Java will convert the value of type int to the corresponding value of type double. The following list shows the type conversions that will be performed for you automatically. An argument in a method invocation that is of any of these types will automatically be converted to any of the types that appear to its right if that is needed to match a formal parameter:[2]

```
byte --> short --> int --> long --> float --> double
```

Note that this is exactly the same as the automatic type casting we discussed in Chapter 2 for storing values of one type in a variable of another type. Thus, we can express both the automatic type casting for arguments and the automatic type casting for variables as one more general rule: You can use a value of any of the listed types anywhere that Java expects a value of a type further down on the list.

All of our examples so far have been methods that return a value, but everything we said about formal parameters and arguments applies to void methods as well: void methods may have formal parameters, and they are handled in exactly the same way as we just described for methods that return a value.

---

2. An argument of type char will also be converted to a matching number type, if the formal parameter is of type int or any type to the right of int in our list of types. However, we do not advocate using this feature.

Quick Reference: Parameters of a Primitive Type

Formal parameters are given in parentheses after the method name at the beginning of a method definition. A formal parameter of a primitive type, such as `int`, `double`, or `char`, is a local variable. When the method is invoked, the parameter is initialized to the value of the corresponding argument in the method invocation. This mechanism is known as the **call-by-value** parameter mechanism. The argument in a method invocation can be a literal constant, like 2 or `'A'`; a variable; or any expression that yields a value of the appropriate type.

Note that if you use a variable of a primitive type as an argument in a method invocation, then the method invocation cannot change the value of this argument variable.

more than one parameter

It is possible, even common, to have more than one formal parameter in a method definition. In that case, each formal parameter is listed in the method heading, and each parameter is preceded by a type. For example, the following might be the heading of a method definition:

```
public void doStuff(int n1, int n2, double cost, char code)
```

Note that each of the formal parameters must be preceded by a type name, even if there is more than one parameter of the same type.

In a method invocation, there must be exactly the same number of arguments in parentheses as there are formal parameters in the method definition heading. For example, the following might be an invocation of our hypothetical method `doStuff`:

```
anObject.doStuff(42, 100, 9.99, 'Z');
```

As suggested by this example, the correspondence is one of order. The first argument in the method call is plugged in for the first parameter in the method definition heading, the second argument in the method call is plugged in for the second parameter in the heading of the method definition, and so forth. Each argument must match its corresponding parameter in type, except for the automatic type conversions that we discussed earlier.

class parameters

One word of warning: Parameters of a class type behave differently from parameters of a primitive type. We will discuss parameters of a class type later in this chapter.

Quick Reference: Correspondence Between Formal Parameters and Arguments

Formal parameters are given in parentheses after the method name at the beginning of a method definition. In a method invocation, **arguments** are given in parentheses after the method name. There must be exactly the same number of arguments in a method invocation as there are formal parameters in the corresponding method definition.

The arguments are plugged in for the formal parameters according to their position in the lists in parentheses. The first argument in the method invocation is plugged in for the first parameter in the method definition, the second argument in the method invocation is plugged in for the second parameter in the method definition, and so forth. Arguments should be of the same types as their corresponding formal parameters, although in some cases, Java will perform an automatic type conversion when the types do not match.

▲ *Gotcha*

Use of the Terms *Parameter* and *Argument*

The use of the terms *formal parameter* and *argument* that we follow in this book is consistent with common usage, but people also often use the terms *parameter* and *argument* interchangeably. Many people use the term *parameter* both for what we call a *formal parameter* and for what we call an *argument*. Other people use the term *argument* both for what we call a *formal parameter* and for what we call an *argument*. When you see the term *parameter* or *argument*, you must determine the exact meaning from the context. △

Summary of Class and Method Definition Syntax

In basic outline, a class definition has the following form:

```
public class Class_Name
{
    Instance_Variable_Declaration_1
    Instance_Variable_Declaration_2
        . . .
    Instance_Variable_Declaration_Last

    Method_Definition_1
    Method_Definition_2
        . . .
    Method_Definition_Last
}
```

This is the form we will use most often, but you are also allowed to intermix the method definitions and the instance variable declarations.

A method definition consist of two parts, in the following order:

Method_Heading
Method_Body

The method headings we have seen thus far are all of the form

```
public Type_Name_Or_void Method_Name(Parameter_List)
```

The *Parameter_List* consists of a list of formal parameter names, each preceded by a type. If the list has more than one entry, the entries are separated by commas. There may be no parameters at all, in which case there is nothing inside the parentheses.

Here are some sample method headings:

```
public double Total(double price, double tax)
public void setValue(int count, char rating)
public void readInput( )
public int projectedPopulation(int years)
```

The *Method_Body* consists of a list of Java statements enclosed in braces `{}`. If the method returns a value, the method definition must include one or more `return` statements.

To see complete examples of class definitions, see Display 4.3 and Display 4.6.

? Self-Test Questions

9. What is the difference between the unqualified term *parameter* and the term *formal parameter*?
10. Define a method called `density` that could be added to the definition of the class `SpeciesSecondTry` in Display 4.6. The method `density` has one parameter of type `double` that is named `area`. The parameter `area` gives the area occupied by the species, expressed in square miles. The method `density` returns a value of type `double` that is equal to the number of individuals per square mile of the species. You can assume that the area is always greater than zero. (*Hint:* The definition is very short.)
11. Define a method called `fixPopulation` that could be added to the definition of the class `SpeciesSecondTry` in Display 4.6. This method has one parameter of type `double` that is named `area`, which gives the area occupied by the species in square miles. The method `fixPopulation` changes the value of the instance variable `population` so that there will be one pair of individuals per square mile.
12. Define a method called `changePopulation` that could be added to the definition of the class `SpeciesSecondTry` in Display 4.6. This method has two parameters. One parameter is of type `double`, is named `area`, and gives the area occupied by the species in square miles. The other parameter is of type `int`, is named `numberPerMile`, and gives the desired number of individuals per square mile. The method `changePopulation` changes the value of the instance variable `population` so that the number of individuals per square mile is (approximately) equal to `numberPerMile`.

4.2 INFORMATION HIDING AND ENCAPSULATION

The cause is hidden, but the result is well known. -Ovid, *Metamorphoses*

Information hiding sounds as though it could be a bad thing to do. What advantage could there be to hiding information? As it turns out, the term *information hiding* as it is used in computer science does indeed refer to a genuine kind of hiding of information, but it is considered a good programming technique. The idea is that, when certain kinds of information are hidden, the programmer's job becomes simpler and the programmer's code becomes easier to understand. It is basically a way to avoid "information overload."

Information Hiding

A programmer who is using a method that you have defined does not need to know the details of the code in the body of the method definition in order to use the method. If a method (or other piece of software) is well written, a programmer who uses the method need only know *what* the method accomplishes and need not worry about *how* the method accomplishes its task. For example, you can use the method `SavitchIn.readlineInt` without even looking at the definition of that method. It is not that the code contains some secret that is forbidden to you. If you really want to see the definition, it is in Appendix 4. The point is that viewing the code will not help you use the method, but it will give you more things to keep track of, which could distract you from your programming tasks.

Designing a method so that it can be used without any need to understand the fine detail of the code is called **information hiding,** to emphasize the fact that the programmer acts as though the body of the method were hidden from view. If the term *information hiding* sounds too negative to you, you can use the term *abstraction*. The two terms *information hiding* and *abstraction* mean the same thing in this context. This use of the term *abstraction* should not be surprising. When you abstract something, you lose some of the details. For example, an abstract of a paper or a book is a brief description of the paper or book, as opposed to the entire book or paper.

information hiding

abstraction

Programming Tip
Parameter Names Are Local to the Method

Methods should be self-contained units that are designed separately from the incidental details of other methods and separately from any program that uses the method. Among the incidental details are the names of the formal parameters. Fortunately, in Java you can choose the formal parameter names without any concern that the name of a formal parameter will be the same as an identifier used in some other method. This is because the formal parameters are really local variables, and so their meanings are confined to their respective method definitions. ○

Precondition and Postcondition Comments

An efficient and standard way to describe what a method does is by means of specific kinds of comments known as preconditions and postconditions. The **precondition** for a method states the conditions that must be true before the method is invoked. The method should not be used, and cannot be expected to perform correctly, unless the precondition is satisfied.

precondition

The **postcondition** describes the effect of the method call. The postcondition tells what will be true after the method is executed in a situation in which the precondition holds. For a method that returns a value, the postcondition will describe the value returned by the method. For a `void` method, the postcondition will, among other things, describe any changes to the calling object. In general, the postcondition describes all the effects produced by a method invocation.

postcondition

For example, the following shows some suitable precondition and postcondition comments for the method `writeOutput` shown in Display 4.3:

```
/**
 Precondition: The instance variables of the calling
 object have values.
 Postcondition: The data stored in (the instance variables
 of) the calling object have been written to the screen.
*/
public void writeOutput()
```

The comment for the method `projectedPopulation` in Display 4.6 can be expressed as follows:

```
/**
 Precondition: years is a nonnegative number.
 Postcondition: Returns the projected population of the
 calling object after the specified number of years.
*/
public int projectedPopulation(int years)
```

If the only postcondition is a description of the value returned, programmers usually omit the word `Postcondition`. The previous comment would typically be written in the following alternative way:

```
/**
 Precondition: years is a nonnegative number.
 Returns the projected population of the calling object
 after the specified number of years.
*/
public int projectedPopulation(int years)
```

Some design specifications may require preconditions and postconditions for all methods. Others omit explicit preconditions and postconditions from certain methods whose names make their action obvious. Names such as `readInput`, `writeOutput`, and `set` are often considered self-explanatory. However, the sound rule to follow is to adhere to whatever guidelines your instructor or supervisor gives you, and when in doubt, add preconditions and postconditions.

Some programmers prefer not to use the words *precondition* and *postcondition* in their comments. However, you should always think in terms of preconditions and postconditions when writing method comments. The really important thing is not the words *precondition* and *postcondition*, but the concepts they name.

■ Java Tip
Assertion Checks

assertion

An **assertion** is a statement that says something about the state of your program. An assertion can be either true or false and should be true if there are no mistakes in your program. Precondition and postcondition commments are examples of assertions. You can have assertion comments at other points in your program as well. For example, all the comments in the following code are assertions:

```
//n == 1
while (n < limit)
{
    n = 2*n;
}
//n >= limit
//n is the smallest power of 2 >= limit.
```

Note that while each of these assertions can be either true or false, depending on the values of `n` and `limit`, they all should be true if the program is performing correctly. An assertion "asserts" that something is true about your program code (when program execution reaches the location of the assertion).

In Java, you can insert a check to see if an assertion is true and to stop the program and output an error message if the assertion is not true. An **assertion check** in Java has the following form:

assertion check

`assert` *Boolean_Expression*;

assert

If you compile and run your program in the proper way, the following happens when the assertion check is executed: If the *Boolean_Expression* evaluates to `true`, nothing happens, but if the *Boolean_Expression* evaluates to `false`, the program ends and outputs an error message saying that an assertion failed.

For example, the previously displayed code can be written as follows, with two of the comments replaced by assertion checks:

```
assert n == 1;
while (n < limit)
{
    n = 2*n;
}
assert n >= limit;
//n is the smallest power of 2 >= limit.
```

Note that we translated only two of the three comments into assertion checks. Not all assertion comments lend themselves to becoming assertion checks. For example, the final comment is an assertion. It is either true or false, and if the program code is correct, it will be true. However, there is no simple way to convert this last comment into a Boolean expression. Doing so would not be impossible, but you would need to use code that would itself be more complicated than what you would be checking. Your decision as to whether to translate a comment like the last one shown here into an assertion check will depend on the details of the particular case.

You can turn assertion checking on and off. You can turn it on when debugging code so that a failed assertion will stop your program and output an error message. Once your code is debugged, you can turn assertion checking off to make your code run more efficiently.

A class containing assertions must be compiled in a different way, even if you do not intend to run it with assertion checking turned on. After all the code is compiled, you can run a program with assertion checking either turned on or turned off.

If you compile your classes using a one-line command, you would compile a class with assertion checking as follows:

```
javac -source 1.4 YourProgram.java
```

You can then run your program with assertion checking turned on or off. The normal way of running a program has assertion checking turned off. To run your program with assertion checking turned on, use the following command:

```
java -enableassertions YourProgram
```

If you are using an IDE, you should have some way to set options for assertion checking. Check the documentation for your IDE. (If you are using TextPad, one way to turn on assertion checking for compiling and running code is as follows: On the Configure menu, choose Preferences, then choose Compile Java from the Tools submenu, and select the check box for the "Prompt for parameters" option. On the same Tools submenu, you will also find the Run Java Application command, and you will need to set the "Prompt for parameters" option for it as well.[3] Then, when you compile a class, a window will appear in which you can enter arguments for the `javac` compile command (for example, `-source 1.4 "YourProgram.java"`). Similarly, when you run a program, a window will appear in which you can enter arguments for the `java` run command (for example, `-enableassertions YourProgram`). The window will already have the last argument in the correct form, such as with or without quotes and full path name or not. You just add `-source 1.4` or `-enableassertions`.) □

Quick Reference: Assertion Checking

An **assertion check** consists of the keyword `assert` followed by a Boolean expression and a semicolon. You can insert an assertion check anywhere in your code. If assertion checking is turned on and the Boolean expression in the assertion check evaluates to `false`, your program will end and output a suitable error message. If assertion checking is not turned on, then the assertion check is treated as a comment.

Syntax:

assert *Boolean_Expression*;

Example:

```
assert n >= limit;
```

The `public` and `private` Modifiers

It is *not* considered good programming practice to make the instance variables of a class `public`. Normally, all instance variables are given the modifier `private`. In this subsection, we explain the differences between the modifiers `public` and `private`.

`public`

As you know, the modifier `public` means that any other class or program can directly access and change the instance variable. For example, the program in Display 4.7 contains the following three lines, which set the values of the `public` instance variables for the object `speciesOfTheMonth`:

```
speciesOfTheMonth.name = "Klingon ox";
speciesOfTheMonth.population = 10;
speciesOfTheMonth.growthRate = 15;
```

The object `speciesOfTheMonth` is an object of the class `SpeciesSecondTry`, the definition for which is given in Display 4.6. As you can see by looking at that class definition, the instance variables `name`, `population`, and `growthRate` all have the modifier `public`, and so the preceding three statements are perfectly valid.

3. If you are running applets, you will also need to select the "Prompt for parameters" option for the Run Java Applet command on the Tools submenu.

Now suppose that we change the modifier `public` before the instance variable `name` in the definition of the class `SpeciesSecondTry` in Display 4.6 to `private` so that the class definition begins as follows:

`private`

```
public class SpeciesSecondTry
{
    private String name;
    public int population;
    public double growthRate;
```

With this change, it is invalid to have the following statement in the program in Display 4.7:

```
speciesOfTheMonth.name = "Klingon ox"; //Invalid when private.
```

The following two statements remain valid, because we left the modifiers of `population` and `growthRate` as `public`:

```
speciesOfTheMonth.population = 10;
speciesOfTheMonth.growthRate = 15;
```

It is considered good programming practice to make all instance variables `private`, as illustrated in Display 4.8. Whenever you place the modifier `private` before an instance variable, that instance variable's *name* is not accessible outside of the class definition. Within any method of the class definition, you can use the instance variable name in any way you wish. In particular, you can directly change the value of the instance variable. However, outside of the class definition, you cannot make any direct reference to the instance variable name.

For example, consider the class `SpeciesThirdTry`, shown in Display 4.8. Because the instance variables are all marked `private`, the last three of the following statements would be invalid in any program (or in any class method definition other than methods of the class `SpeciesThirdTry`):

```
SpeciesThirdTry secretSpecies = new SpeciesThirdTry();//Valid
secretSpecies.readInput();//Valid
secretSpecies.name = "Aardvark";//Invalid. name is private.
System.out.println(secretSpecies.population);//Invalid
                                //population is private.
System.out.println(secretSpecies.growthRate);//Invalid.
                                //growthRate is private.
```

Notice that the invocation of the method `readInput` is valid. So there is still a way to set the instance variables of an object, even though those instance variables are `private`. Making an instance variable `private` does not mean that there is no way to change it. It means only that you cannot use the *instance variable name* to refer directly to the variable (except within the class definition that includes the instance variable).

Within the definition of methods in the same class, you can access private instance variables in any way you want. Notice the definition of the method `readInput`, which is shown in Display 4.8. It sets the value of instance variables with assignment statements such as

```
name = SavitchIn.readLine();
```

and

```
population = SavitchIn.readLineInt();
```

DISPLAY 4.8 A Class with Private Instance Variables

```
public class SpeciesThirdTry
{
    private String name;
    private int population;
    private double growthRate;

    public void readInput()
    {
        System.out.println("What is the species' name?");
        name = SavitchIn.readLine();
        System.out.println(
                    "What is the population of the species?");
        population = SavitchIn.readLineInt();
        while (population < 0)
        {
            System.out.println("Population cannot be negative.");
            System.out.println("Reenter population:");
            population = SavitchIn.readLineInt();
        }
        System.out.println(
                "Enter growth rate (percent increase per year):");
        growthRate = SavitchIn.readLineDouble();
    }

    public void writeOutput()
    <The definition of the method writeOutput is the same as in Display 4.3.>

    /**
     Precondition: years is a nonnegative number.
     Returns the projected population of the calling object
     after the specified number of years.
    */
    public int projectedPopulation(int years)

        <The definition of the method projectedPopulation is the same as in Display 4.6.>
}
```

We will give an even better version of this class later in the chapter.

Within any class method, you can access all the instance variables of that class in any way you want, even if the instance variables are marked `private`.

private methods

Class methods can also be `private`. If a method is marked `private`, then it cannot be invoked outside of the class definition, but it can still be invoked within the definition of any other method in that same class. Most methods are marked `public`, but if you have a method whose only purpose is to be used within the definition of other methods of that class, it makes sense to mark this "helping" method `private`.

Quick Reference: The `public` and `private` Qualifiers

Within a class definition, each instance variable declaration and each method definition can be preceded with either `public` or `private`. If an instance variable is preceded with `private`, then it cannot be referred to by name anyplace except within the definitions of methods of the same class. If it is preceded by `public`, there are no restrictions on the use of the instance variable name. If a method definition is preceded with `private`, then the method cannot be invoked outside of the class definition. If the method is preceded by `public`, there are no restrictions on the method's use.

Normally, all instance variables are marked `private` and most or all methods are marked `public`.

Programming Tip

Instance Variables Should Be `private`

You should make all the instance variables in a class `private`. The reason for this is that it forces the programmer who uses the class (whether that is you or somebody else) to access the instance variables only via methods. This allows the class to control how a programmer accesses the instance variables.

Making all instance variables `private` does control access to them, but what if you have a legitimate reason to access an instance variable? For these cases, you should provide accessor methods. An **accessor method** is simply a method that allows you to read data contained in one or more instance variables. In Display 4.9, we have rewritten the class for a species yet another time. This version has accessor methods for obtaining the value of each instance variable. They are the methods that start with the word `get`, as in `getName`.

accessor method

Accessor methods allow you to read the data in a private instance variable. Other methods, known as **mutator methods**, allow you to change the data stored in private instance variables. Our class definition has a mutator method, called `set`, for setting the instance variables to new values. The program in Display 4.10 illustrates the use of the mutator method `set`. That program is similar to the one in Display 4.7, but because this version of our species class has private instance variables, we must use the mutator method `set` to reset the values of the instance variables.

mutator method

It may seem that accessor methods and mutator methods defeat the purpose of making instance variables `private`, but there is a method to this madness. (No pun intended, I think.) A mutator method can check that any change is appropriate and warn the user if there is a problem. For example, the mutator method `set` checks to see if the program inadvertently sets `population` equal to a negative number. ○

Quick Reference: Accessor and Mutator Methods

A public method that reads and returns data from one or more private instance variables is called an **accessor method.** The names of accessor methods typically begin with `get`.

A public method that changes the data stored in one or more private instance variables is called a **mutator method.** The names of mutator methods typically begin with `set`.

DISPLAY 4.9 A Class with Accessor and Mutator Methods

```
public class SpeciesFourthTry
{
    private String name;
    private int population;
    private double growthRate;
```

Yes, we will define an even better version of this class later.

<The definition of the methods `readInput`, `writeOutput`, and `projectedPopulation` go here. They are the same as in Display 4.3 and Display 4.6.>

```
    public void set(String newName,
                    int newPopulation, double newGrowthRate)
    {
        name = newName;
        if (newPopulation >= 0)
            population = newPopulation;
        else
        {
            System.out.println(
                         "ERROR: using a negative population.");
            System.exit(0);
        }
        growthRate = newGrowthRate;
    }
```

An accessor method can check to make sure that instance variables are not set to improper values.

```
    public String getName()
    {
        return name;
    }

    public int getPopulation()
    {
        return population;
    }

    public double getGrowthRate()
    {
        return growthRate;
    }
}
```

DISPLAY 4.10 Using a Mutator Method *(Part 1 of 2)*

```
/**
 Demonstrates the use of the mutator method set.
*/
public class SpeciesFourthTryDemo
{
    public static void main(String[] args)
    {
        SpeciesFourthTry speciesOfTheMonth =
                                        new SpeciesFourthTry( );
        int numberOfYears, futurePopulation;


        System.out.println("Enter number of years to project:");
        numberOfYears = SavitchIn.readLineInt( );


        System.out.println(
                    "Enter data on the Species of the Month:");
        speciesOfTheMonth.readInput( );
        speciesOfTheMonth.writeOutput( );


        futurePopulation =
            speciesOfTheMonth.projectedPopulation(numberOfYears);
        System.out.println("In " + numberOfYears
                               + " years the population will be "
                               + futurePopulation);


        speciesOfTheMonth.set("Klingon ox", 10, 15);


        System.out.println("The new Species of the Month:");
        speciesOfTheMonth.writeOutput( );
        System.out.println("In " + numberOfYears
           + " years the population will be "
           + speciesOfTheMonth.projectedPopulation(numberOfYears));
    }
}
```

DISPLAY 4.10 Using a Mutator Method *(Part 2 of 2)*

Sample Screen Dialog

```
Enter number of years to project:
10
Enter data on the Species of the Month:
What is the species' name?
Ferengie fur ball
What is the population of the species?
1000
Enter growth rate (percent increase per year):
-20.5
Name = Ferengie fur ball
Population = 1000
Growth rate = -20.5%
In 10 years the population will be 100
The new Species of the Month:
Name = Klingon ox
Population = 10
Growth rate = 15.0%
In 10 years the population will be 40
```

? Self-Test Questions

13. In Display 4.10, we set the data for the object `speciesOfTheMonth` as follows:

```
speciesOfTheMonth.set("Klingon ox", 10, 15);
```

Could we have used the following code instead?

```
speciesOfTheMonth.name = "Klingon ox";
speciesOfTheMonth.population = 10;
speciesOfTheMonth.growthRate = 15;
```

If we could have used this alternative code, why didn't we? If we could not have used this alternative code, explain why we cannot use it.

14. Give preconditions and postconditions for the following method, which is intended to be added to the class `SpeciesFourthTry` in Display 4.9:

```
public void updatePopulation()
{
    population = (int)(population
                        + (growthRate/100)*population);
}
```

15. What is an assertion? Give examples of assertions.

16. Suppose that you did not have assertion checking in Java. (Earlier versions of Java did not.) Write some code to simulate the following assertion check:

```
assert balance > 0;
```

`balance` is a variable of type `double`.

17. What is an accessor method? What is a mutator method?

18. Give the complete definition of a class called `Person` that has two instance variables, one for the person's name and the other for the person's age. Include accessor methods and mutator methods, following the model in Display 4.9. Also include methods for input and output. There are no other methods.

Programming Example

A Purchase Class

Display 4.11 contains a class for a single purchase, such as 12 apples or 2 quarts of milk. It is designed to be part of a program to be used at the checkout stand of a supermarket. Recall that supermarkets often give prices not in unit costs, that is, not as the price for one, but as the price for some number, such as 5 for $1.25 or 3 for $1.00. They hope that if they price apples at 5 for $1.25, you will buy 5 apples instead of 2. But 5 for $1.25 is really $0.25 each, and if you buy 2 apples, they charge you only $0.50.

The instance variables are as follows:

```
private String name;
private int groupCount; //Part of price,
                        //like the 2 in 2 for $1.99.
private double groupPrice; //Part of price,
                           //like the $1.99 in 2 for $1.99.
private int numberBought; //Total number being purchased.
```

It is easiest to explain the meaning of these instance variables with an example. If you buy 12 apples at 5 for $1.25, then `name` has the value `"apples"`, `groupCount` has the value `5`, `groupPrice` has the value `1.25`, and `numberBought` has the value `12`. Note that the price of 5 for $1.25 is stored in the two instance variables `groupCount` (for the 5) and `groupPrice` (for the $1.25).

Consider the method `getTotalCost`, for example. The total cost of the purchase is calculated as

```
(groupPrice/groupCount)*numberBought
```

Or, to be very specific, if this purchase is 12 apples at 5 for $1.25, the total cost is

```
(1.25 / 5) * 12
```

Also notice the methods `readInput`, `setPrice`, and `setNumberBought`. All of these methods check for negative numbers when it does not make sense to have a negative number, such as when the user enters the number purchased. A simple demonstration program that uses this class is given in Display 4.12. ■

DISPLAY 4.11 `Purchase` **Class** *(Part 1 of 3)*

```
/**
 Class for the purchase of one kind of item, such as 3 oranges.
 Prices are set supermarket style, such as 5 for $1.25.
*/
public class Purchase
{
    private String name;
    private int groupCount; //Part of price, like the 2 in 2 for $1.99.
    private double groupPrice;
                    //Part of price, like the $1.99 in 2 for $1.99.
    private int numberBought; //Total number being purchased.

    public void setName(String newName)
    {
        name = newName;
    }

    /**
     Sets price to count pieces for $costForCount.
     For example, 2 for $1.99.
    */
    public void setPrice(int count, double costForCount)
    {
        if ((count <= 0) || (costForCount <= 0))
        {
            System.out.println("Error: Bad parameter in setPrice.");
            System.exit(0);
        }
        else
        {
            groupCount = count;
            groupPrice = costForCount;
        }
    }

    public void setNumberBought(int number)
    {
        if (number <= 0)
        {
            System.out.println("Error: Bad parameter in setNumberBought.");
            System.exit(0);
        }
        else
            numberBought = number;
    }
```

■ DISPLAY 4.11 Purchase Class *(Part 2 of 3)*

```
/**
 Gets price and number being purchased from keyboard.
*/
public void readInput( )
{
    System.out.println("Enter name of item you are purchasing:");
    name = SavitchIn.readLine( );
    System.out.println("Enter price of item on two lines.");
    System.out.println("For example, 3 for $2.99 is entered as");
    System.out.println("3");
    System.out.println("2.99");
    System.out.println("Enter price of item on two lines, now:");
    groupCount = SavitchIn.readLineInt( );
    groupPrice = SavitchIn.readLineDouble( );

    while ((groupCount <= 0) || (groupPrice <= 0))
    {//Try again:
        System.out.println(
               "Both numbers must be positive. Try again.");
        System.out.println("Enter price of item on two lines.");
        System.out.println(
                       "For example, 3 for $2.99 is entered as");
        System.out.println("3");
        System.out.println("2.99");
        System.out.println(
                     "Enter price of item on two lines, now:");
        groupCount = SavitchIn.readLineInt( );
        groupPrice = SavitchIn.readLineDouble( );
    }

    System.out.println("Enter number of items purchased:");
    numberBought = SavitchIn.readLineInt( );

    while (numberBought <= 0)
    {//Try again:
        System.out.println(
                   "Number must be positive. Try again.");
        System.out.println("Enter number of items purchased:");
        numberBought = SavitchIn.readLineInt( );
    }
}
```

DISPLAY 4.11 `Purchase` Class *(Part 3 of 3)*

```
    /**
     Outputs price and number being purchased to screen.
    */
    public void writeOutput()
    {
        System.out.println(numberBought + " " + name);
        System.out.println("at " + groupCount
                                 + " for $" + groupPrice);
    }

    public String getName()
    {
        return name;
    }

    public double getTotalCost()
    {
        return ((groupPrice/groupCount)*numberBought);
    }

    public double getUnitCost()
    {
        return (groupPrice/groupCount);
    }

    public int getNumberBought()
    {
        return numberBought;
    }
}
```

DISPLAY 4.12 Use of the `Purchase` Class *(Part 1 of 2)*

```
public class PurchaseDemo
{
    public static void main(String[] args)
    {
        Purchase oneSale = new Purchase();

        oneSale.readInput();
        oneSale.writeOutput();
        System.out.println("Cost each $" + oneSale.getUnitCost());
        System.out.println("Total cost $"
                                  + oneSale.getTotalCost());
    }
}
```

DISPLAY 4.12 Use of the `Purchase` Class *(Part 2 of 2)*

Sample Screen Dialog

```
Enter name of item you are purchasing:
grapefruit
Enter price of item on two lines.
For example, 3 for $2.99 is entered as
3
2.99
Enter price of item on two lines, now:
4
5.00
Enter number of items purchased:
0
Number must be positive. Try again.
Enter number of items purchased:
2
2 grapefruit
at 4 for $5.0
Cost each $1.25
Total cost $2.5
```

Encapsulation

In Chapter 1, we said that **encapsulation** is the process of hiding all the details of a class definition that are not necessary to understanding how objects of the class are used. For encapsulation to be useful, the class definition must be given in such a way that the programmer is spared the bother of worrying about the internal details of the class definition. We have already discussed some of the techniques for doing this under the topic of information hiding. Encapsulation is a form of information hiding. Encapsulation, when done correctly, neatly divides a class definition into two parts, which we will call the user interface[4] and the implementation. The **user interface** tells a programmer all that she or he needs to know in order to use the class. The user interface consists of the headings for the public methods and the defined constants of the class, along with comments that tell a

encapsulation

user interface

4. The word *interface* also has a technical meaning in the Java language. We are using the word slightly differently when we say *user interface*, although in spirit, the two uses of the word *interface* are the same.

programmer how to use these public methods and the public defined constants of the class. The user interface part of the class definition should be all you need to know in order to use the class in your program.

implementation

The **implementation** consists of all private elements of the class definition, principally the private instance variables of the class, along with the definitions of both the public and private methods. Note that the user interface and implementation of a class definition are not separated in your Java code. They are mixed together. For example, the user interface for the class `Purchase` in Display 4.11 is highlighted. Although you need the implementation in order to run a program that uses the class, you should not need to know anything about the implementation in order to write the code that uses the class.

When defining a class using the principle of encapsulation, you must define the class in such a way that the user interface and the implementation do indeed neatly separate conceptually, so that the interface is a simplified and safe description of the class. One way to think of this is to imagine that there is a wall between the implementation and the interface, with well-regulated communication across the wall. This is shown graphically in Display 4.13. When a class is defined in this way, using encapsulation to neatly separate the implementation and the user interface, we say that the class is **well encapsulated.**

well encapsulated

DISPLAY 4.13 Encapsulation

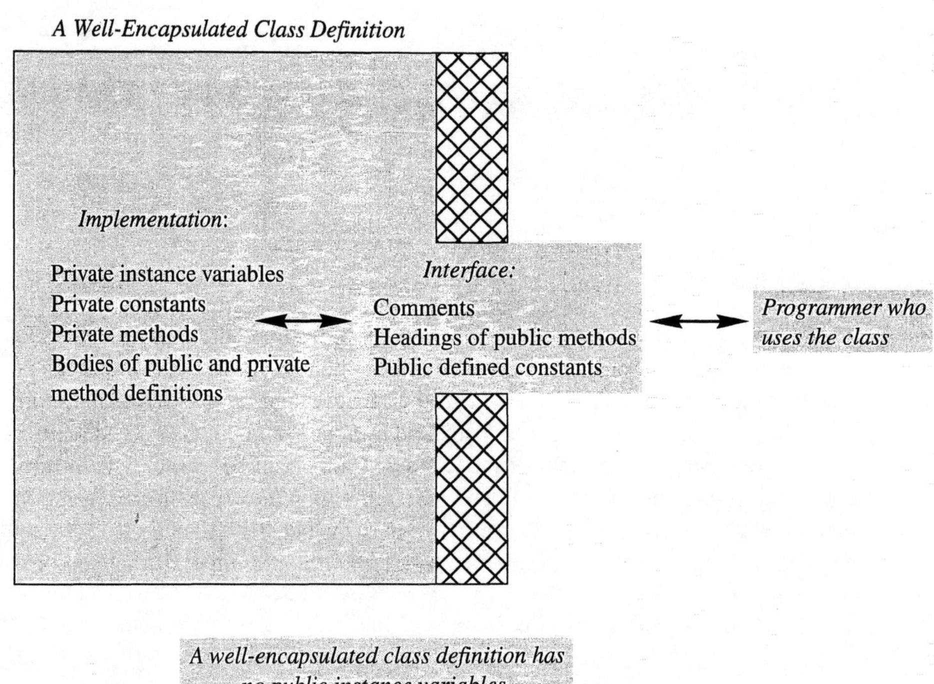

Some of the most important guidelines for defining a well-encapsulated class are the following:

encapsulation guidelines

1. Place a comment before the class definition that describes how the programmer should think about the class data and methods. (Note that this need not be a list of instance variables. If the class describes an amount of money, the programmer should think in terms of dollars and cents and not in terms of an instance variable of type `double`, if that is what is used to record the amount of money, nor should the programmer think in terms of two instance variables of type `int` for dollars and cents, if that is what is used to record the amount of money. In fact, the programmer using the class should not care whether the money is represented as an instance variable of type `double` or as two instance variables of type `int`, or is represented in some other way.)
2. All the instance variables in the class should be marked `private`.
3. Provide public accessor and mutator methods to read and change the data in an object. Also, provide public methods for any other basic methods that a programmer needs in order to manipulate the data in the class; for example, you should provide input and output methods.
4. Fully specify how to use each public method with a comment placed before the method heading.
5. Make any helping methods `private`.
6. Some of the comments in a class definition are part of the user interface, describing how to use the class. These comments are usually placed before the class definition to describe general properties and before particular method definitions to explain how to use that particular method. Other comments are needed only to understand the implementation. A good rule to follow is to use the `/**/` types of comments for user-interface comments and the `//` types of comments for implementation comments. In Display 4.11, the user-interface comments are highlighted.

comments

When you use encapsulation to define your class, you should be able to go back and change the implementation details of the class definition without requiring changes in any program that uses the class. This is a good way to test whether you have written a well-encapsulated class definition. There are often very good reasons for changing the implementation details of a class definition. For example, you may come up with a more efficient way to implement a method so that the method invocations run faster. You may even decide to change some details of what the implementation does without changing the way the methods are invoked and the basic things they do. For example, if you have a class for bank account objects, you might change the amount of the penalty charged to an account that is overdrawn.

FAQ: What Is an API?

The term **API** stands for *application programming interface.* The API for a class is essentially the same thing as the user interface for the class. You will often see the term *API* when reading the documentation for class libraries.

FAQ: What is an ADT?

The term **ADT** is short for *abstract data type*. An ADT is a data type that is written using good information hiding techniques. Thus in Java, an ADT is basically the same thing as a well-encapsulated class definition.

Quick Reference: Encapsulation

Encapsulation is a term often heard when describing modern programming techniques. **Encapsulation** means that the data and the actions are combined into a single item (in our case, a class object) and that the details of the implementation are hidden. Thus, the terms *information hiding, ADT,* and *encapsulation* all refer to basically the same general idea: In very operational terms, the idea is to spare the programmer who uses your class from needing to read the details of how your class is implemented.

Automatic Documentation with `javadoc`

If your copy of Java came from Sun Microsystems (or even from certain other places), it includes a program named `javadoc` that will automatically generate documentation for the user interfaces to your classes. This documentation tells somebody who uses your program or class what she or he needs to know in order to use it. To get a more useful `javadoc` document, you must write your comments in a particular way. All the classes in this book have been commented for use with `javadoc` (although because of space constraints, the comments are a little sparser than would be ideal). If you comment your class definition correctly, such as the way the class in Display 4.11 is commented, `javadoc` will take your class definition as input and produce a nicely formatted display of the user interface for your class. For example, if `javadoc` is run on the class definition in Display 4.11, the output will consist only of the highlighted text. (It will also adjust spacing and line breaks and such.)

You do not need to use `javadoc` in order to understand this book. Nor do you do need to use `javadoc` in order to write Java programs. Moreover, in order to read the documents produced by `javadoc`, you must use a Web browser (or other HTML viewer). However, if you are already using a Web browser, such as Netscape Navigator or Microsoft's Internet Explorer, you are likely to find `javadoc` both easy to use and very useful. Appendix 9 covers `javadoc`.

UML Class Diagrams

We gave an example of a class diagram at the start of the chapter (Display 4.2). You now know enough to understand all the notation in that diagram. However, rather than looking at that class diagram, let's look at a new one. Display 4.14 contains a UML class diagram for the class `Purchase` from Display 4.11. The details are pretty much self-explanatory, except for the plus and minus signs. A plus sign (+) before an instance variable or method means the member is public. A minus sign (–) before an instance variable or method means the member is private.

Notice that the class diagram contains more than the interface for the class and less than a full implementation. Normally, the class diagram is done before the class is defined. It is an outline of both the interface and the implementation. The class diagram is primarily for the programmer defining the class. The interface is for the programmer who will use the class when producing additional software.

DISPLAY 4.14 UML Class Diagram

This is the class diagram for the class Purchase *in Display* 4.11.

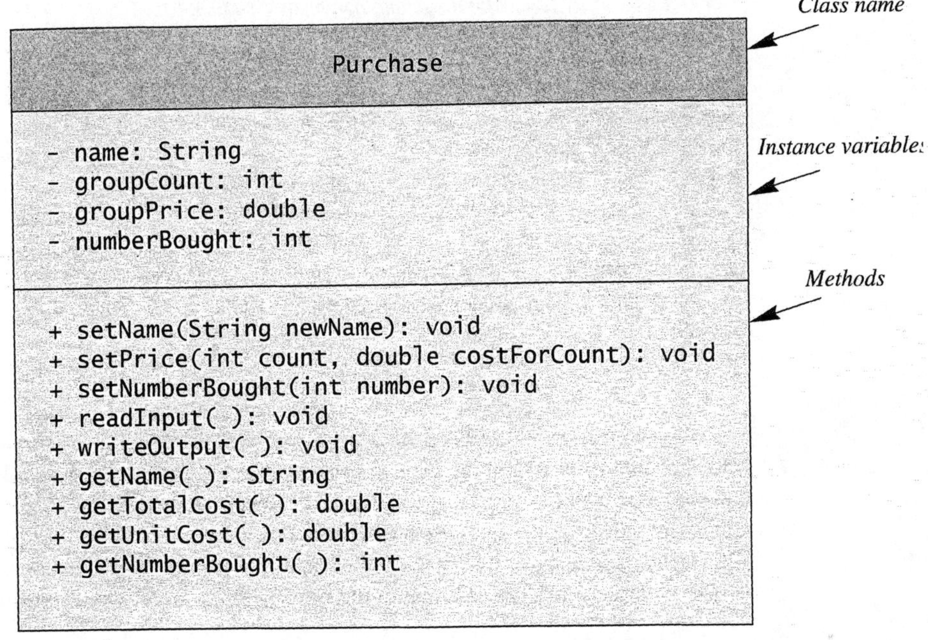

A minus sign (−) means the member is private.
A plus sign (+) means the member is public.

? Self-Test Questions

19. What is a well-encapsulated class definition?

20. When should an instance variable in a class definition be labeled private and when should it be labeled public?

21. Why would you ever label a method private?

22. In a class definition, is anything labeled private ever part of the user interface?

23. In a class definition, is the body of any method definition ever part of the user interface?

4.3 OBJECTS AND REFERENCE

"You are sad," the Knight said in anxious tone: "let me sing you a song to comfort you."
"Is it very long?" Alice asked, for she had heard a good deal of poetry that day.
"It's long," said the Knight, "but it's very, very beautiful. Everybody that hears me sing it—either it brings the tears into their eyes, or else—"
"Or else what?" said Alice, for the Knight had made a sudden pause.
"Or else it doesn't, you know. The name of the song is called 'Haddocks' Eyes.' *"*
"Oh, that's the name of the song, is it?" Alice asked, trying to feel interested.
"No, you don't understand," the Knight said, looking a little vexed. "That's what the name is called. The name really is 'The Aged Aged Man.' *"*
"Then I ought to have said 'That's what the song is called'?" Alice corrected herself.
"No, you oughtn't: that's quite another thing! The song is called 'Ways and Means': *but that's only what it's called, you know!"*
"Well, what is the song, then?" said Alice, who was by this time completely bewildered.
"I was coming to that," the Knight said. "The song really is 'A-sitting On A Gate': *and the tune's my own invention."* -Lewis Carroll, *Through the Looking-Glass*

Variables of a class type, such as the variable `oneSale` in Display 4.12, behave very differently from variables of the primitive types, such as `int`, `double`, and `char`. Variables of a class type are names for objects of their class, but the objects are not the values of the variables in the same way that, say, the number 6 can be the value of a variable of type `int`. A variable of a class type can name an object, but the naming process is a bit subtle. In this section, we discuss how a variable of a class type names objects, and we also discuss the related topic of how method parameters of a class type behave in Java.

Variables of a Class Type and Objects

Variables of a class type name objects in a way that is different from how variables of primitive types, such as `int` or `char`, store their values. Every variable, whether of a primitive type or a class type, is implemented as a memory location. (If this sounds unfamiliar, read Chapter 1.) If the variable is of a primitive type, the value of the variable is stored in the memory location assigned to the variable. However, if the variable is of a class type, then an object named by the variable is stored in some other location in memory, and the memory address of where the object is located is what is stored in the variable that names the object.

memory addresses

There is a reason why variables of a primitive type and variables of a class type name values in different ways. A value of a primitive type, such as the type `int`, always requires the same amount of memory to store one value. In Java, there is a maximum value of type `int`, and so values of type `int` have a limit on their size. However, an object of a class type, such as an object of the class `String`, might be of any size. The memory location for a variable of type `String` is of a fixed size, so it cannot store an arbitrarily long string. It can, however, store the address of any string, since there is always a last address and thus a limit on the size of an address.

reference

The memory address of where an object is stored is called a **reference** to the object, and that is why this section is named "Objects and Reference."

The fact that variables of a class type contain references can produce some surprising results. Variables of a class type behave very differently from variables of a primitive type. Consider the following lines of code that might begin the `main` part of a program:

```
SpeciesFourthTry klingonSpecies, earthSpecies;
klingonSpecies = new SpeciesFourthTry();
earthSpecies = new SpeciesFourthTry();
int n, m;
n = 42;
m = n;
```

As you would expect, there are two variables of type `int`: `n` and `m`. Both have a value of `42`, but if you change one, the other still has a value of `42`. For example, if the program continues with

```
n = 99;
System.out.println(n + " and " + m);
```

then the output produced will be

```
99 and 42
```

No surprises so far, but let's suppose the program continues as follows:

assignment with variables of a class type

```
klingonSpecies.set("Klingon ox", 10, 15);
earthSpecies.set("Black rhino", 11, 2);
earthSpecies = klingonSpecies;
earthSpecies.set("Elephant", 100, 12);
System.out.println("earthSpecies:");
earthSpecies.writeOutput();
System.out.println("klingonSpecies:");
klingonSpecies.writeOutput();
```

You might think that the `klingonSpecies` is the Klingon ox and the `earthSpecies` is the elephant, but the output produced may surprise you. It is the following:

```
earthSpecies:
Name = Elephant
Population = 100
Growth rate = 12%
klingonSpecies:
Name = Elephant
Population = 100
Growth rate = 12%
```

What has happened? You have two variables, `klingonSpecies` and `earthSpecies`, but you have only one object. Both variables contain the same reference, and so both variables name the same object. When you change `klingonSpecies`, you also change `earthSpecies`, and when you change `earthSpecies`, you also change `klingonSpecies`, because they are the same object.

Each object is stored in the computer's memory in some location, and that location has an address. The variables `earthSpecies` and `klingonSpecies` are really just ordinary variables (like the kind we use for `int` variables), but they store memory addresses for objects of the class `SpeciesFourthTry`. *When we say that a variable of a class type names an object, we mean that the variable contains the memory address of that object.* This is illustrated in Display 4.15.

■ DISPLAY 4.15 Class Variables *(Part 1 of 2)*

```
SpeciesFourthTry klingonSpecies, earthSpecies;
```

```
klingonSpecies = new SpeciesFourthTry();
earthSpecies = new SpeciesFourthTry();
```

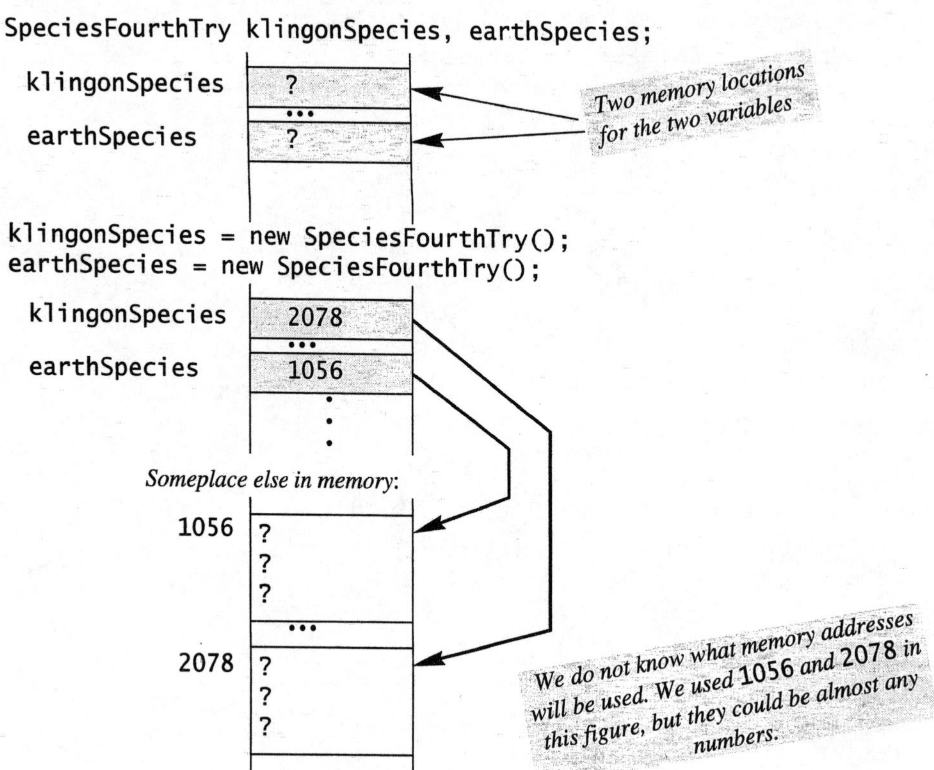


```
klingonSpecies.set("Klingon ox", 10, 15);
earthSpecies.set("Black rhino", 11, 2);
```

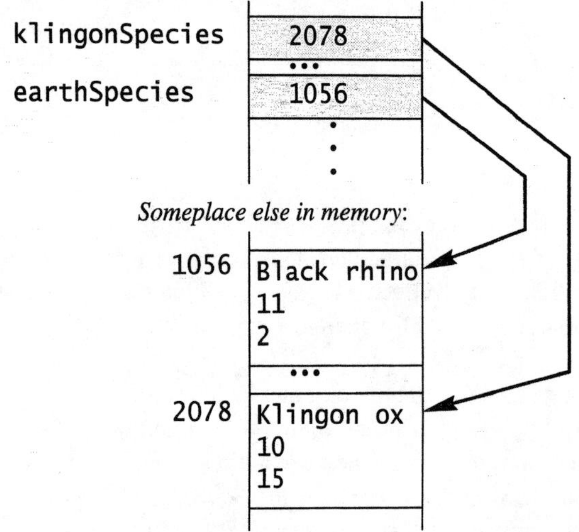

■ DISPLAY 4.15 Class Variables *(Part 2 of 2)*

```
earthSpecies = klingonSpecies;
```

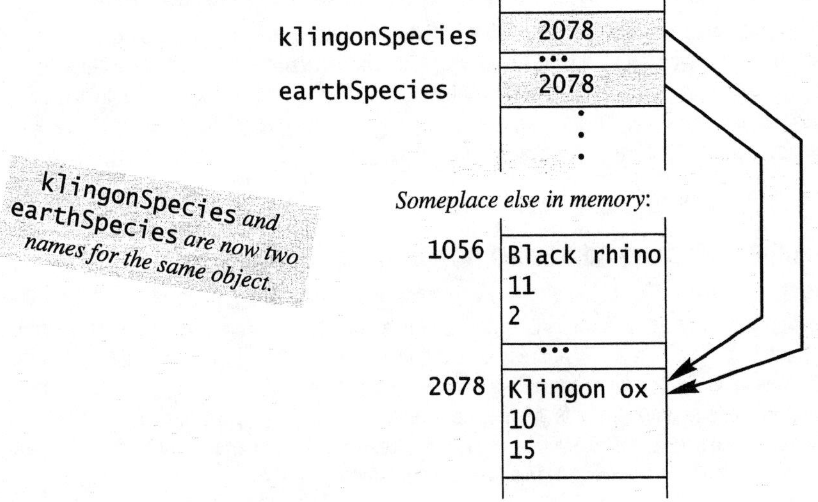


```
earthSpecies.set("Elephant", 100, 12);
```

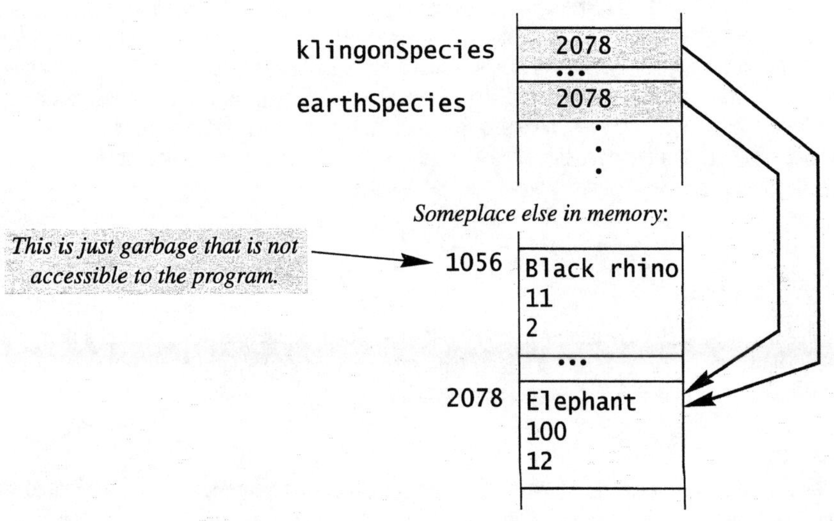

When we have an assignment statement such as

```
earthSpecies = klingonSpecies;
```

it just copies the memory address in `klingonSpecies` into the variable `earthSpecies`, so that they both have the same memory address and so both name the same object.

One word of warning about memory addresses: A memory address is a number, but it is not the same kind of number as an `int` value. So do not try to treat it as an ordinary integer.

Remember: Variables of a Class Type Store Memory Addresses

A variable of a primitive type stores a value of that type. Variables of a class type behave differently. A variable of a class type does not store an object of that class. A variable of a class type stores the memory address of where the object is located in the computer's memory. This allows a variable of a class type to be used as a name for an object of that class. However, some operations, such as = and ==, behave quite differently for variables of a class type than they do for variables of a primitive type.

Remember: Memory Addresses Are and Are Not Numbers

A variable of a class type stores a memory address. A memory address is a number. But a variable of class type cannot be used like a variable that stores a number. This is not crazy. This is abstraction. The important property of a memory address is that it identifies a memory location. The fact that the implementors used numbers, rather than letters or colors or something else, to identify memory locations is an accidental property. Java prevents you from using this accidental property. It does so to keep you from doing things you should not do, such as obtaining access to restricted memory or otherwise screwing up the computer. It also makes your code easier to understand.

Quick Reference: Class Types and Reference Types

A variable of a class type does not actually hold an object of that class. A variable of a class type holds only the address of where that object is stored in memory. This memory address is often called a **reference** to the object in memory. For this reason, class types are often called reference types. A **reference type** is just a type whose variables hold references (that is, hold memory addresses), as opposed to actual values of objects. However, there are reference types other than class types, so we will use the term *class type* when referring to the name of a class. All class types are reference types, but as you will see in Chapter 6, there are reference types that are not class types.

FAQ: What's `new`?

Variables of a class type work differently than variables of a primitive type. A variable of a primitive type holds a value of that type. A variable of a class type does not actually hold an object of that class. Instead, it holds the address of where that object is stored in memory. The declaration

```
SpeciesFourthTry s;
```

creates a variable `s` that can hold a memory address. At this point, your program has a place to store a memory address, but no place to store the data in the instance variables of an object of type `SpeciesFourthTry`. To get a memory location to store the values of instance variables, your program needs to use `new`. The following assigns a memory location to an object of type `SpeciesFourthTry` and places the address of that memory location in the variable `s`:

```
s = new SpeciesFourthTry();
```

In a very informal sense, you can think of `new` as creating the instance variables of the object.

▲ Gotcha

Use of = and == with Variables of a Class Type

In the previous subsection, you saw some of the surprises you can get when using the assignment operator with variables of a class type. The test for equality also behaves in what may seem like a peculiar way. Suppose the class SpeciesFourthTry is defined as shown in Display 4.9, and suppose you have the following in a program:

== with variables of a class type

```
SpeciesFourthTry klingonSpecies = new SpeciesFourthTry();
SpeciesFourthTry earthSpecies = new SpeciesFourthTry();
klingonSpecies.set("Klingon ox", 10, 15);
earthSpecies.set("Klingon ox", 10, 15);
if (klingonSpecies == earthSpecies)
    System.out.println("They are EQUAL.");
else
    System.out.println("They are NOT equal.");
```

This will produce the output

```
They are NOT equal.
```

Display 4.16 illustrates the execution of this code.

The problem is that, although, the two species are equal in an intuitive sense, a variable of a class type really contains only a memory address. There are two objects of type SpeciesFourthTry in memory. Both of them represent the same species in the real world, but they have different memory addresses, and the == operator checks only to see if the memory addresses are equal. The == operator tests for a kind of equality, but it is not the kind of equality you usually care about. When defining a class, you should normally define a method for the class that is called equals and that tests objects to see if they are equal. △

■ Java Tip

Define an equals Method for Your Classes

When you compare two objects using the == operator, you are checking to see whether they have the same address in memory. You are not testing for what you would intuitively call "being equal." To test for your intuitive notion of equality, you should define a method called equals. In Display 4.17, we have redefined our definition of a class for species one last time. This time, we have added a method called equals. This method equals is used with objects of the class Species in exactly the same way that we used the String method equals with objects of type String. The program in Display 4.18 demonstrates the use of the method equals.

Our definition of the method equals for the class Species uses the method equalsIgnoreCase of the class String. As we pointed out in Chapter 2, this method is automatically provided as part of the Java language. The method equalsIgnoreCase returns true if the two strings being compared are the same except that some letters might differ by being uppercase in one string and lowercase in the other string; otherwise, it returns false. □

equals-IgnoreCase

DISPLAY 4.16 Dangers of == with Objects

```
klingonSpecies = new SpeciesFourthTry();
earthSpecies = new SpeciesFourthTry();
```

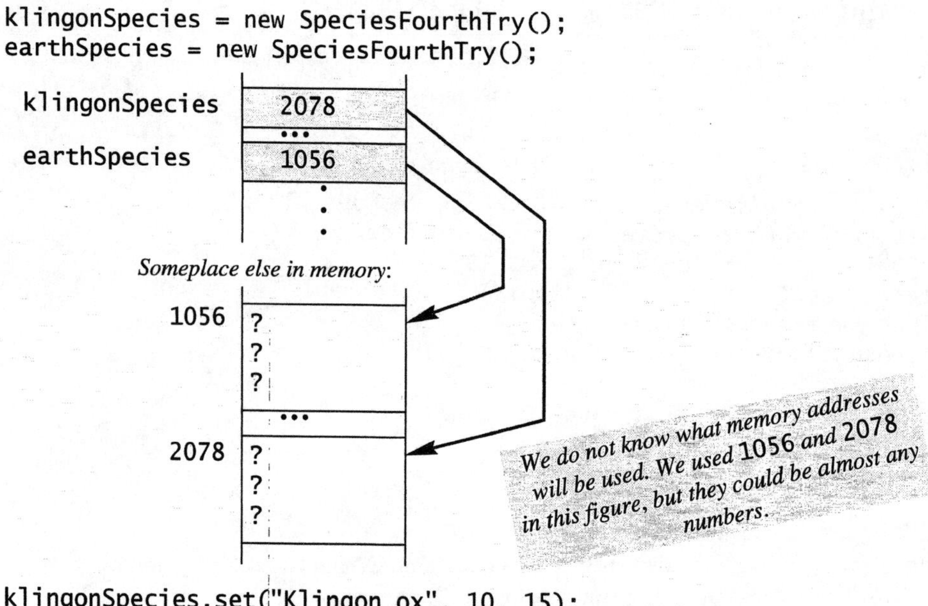

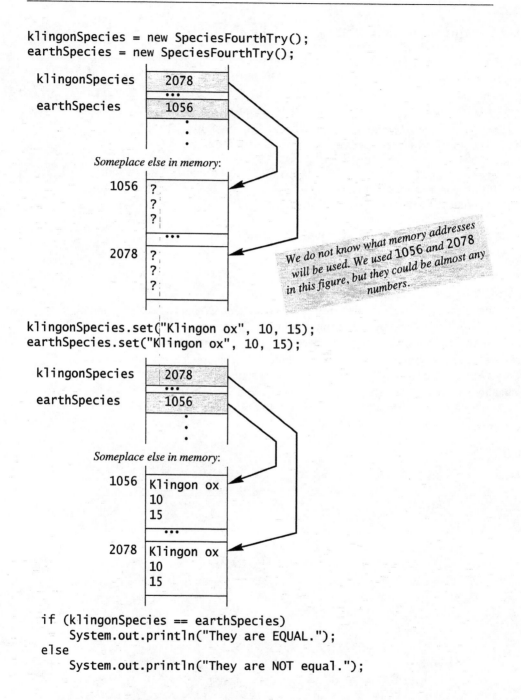

```
klingonSpecies.set("Klingon ox", 10, 15);
earthSpecies.set("Klingon ox", 10, 15);
```

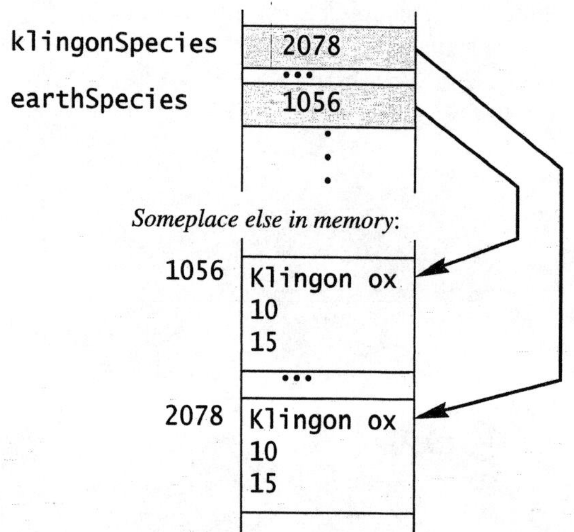


```
if (klingonSpecies == earthSpecies)
    System.out.println("They are EQUAL.");
else
    System.out.println("They are NOT equal.");
```

The output is `They are Not equal`, *because* `2078` *is not equal to* `1056`.

DISPLAY 4.17 Defining an `equals` Method

```
public class Species
{
    private String name;
    private int population;
    private double growthRate;

    <The definition of the methods readInput, writeOutput, and projectedPopulation
            go here. They are the same as in Display 4.3 and Display 4.6.>

     <The definition of the methods set, getName, getPopulation,
          and getGrowthRate go here. They are the same as in Display 4.9.>

     public boolean equals(Species otherObject)
     {
         return ((this.name.equalsIgnoreCase(otherObject.name))
                 && (this.population == otherObject.population)
                 && (this.growthRate == otherObject.growthRate));
     }
}
```

`equalsIgnoreCase` is a method of the class `String` and is automatically provided as part of the Java language.

Notice that the method `equals` in Display 4.17 always returns either `true` or `false`, and so the type for the value returned is `boolean`. The `return` statement may seem a bit strange, but it is nothing other than a boolean expression of the kind you might use in an `if-else` statement. It may help you to understand things if you note that the definition of `equals` in Display 4.17 can be expressed by the following pseudocode:

returning a `boolean` value

```
if ((this.name.equalsIgnoreCase(otherObject.name))
            && (this.population == otherObject.population)
            && (this.growthRate == otherObject.growthRate))
then return true
otherwise return false
```

Therefore, the following (from the program in Display 4.18):

```
if (s1.equals(s2))
   System.out.println("Match with the method equals.");
else
   System.out.println("Do Not match with the method equals.");
```

■ DISPLAY 4.18 Demonstrating an `equals` Method

```
public class SpeciesEqualsDemo
{
    public static void main(String[] args)
    {
        Species s1 = new Species(), s2 = new Species();

        s1.set("Klingon Ox", 10, 15);
        s2.set("Klingon Ox", 10, 15);

        if (s1 == s2)
            System.out.println("Match with ==.");
        else
            System.out.println("Do Not match with ==.");

        if (s1.equals(s2))
            System.out.println("Match with the method equals.");
        else
            System.out.println(
                                "Do Not match with the method equals.");

        System.out.println(
                      "Now we change one Klingon Ox to all lowercase.");
        s2.set("klingon ox", 10, 15);
        if (s1.equals(s2))
            System.out.println("Still match with the method equals.");
        else
            System.out.println(
                                "Do Not match with the method equals.");
    }
}
```

Screen Output

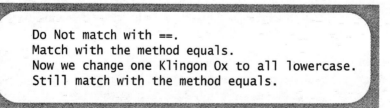

```
Do Not match with ==.
Match with the method equals.
Now we change one Klingon Ox to all lowercase.
Still match with the method equals.
```

is equivalent to the following pseudocode:

```
if it is true that
        (s1.name.equalsIgnoreCase(s2.name))
         && (s1.population == s2.population)
         && (s1.growthRate == s2.growthRate), then
```

```
        System.out.println("Match with the method equals.");
    else
        System.out.println("Do Not match with the method equals.");
```

We did not need to use the `this` parameter in the definition of `equals` in Display 4.17. The definition given there is equivalent to the following:

use of `this` is optional

```
public boolean equals(Species otherObject)
{
    return ((name.equalsIgnoreCase(otherObject.name))
            && (population == otherObject.population)
            && (growthRate == otherObject.growthRate))
}
```

The instance variable `population` by itself always means the same as `this.population`. Similarly, any other instance variable by itself is treated as though it were preceded by `this` and a dot.

We will say more about methods that return a value of type `boolean` in the subsection "Boolean-Valued Methods" a little later in the chapter.

There is no unique definition of `equals` that has been handed down by the gods for all time. The definition of `equals` that you write will depend on how you intend to use the class. The definition in Display 4.17 says that two objects of the class `Species` are equal if they represent the same records—that is, the same species name, the same population size, and the same growth rate. In some other context, you might want to define `equals` to mean that two objects are equal if they have the same species name, but possibly different populations or different growth rates. This would correspond to considering two objects to be equal if they are records for the same species, even if they are records for the same species at different times.

You should always use the identifier `equals` for the name of the method you create to test whether two objects are equal. Do not use some other identifier, such as `same`; do not even use `equal` (without an `s`). This is because certain software that is part of Java depends on your using the exact name `equals` to test for equality of objects. This software invokes a method named `equals`, so your method had better be named `equals`.

If you do not define an `equals` method for your class, Java will automatically create a default definition of `equals`, but it is unlikely to behave the way you want it to. Thus, it is best to define your own `equals` method.

Programming Example

A Species Class

The final version of our class for species objects is given in Display 4.19. It is the same definition as the one in Display 4.17, but this time we have included all of the details so that you can see a complete example. We have also written the definition of the method `equals` without using the `this` parameter, since that is the form most programmers use. The definition of `equals` in Display 4.19 is completely equivalent to the definition in Display 4.17. Display 4.20 contains the class diagram for this class `Species`. ■

DISPLAY 4.19 A Complete `Species` Class *(Part 1 of 3)*

```
/**
 Class for data on endangered species.
*/
public class Species
{
    private String name;
    private int population;
    private double growthRate;

    public void readInput()
    {
        System.out.println("What is the species' name?");
        name = SavitchIn.readLine();
        System.out.println(
                      "What is the population of the species?");
        population = SavitchIn.readLineInt();
        while (population < 0)
        {
            System.out.println("Population cannot be negative.");
            System.out.println("Reenter population:");
            population = SavitchIn.readLineInt();
        }
        System.out.println(
               "Enter growth rate (percent increase per year):");
       growthRate = SavitchIn.readLineDouble();
    }

    public void writeOutput()
    {
         System.out.println("Name = " + name);
         System.out.println("Population = " + population);
         System.out.println("Growth rate = " + growthRate + "%");
    }

    /**
     Precondition: years is a nonnegative number.
     Returns the projected population of the calling object
     after the specified number of years.
    */
    public int projectedPopulation(int years)
    {
        double populationAmount = population;
        int count = years;
```

This is the same class definition as in Display 4.17, but with all the details shown.

<Definition of `projectedPopulation` continued on next page.>

■ DISPLAY 4.19 A Complete Species Class *(Part 2 of 3)*

```
        while ((count > 0) && (populationAmount > 0))
        {
            populationAmount = (populationAmount +
                         (growthRate/100) * populationAmount);
            count--;
        }
        if (populationAmount > 0)
            return (int)populationAmount;
        else
            return 0;
    }

    public void set(String newName, int newPopulation,
                                    double newGrowthRate)
    {
        name = newName;
        if (newPopulation >= 0)
            population = newPopulation;
        else
        {
            System.out.println("ERROR: using a negative population.");
            System.exit(0);
        }
        growthRate = newGrowthRate;
    }

    public String getName()
    {
        return name;
    }

    public int getPopulation()
    {
        return population;
    }

    public double getGrowthRate()
    {
        return growthRate;
    }
```

DISPLAY 4.19 A Complete Species Class *(Part 3 of 3)*

```
    public boolean equals(Species otherObject)
    {
        return ((name.equalsIgnoreCase(otherObject.name))
                && (population == otherObject.population)
                && (growthRate == otherObject.growthRate));
    }
}
```

This version of `equals` *is equivalent to the version in Display 4.17. In Display 4.17, we explicitly used the* `this` *parameter. This version, omits the* `this` *parameter, but it is understood to be there implicitly.*

DISPLAY 4.20 Class Diagram for the Class `Species` in Display 4.19

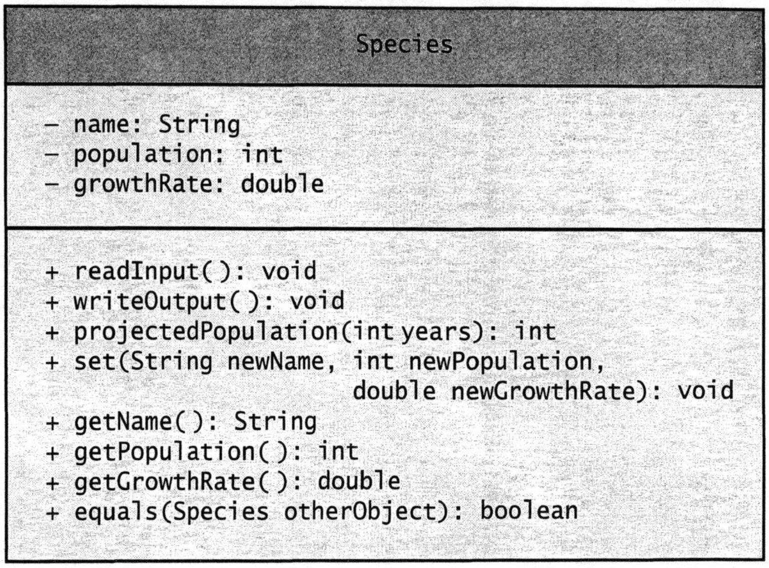

```
Species
-------------------------------------------
- name: String
- population: int
- growthRate: double
-------------------------------------------
+ readInput( ): void
+ writeOutput( ): void
+ projectedPopulation(int years): int
+ set(String newName, int newPopulation,
                  double newGrowthRate): void
+ getName( ): String
+ getPopulation( ): int
+ getGrowthRate( ): double
+ equals(Species otherObject): boolean
```

Boolean-Valued Methods

Methods can return a value of type `boolean`. There is really nothing new about this: You just specify a return type of `boolean` and use a boolean expression in the `return` statement. You have already seen one such method, namely the `equals` method for the class `Species` in Display 4.19, reproduced in what follows: `equals`

```
public boolean equals(Species otherObject)
{
    return ((name.equalsIgnoreCase(otherObject.name))
                && (population == otherObject.population)
                && (growthRate == otherObject.growthRate));
}
```

This method simply evaluates the boolean expression in the `return` statement. That boolean expression produces a value of `true` or `false`. The method `equals` returns this value.

As you have already seen, you can use an invocation of the method `equals` in an `if-else` statement, a `while` statement, or another statement that requires a boolean expression. You can also store the value returned by the method `equals`, or any other boolean-valued method, in a variable of type `boolean`. For example,

```
Species s1 = new Species(), s2 = new Species();
<Some code to set the values of s1 and s2.>
boolean areEqual;
areEqual = s1.equals(s2);
<Some more code.>
if (areEqual)
    System.out.println("They are equal.");
else
    System.out.println("They are not equal.");
```

As another example of a boolean-valued method, you might add the following method to the definition of the class `Species` in Display 4.19: examples

```
/**
 Precondition: The calling object and the argument
 otherSpecies both have values for their population.
 Returns true if the population of the calling object
 is greater than the population of otherSpecies;
 otherwise, returns false.
*/
public boolean largerPopulationThan(Species otherSpecies)
{
    return (population > otherSpecies.population);
}
```

You can then use the method `largerPopulationThan` in the same sorts of ways that you use the method `equals`. For example, the following might appear in some program:

```
Species s1 = new Species(), s2 = new Species();
<Some code to set the values of s1 and s2.>
if (s1.largerPopulationThan(s2))
    System.out.println(s1.getName()
                            + " has the larger population.");
else
    System.out.println(s2.getName()
                            + " has the larger population.");
```

As an additional example, you might also add the following method to the definition of the class Species in Display 4.19:

```
/**
 Precondition: The calling object has a value for
 its population.
 Returns true if the population of the calling object
 is zero; otherwise, returns false.
*/
public boolean isExtinct()
{
    return (population == 0);
}
```

The following sample code might then appear in a program:

```
Species s1 = new Species();
<Some code to set the value of s1.>
if (s1.isExtinct())
    System.out.println(s1.getName() + " is extinct.");
else
    System.out.println(s1.getName() + " is still with us.");
```

? Self-Test Questions

24. What is a reference type? Are class types reference types? Are primitive types (like int) reference types?
25. When comparing two objects of a class type to see if they are "equal" or not, should you use == or the method equals?
26. When comparing two objects of a primitive types (like int) to see if they are "equal" or not, should you use == or the method equals?
27. Write a method definition for a method called largerGrowthRateThan that could be added to the class Species in Display 4.19. The method larger-GrowthRateThan has one argument of type Species. The method returns true if the calling object has a larger growth rate than the growth rate of the one argument; otherwise, it returns false.

Class Parameters

Parameters of a class type are treated differently than parameters of a primitive type. In a sense, we have already discussed this difference when we discussed using the assignment operator with objects of a class type. Recall the following two points, which will help us describe how class parameters work:

1. First, recall how the assignment operator works with classes:
   When you use an assignment operator with objects of a class type, you are actually copying a memory address. Suppose that Species is the class defined in Display 4.19, and consider the following code:

```
Species species1 = new Species();
Species species2 = new Species();
```

```
species2.readInput();
species1 = species2;
```

As we discussed in the previous section, `species1` and `species2` are now two names for the same object.

2. Now consider how parameters *of a primitive type* work. For example, consider the following call to the method `projectedPopulation` that we used in Display 4.10:

```
futurePopulation =
  speciesOfTheMonth.projectedPopulation(numberOfYears);
```

The method definition for `projectedPopulation` is in Display 4.19. The definition begins as follows:

```
public int projectedPopulation(int years)
{
    double populationAmount = population;
    int count = years;
    while ((count > 0) && (populationAmount > 0))
    {
        .
        .
        .
```

Recall that the formal parameter `years` is actually a local variable. When the method `projectedPopulation` is invoked, this local variable `years` is initialized to the value of the argument `numberOfYears`. So when the method is called, it is as if the following assignment statement were temporarily inserted into the method definition:

```
years = numberOfYears;
```

In other words, it is as if the definition of the method `projectedPopulation` was, for the duration of this method invocation, changed as follows:

```
public int projectedPopulation(int years)
{
    years = numberOfYears;
    double populationAmount = population;
    int count = years;
    while ((count > 0) && (populationAmount > 0))
    {
        .
        .
        .
```

Wow—that's a long preamble, but if you understand these two points, it will be very easy to explain how parameters of a class type work. Parameters of a class type work the same as described in point 2 for parameters of a primitive type, *but because the assignment operator means something different for variables of a class type, the effect is very different!* [5]

Let's go through that explanation again with slightly different words (but the same message). Consider the following call to the method `equals` that was used in Display 4.18:

```
if (s1.equals(s2))
    System.out.println("Match with the method equals.");
else
    System.out.println("Do Not match with the method equals.");
```

In this call, `s2` is an argument of the class type `Species` defined in Display 4.19. We reproduce here the definition for the method `equals`. (This version of `equals` was given in Display 4.17 and is equivalent to the version in Display 4.19):

```
public boolean equals(Species otherObject)
{
     return ((this.name.equalsIgnoreCase(otherObject.name))
              && (this.population == otherObject.population)
              && (this.growthRate == otherObject.growthRate))
}
```

When the method `equals` is called in `s1.equals(s2)`, it is as if the following assignment statement was temporarily inserted at the start of the method definition:

```
otherObject = s2;
```

In other words, the method definition, for the duration of this call to `equals`, is equivalent to

```
public boolean equals(Species otherObject)
{
     otherObject = s2;//You cannot do this, but
                      //Java acts as if you could and did do this.
     return ((this.name.equalsIgnoreCase(otherObject.name))
              && (this.population == otherObject.population)
              && (this.growthRate == otherObject.growthRate))
}
```

Recall, however, that this assignment statement merely copies the memory address of `s2` into the variable `otherObject`, so `otherObject` becomes just another name for the object named by `s2`. Thus, anything done with the object named `otherObject` will in

---

5. Some programmers refer to the parameter mechanism for class parameters as **call-by-reference** parameter passing. Others say that this terminology is incorrect. The problem is that there is more than one commonly used definition of *call-by-reference*. One point is clear, however: class parameters in Java behave a bit differently than what is known as call-by-reference parameters in other languages. So we will not use the term *call-by-reference* here. In any event, the important thing is to understand how class parameters work, no matter what you call them.

fact be done with the object named s2. Thus, it is as if the method performed the following action:

```
return ((this.name.equalsIgnoreCase(s2.name))
          && (this.population == s2.population)
         && (this.growthRate == s2.growthRate))
```

Notice that with a parameter of a class type, whatever action is taken with the formal parameter (in this example, otherObject) is actually taken with the argument used in the method call (in this case, s2). So the argument used in the method call is actually acted upon and can be changed by the method call.

In the case of the method equals, the effect of this parameter-passing mechanism for parameters of a class type is not so different from what happens with parameters of a primitive type. With some other methods, however, the difference is more dramatic. The next subsection gives a more dramatic example of how parameters of a class type differ from parameters of a primitive type.

Quick Reference: Parameters of a Class Type

Formal parameters are given in parentheses after the method name at the beginning of a method definition. A formal parameter of a class type is a local variable that holds the memory address of an object of that class type. When the method is invoked, the parameter is initialized to the address of the corresponding argument in the method invocation. In less technical terms, this means that the formal parameter will serve as an alternative name for the object given as the corresponding argument in a method invocation.

Note that this means that if you use an argument of a class type in a method invocation, then the method invocation can change the argument.

Comparing Class Parameters and Primitive-Type Parameters

Suppose we add a method named makeEqual to the class Species to form a new class called DemoSpecies, as shown in Display 4.21. This class is only for our demonstration, so do not worry about the rest of the class definition. Notice that the method makeEqual has parameters of type DemoSpecies, and that makeEqual changes the parameter. Let's play with this toy class.

Look at the demonstration program in Display 4.22. The call to makeEqual has an argument s2 of type DemoSpecies. Note that the change performed in the method body is actually performed on the argument s2. A method can actually change the value of an argument of a class type.

Now look at the method named tryToMakeEqual, also in Display 4.21. Notice that tryToMakeEqual has a parameter of the primitive type int and that tryToMakeEqual changes the formal parameter. The demonstration program in Display 4.22 calls tryToMakeEqual using the argument aPopulation of type int. Note that the change performed in the method body has no effect on the argument aPopulation. This is because, with arguments of a primitive type, Java uses the call-by-value parameter mechanism, and because variables of a primitive type hold actual values, not memory addresses. Thus, the parameter is a local variable that holds the value of the argument, and any changes are made to this local variable and not to the argument.

Parameters of a class type are more versatile than parameters of a primitive type. Parameters of a primitive type can be used to give values to a method, but a method cannot change the value of any primitive-type variable that is given to it as an argument. On the other hand, not only can parameters of a class type be used to give information to a method, but the method can also change the object named by an argument of a class type.

DISPLAY 4.21 Just a Demonstration Class

```
/**
 This is a version of the class Species, but is only a toy
 example designed to demonstrate the difference between
 parameters of a class type and parameters of a primitive type.
*/
public class DemoSpecies
{
    private String name;
    private int population;
    private double growthRate;

    /**
     Precondition: Calling object has been given values.
     Postcondition: otherObject has the same data as the
     calling object. The calling object is unchanged.
    */
    public void makeEqual(DemoSpecies otherObject)
    {
        otherObject.name = this.name;
        otherObject.population = this.population;
        otherObject.growthRate = this.growthRate;
    }

    /**
     Tries to set intVariable equal to the population of
     the calling object. But it cannot succeed, because
     arguments of a primitive type cannot be changed.
    */
    public void tryToMakeEqual(int intVariable)
    {
        intVariable = this.population;
    }

    public boolean equals(DemoSpecies otherObject)
    <The rest of the class definition of the method equals is the same as in Display 4.19.>

    <The rest of the class definition is the same as that of the class Species in Display 4.19.>

}
```

DISPLAY 4.22 Comparing Parameters of a Class Type and a Primitive Type

```
public class ParametersDemo
{
    public static void main(String[] args)
    {
        DemoSpecies s1 = new DemoSpecies(),
                    s2 = new DemoSpecies();

        s1.set("Klingon Ox", 10, 15);
        s2.set("Ferengie Fur Ball", 90, 56);
        System.out.println("Value of s2 before call to method:");
        s2.writeOutput( );
        s1.makeEqual(s2);
        System.out.println("Value of s2 after call to method:");
        s2.writeOutput();

        int aPopulation = 42;
        System.out.println(
                    "Value of aPopulation before call to method: "
                   + aPopulation);
        s1.tryToMakeEqual(aPopulation);
        System.out.println(
                    "Value of aPopulation after call to method: "
                   + aPopulation);
    }
}
```

Screen Output

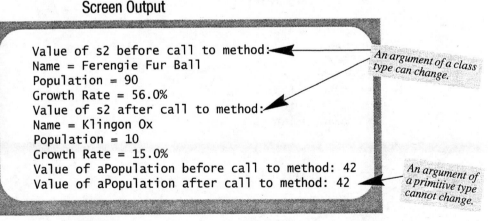

```
Value of s2 before call to method:
Name = Ferengie Fur Ball
Population = 90
Growth Rate = 56.0%
Value of s2 after call to method:
Name = Klingon Ox
Population = 10
Growth Rate = 15.0%
Value of aPopulation before call to method: 42
Value of aPopulation after call to method: 42
```

An argument of a class type can change.

An argument of a primitive type cannot change.

Remember: Differences Between Primitive and Class-Type Parameters

A method cannot change the value of a variable of a primitive type that is an argument to the method. On the other hand, a method can change the values of the instance variables of an argument of a class type.

? Self-Test Questions

28. What is wrong with a program that starts as follows (the class Species is defined in Display 4.19)?

```
public class SpeciesEqualsDemo
{
    public static void main(String[] args)
    {
        Species s1, s2;

        s1.set("Klingon Ox", 10, 15);
        s2.set("Klingon Ox", 10, 15);

        if (s1 == s2)
            System.out.println("Match with ==.");
        else
           System.out.println("Do Not match with ==.");
    }
}
```

29. What is the biggest difference between a parameter of a primitive type and a parameter of a class type?

30. What is the output produced by the following program (the class Species is defined in Display 4.19)?

```
public class ExerciseProgram
{
    public static void main(String[] args)
    {
        Species s1 = new Species();
        ExerciseClass mysteryMaker = new ExerciseClass();
        int n = 0;
        s1.set("Hobbit", 100, 2);
        mysteryMaker.mystery(s1, n);
        s1.writeOutput();
        System.out.println("n = " + n);
    }
}
```

The class ExerciseClass is as follows:

```
public class ExerciseClass
{
    public void mystery(Species s, int m)
    {
        s.set("Klingon Ox", 10, 15);
        m = 42;
    }
}
```

31. Redefine the class Person from Self-Test Question 18 so that it includes an equals method.

CHAPTER SUMMARY

- Classes have instance variables to store data and methods to perform actions.
- All instance variables in a class should be declared to be `private`. When they are declared `private`, they cannot be accessed by name except within the definition of a method of the same class.
- Encapsulation means that the data and the actions are combined into a single item (in our case, a class object) and that the *details of the implementation are hidden.* Making all instance variables `private` is part of the encapsulation process.
- A variable of a class type is a reference variable. This means that a variable of a class type holds the memory address of where the object it names is stored in memory.
- There are two kinds of methods: methods that return a value and `void` methods.
- Methods can have parameters of a primitive type or parameters of a class type, but the two types of parameters behave differently.
- A parameter of a primitive type is a local variable that is initialized to the value of the corresponding argument when the method is called. This mechanism of substituting arguments for formal parameters is known as the call-by-value mechanism.
- A parameter of a class type becomes another name for the corresponding argument in a method invocation. Thus, any change that is made to the parameter will be made to the corresponding argument.
- The operators = and ==, when used on objects of a class, do not behave the same as they do when used on primitive types.
- You usually want to define an `equals` method for the classes you define.

✔ Answers to Self-Test Questions

1.

```
SpeciesFirstTry speciesOfTheYear = new SpeciesFirstTry();
System.out.println("Enter data for Species of the Year:");
speciesOfTheYear.readInput();
```

2. `dilbert.readInput();`

3.

```
public class SpeciesFirstTry
{
    public String name;
    public int number;
```

```
    public int population;
    public double growthRate;
    public void readInput( )
    {
        System.out.println("What is the species' name?");
        name = SavitchIn.readLine( );
        System.out.println("What is the species' number?");
        number = SavitchIn.readLineInt( );
        while (number < 0)
        {
            System.out.println(
                     "Number cannot be negative.");
            System.out.println("Reenter number:");
            number = SavitchIn.readLineInt( );
        }
        System.out.println(
                    "What is the population of the species?");
        population = SavitchIn.readLineInt( );
        while (population < 0)
        {
            System.out.println(
                      "Population cannot be negative.");
            System.out.println("Reenter population:");
            population = SavitchIn.readLineInt( );
        }
       System.out.println(
            "Enter growth rate (percent increase per year):");
        growthRate = SavitchIn.readLineDouble( );
    }

    public void writeOutput( )
    {
       System.out.println("Name = " + name);
       System.out.println("Number = " + number);
       System.out.println("Population = " + population);
       System.out.println("Growth rate = " + growthRate + "%");
    }

    public int populationIn10( )
     <This method does not change.>
}
```

4.

```
   public int femalePopulation( )
   {
       return (population/2 + population%2);
   }

   public int malePopulation( )
   {
       return population/2;
   }
```

5.

```
public void writeOutput()
{
    System.out.println("Name = " + this.name);
    System.out.println("Population = " + this.population);
    System.out.println("Growth rate = "
                          + this.growthRate + "%");
}
```

6.

```
public void readInput()
{
    System.out.println("What is the species' name?");
    this.name = SavitchIn.readLine();

    System.out.println(
            "What is the population of the species?");
    this.population = SavitchIn.readLineInt();
    while (this.population < 0)
    {
        System.out.println(
                "Population cannot be negative.");
        System.out.println("Reenter population:");
        this.population = SavitchIn.readLineInt();
    }

    System.out.println(
        "Enter growth rate (percent increase per year):");
    this.growthRate = SavitchIn.readLineDouble();
}
```

7.

```
public int populationIn10()
{
    double populationAmount = this.population;
    int count = 10;
    while ((count > 0) && (populationAmount > 0))
    {
        populationAmount = (populationAmount +
                (this.growthRate/100) * populationAmount);
        count--;
    }
    if (populationAmount > 0)
        return (int)populationAmount;
    else
        return 0;
}
```

8. The expression `(int)` is a type cast. It is needed because the method heading specifies that the type of the returned value is `int`, and so the value of `populationAmount` must be changed from `double` to `int` before it is returned.

9. In this book the terms *parameter* and *formal parameter* mean the exact same thing.

10.

```
public double density(double area)
{
    return population/area;
}
```

11.

```
public void fixPopulation(double area)
{
     population = (int)(2*area);
}
```

12.

```
public void changePopulation(double area,
                                           int numberPerMile)
{
     population = (int)(numberPerMile*area);
}
```

13. We cannot use the alternative code because the instance variables are labeled `private` in the class definition and so cannot be accessed directly except within a method definition of the class `SpeciesFourthTry`.

14.

```
/**
 Precondition: Calling object's population and growth
 rate have been given values.
 Postcondition: Calling object's population was updated to
 reflect one year's change.
 Other data values are unchanged.
*/
```

15. An assertion is a statement that says something about the state of your program. An assertion can be either true or false and should be true if there are no mistakes in the program. Precondition and postcondition statements are examples of assertions. The following is another example of an assertion given two times, once as a comment and once as an assertion check:

```
// (timeLeft > 30) && (points < 10)
assert (timeLeft > 30) && (points < 10);
```

16.

```
if (balance <= 0) //if (balance > 0) is false.
{
   System.out.println("Assertion (balance > 0) failed.");
   System.out.println("Aborting program.");
   System.exit(0);
}
```

17. An accessor method is a public method that reads and returns data from one or more private instance variables. (The names of accessor methods typically begin with `get`.) A mutator method is a public method that changes the data stored in one or more private instance variables. (The names of mutator methods typically begin with `set`.)

18.

```
public class Person
{
    private String name;
    private int age;

    public void readInput()
    {
        System.out.println("What is the person's name?");
        name = SavitchIn.readLine();

        System.out.println("What is the person's age?");
        age = SavitchIn.readLineInt();
        while (age < 0)
        {
            System.out.println("Age cannot be negative.");
            System.out.println("Reenter age:");
            age = SavitchIn.readLineInt();
        }
    }

    public void writeOutput()
    {
        System.out.println("Name = " + name);
        System.out.println("Age = " + age);
    }

    public void set(String newName, int newAge)
    {
        name = newName;
        if (newAge >= 0)
            age = newAge;
        else
        {
            System.out.println("ERROR: Used a negative age.");
            System.exit(0);
        }
    }

    public String getName()
    {
        return name;
    }

    public int getAge()
    {
        return age;
    }
}
```

19. A well-encapsulated class definition is one written so that it neatly separates into user interface and implementation. A programmer who uses the class should need to know only about the user interface without being concerned with the implementation details.

20. Instance variables should always be labeled `private`.

21. If a method is a helping method that is used only in the definitions of other methods, it should be labeled `private`.

22. No, it is part of the implementation.

23. No, it is part of the implementation.

24. A reference type is a type whose variables hold references (that is, hold memory addresses), as opposed to actual values of objects. Class types are reference types. (There are reference types other than class types, but we will not see any until later in the book.) Primitive types are not reference types.

25. Normally, you use the method `equals` when testing two objects to see if they are "equal" or not. (The only time you would use == is if you wanted to see whether the objects were in the same place in memory, and it is unlikely that you would want to make such a test.)

26. You use == when comparing two objects of a primitive type (like `int`) to see if they are "equal" or not. In fact, there normally is no `equals` method for primitive types.

27.

```
/**
 Precondition: The calling object and the argument
 otherSpecies both have values for their growth rates.
 Returns true if the growth rate of the calling object is
 greater than the growth rate of otherSpecies;
 otherwise, returns false.
*/
public boolean largerGrowthRateThan(Species otherSpecies)
{
    return (growthRate > otherSpecies.growthRate);
}
```

28. The variables `s1` and `s2` are names for object of type `Species`, but this program does not create any objects for them to name. They are just names, not yet objects. The program should begin as follows:

```
public class SpeciesEqualsDemo
{
    public static void main(String[] args)
    {
        Species s1 = new Species(), s2 = new Species();
         <The rest of the code is OK.>
```

29. The biggest difference is in how a method handles arguments that correspond to the different kinds of parameters. A method cannot change the value of a variable of a primitive type that is an argument to the method. On the other hand, a method can change the values of the instance variables of an object of a class type whose name is an argument to the method.

30.

```
Name = Klingon ox
Population = 10
Growth rate = 15.0%
n = 0
```

31. The class definition is the same as before except for the addition of the method `equals`. The following are two possible definitions of `equals`. The first corresponds to saying that a person at one age is equal to the same person at another (possibly different) age. The second one corresponds to saying that a person at one age is not equal to what she or he will be at another age.

```
public boolean equals(Person otherObject)
{
     return (this.name.equalsIgnoreCase(otherObject.name));
}
public boolean equals(Person otherObject)
{
    return ((this.name.equalsIgnoreCase(otherObject.name))
                 && (this.age == otherObject.age) );
}
```

They are also correct if you omit all the occurrences of `this` and the following dot.

Programming Projects

1. Write a program to answer questions like the following: Suppose the species Klingon ox has a population of 100 and a growth rate of 15 percent, and the species elephant has a population of 10 and a growth rate of 35 percent. How many years will it take for the elephant population to exceed the Klingon ox population? Use the class `Species` in Display 4.19. Your program will ask for the data on both species and will respond by telling how many years it will take for the populations to change so that the species that starts with the lower population outnumbers the species that starts with the higher population. The two species may be entered in any order. Note that it is possible that the species with the smaller population will never outnumber the other species. In this case, your program should output a suitable message stating this fact.
2. Define a class called `Counter`. An object of this class is used to count things, so it records a count that is a nonnegative whole number. Include methods to set the counter to 0, to increase the count by 1, and to decrease the count by 1. Be sure that no method allows the value of the counter to become negative. Also include an accessor method that returns the current count value, as well as a method that outputs the count to the screen. There will be no input method. The only method that can set the counter is the one that sets it to zero. Write a program to test your class definition. *Hint:* You need only one instance variable.

3. Write a grading program for a class with the following grading policies:

   a. There are two quizzes, each graded on the basis of 10 points.

   b. There is one midterm exam and one final exam, each graded on the basis of 100 points.

   c. The final exam counts for 50 percent of the grade, the midterm counts for 25 percent, and the two quizzes together count for a total of 25 percent. (Do not forget to normalize the quiz scores. They should be converted to percentages before they are averaged in.)

   Any grade of 90 or more is an A, any grade of 80 or more (but less than 90) is a B, any grade of 70 or more (but less than 80) is a C, any grade of 60 or more (but less than 70) is a D, and any grade below 60 is an F. The program will read in the student's scores and output the student's record, which consists of two quiz scores and two exam scores as well as the student's overall numeric score for the entire course and final letter grade.

   Define and use a class for the student record. The class should have instance variables for the quizzes, midterm, final, overall numeric score for the course, and final letter grade. The overall numeric score is a number in the range 0 to 100, which represents the weighted average of the student's work. The class should have input and output methods. The input method should not ask for the final numeric grade, nor should it ask for the final letter grade. The class should have methods to compute the overall numeric grade and the final letter grade. These last two methods will be `void` methods that set the appropriate instance variables. Remember, one method can call another method. If you prefer, you can define a single method that sets both the overall numeric score and the final letter grade, but if you do this, use a helping method. Your program should use all the methods we discussed. Your class should have a reasonable set of accessor and mutator methods, whether or not your program uses them. You may add other methods if you wish.

4. Add methods to the `Person` class from Self-Test Question 18 to set just the name attribute of a `Person`, to set just the age attribute of a `Person`, to test whether two `Persons` are equal (have the same name and age), to test whether two `Persons` have the same name, to test whether two `Persons` are the same age, to test whether one `Person` is older than another, and to test whether one `Person` is younger than another. Write a driver (test) program that demonstrates each method, with at least one true and one false case for each of the test methods.

5. Create a class that graphs a grade distribution (number of A's, B's, C's, D's, and F's) horizontally by printing lines with proportionate numbers of asterisks corresponding to the percentage of grades in each category. Write methods to set the number of each letter grade; read the number of each letter grade; return the total number of grades; return the percentage of each letter grade as a whole number between 0 and 100, inclusive; and draw the graph. Set it up so that 50 asterisks correspond to 100 percent (each one corresponds to 2 percent), include a scale on the horizontal axis indicating each 10 percent increment from 0 to 100 percent, and label each line with its letter grade. For example, if there are 1 A, 4 B's, 6 C's, 2 D's, and 1 F, the total number of grades is 14, the percentage of A's is 7, the percentage of B's is 29, the percentage of C's is 43, the percentage of D's is 14, and

the percentage of F's is 7. The A row would contain 4 asterisks (7 percent of 50 rounded to the nearest integer), the B row 14, the C row 21, the D row 7, and the F row 4, so the graph would look like this:

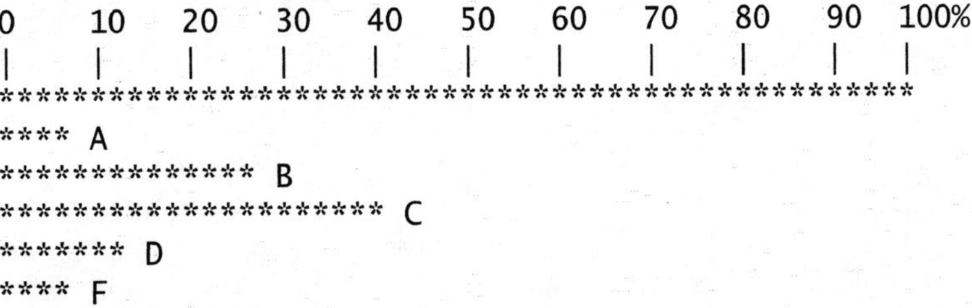

```
0    10   20   30   40   50   60   70   80   90   100%
|    |    |    |    |    |    |    |    |    |    |
**************************************************
**** A
************** B
********************* C
******* D
**** F
```

6. Write a program that uses the Purchase class (Display 4.11) to set the following prices:
   Oranges: 10 for 2.99
   Eggs: 12 for 1.69
   Apples: 3 for 1.00
   Watermelons: 4.39 each
   Bagels: 6 for 3.50

   Then calculate the total bill and subtotals for each item for the following:
   2 dozen oranges
   3 dozen eggs
   20 apples
   2 watermelons
   1 dozen bagels

7. Write a program to answer questions like the following: Suppose the species Klingon ox has a population of 100 and a growth rate of 15 percent, and it lives in an area of 1500 square miles. How long would it take for the population density to exceed 1 per square mile? Use the class Species in Display 4.19 with the addition of the density method from Self-Test Question 10.

Chapter 5

Applets and HTML

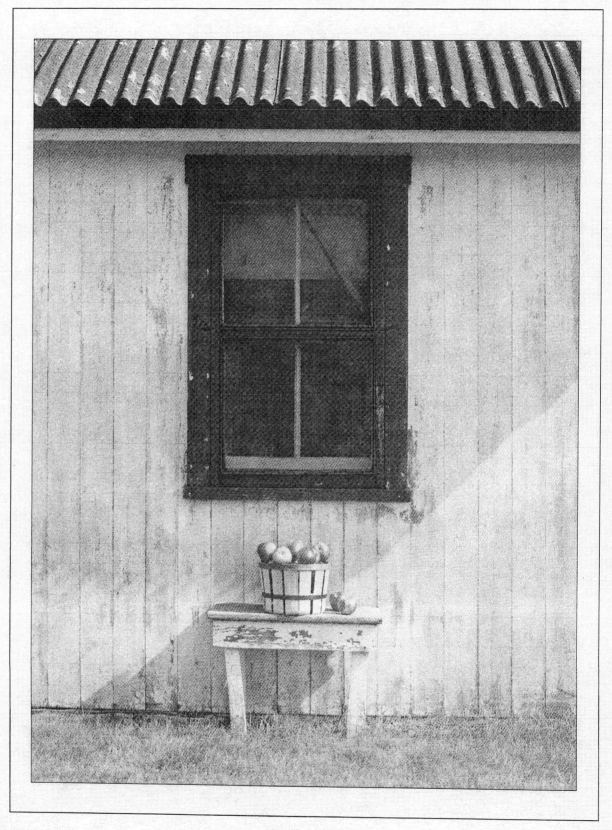

Chapter 13

Applets and HTML

13

Visit our Web site. -Common advertisement copy

All that has come before this chapter is important in learning how to program and in learning the Java language. However, we have not yet touched on what initially made Java famous. Java became famous due in large part to its connection to the Internet.

In this chapter, we describe a version of Java programs that can be run across the Internet. The World Wide Web (the Web, for short) is the collection of locations on the Internet that you can view with a Web browser. Applets are simply Java programs that are designed to run from a document (page) on the Web. HTML is a language used to create Web documents. Although Java applets were designed to run from within HTML documents, you can run an applet as a stand-alone program without any reference to HTML or the Internet. So we will discuss applets first and then discuss HTML.

OBJECTIVES

Find out how to write applets.

Learn to write a simple HTML document.

Learn how to embed an applet in an HTML document.

PREREQUISITES

Section	Prerequisite
Section 13.1 Writing applets	Chapter 12 (and its prerequisites)
Section 13.2 Introduction to HTML	None, not even Section 13.1
Section 13.3 Applets in HTML	Sections 13.1 and 13.2

If you wish to skip or delay reading this chapter, you can. Chapter 14 does not use any material from this chapter.

If you want to learn only how to write applets, and you will not be running them from an HTML document (a Web page), then Section 13.1 will give you all the information you need.

If you already know HTML, but do not know about applets, you can skip Section 13.2 and go from Section 13.1 to Section 13.3.

Web browser

To really get much benefit from Sections 13.2 and 13.3, you should know how to use a Web browser such as the Netscape Navigator or Microsoft's Internet Explorer. All the constructs discussed in this chapter produce things to be viewed via a Web browser. We will assume that you have used a Web browser to read something on the Web, but we will not assume that you know how to create things to be viewed on the Web. Most readers could get sufficient experience simply by playing with a Web browser without any instruction or reading. To get the full benefit of this chapter, you should also understand how path names are used on your operating system, so that you can name a file that is contained in a different directory (different folder).

13.1 APPLETS

An applet a day keeps the doctor away. -Anonymous

The word *applet* sounds as though it might refer to a small apple, but it is supposed to sound like a small application. Thus, applets are just "little Java programs," in some sense of the word *little*. However, the character of applets comes not from their size, but from how and where they are run. Applets are Java programs that can be displayed on a Web site and viewed over the Internet. They can also be run on your local computer, without any connection to the Internet. In this section, we will describe how you write applets and how to view them without any connection to the Internet. In Section 13.3, we will describe one simple way to view an applet over the Internet.

An applet is very much like a Swing GUI, and if you understand some details about Swing, then you will find it very easy to write applets. In this section, we will assume that you are already familiar with the Swing material given in Chapter 12. We will show you how to write simple applets that do the same thing as the windowing systems we covered there. If you go on to learn more about Swing, you can use almost all of your new Swing techniques in your applets.

Applet Basics

An applet is a derived class of the class `JApplet` (actually, of any descendant class, but typically it is a directly derived class). The class `JApplet` is a class in the Swing library, so you need the following `import` statement when using the class `JApplet`:

```
import javax.swing.*;
```

import

When you are writing an applet, you may also need the AWT library, so your full list of `import` statements is likely to be the following:

```
import javax.swing.*;
import java.awt.*;
import java.awt.event.*;
```

Display 13.1, shows a part of the class hierarchy to help you put the class `JApplet` in context. Note that a `JApplet` is a `Container`. Thus, you can add things to an applet. You add components to an applet in the same way that you add components to a `JFrame`.

In Display 13.1, you might notice the class `Applet`. This class is an older version of the class `JApplet`. The `Applet` class was used to create applets before the introduction of `JApplet`.

You can design an applet class in much the same way that you design a windowing system, using Swing, as in Chapter 12. The main difference is that you derive an applet class from the class `JApplet` instead of the class `JFrame`. Other differences between an applet class and a regular Swing windowing class consist mostly of things that are omitted from the definition of the applet class.

DISPLAY 13.1 Placing Applets in the Class Hierarchy

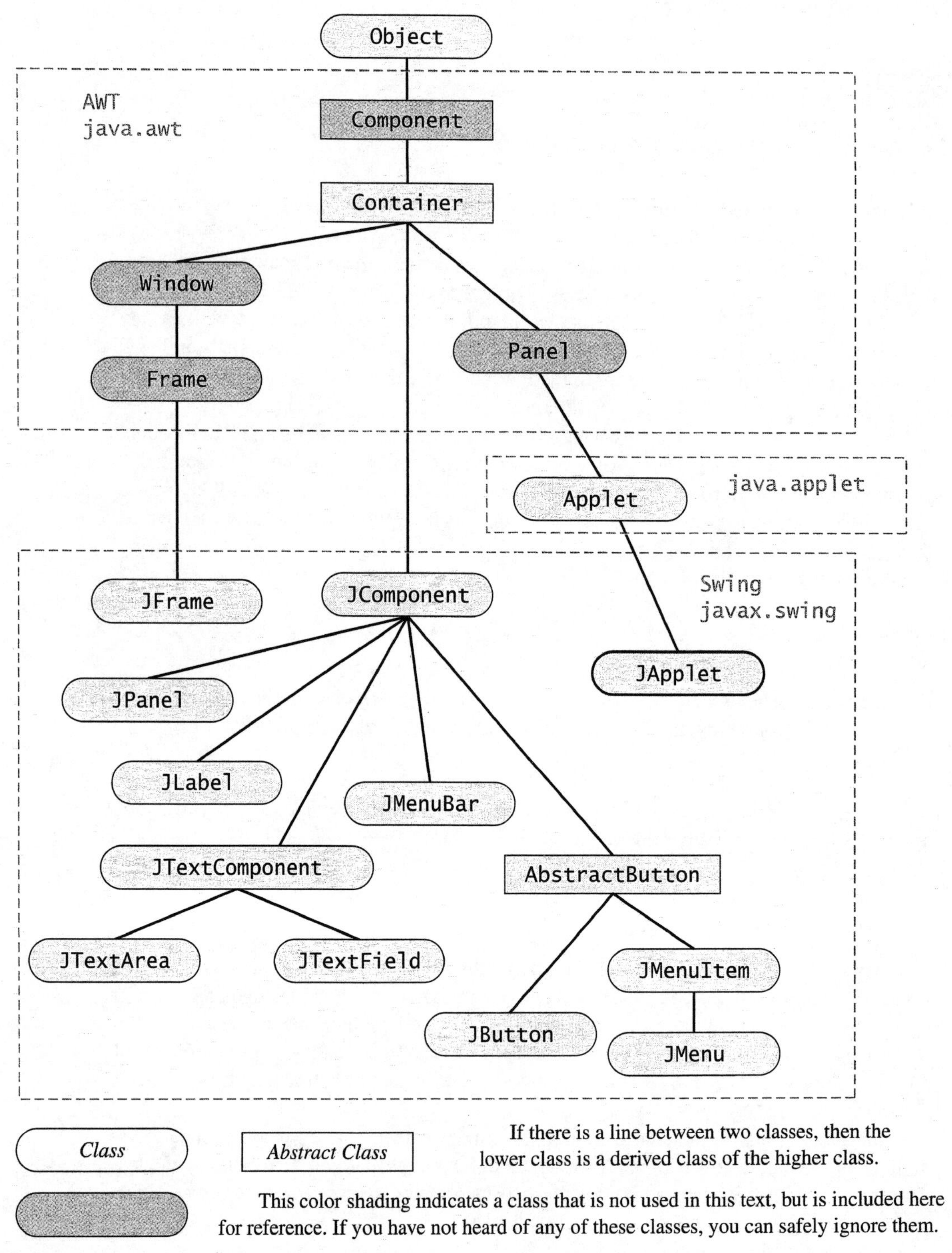
Object
AWT
java.awt
Component
Container
Window
Frame
Panel
Applet
java.applet
JFrame
JComponent
Swing
javax.swing
JApplet
JPanel
JLabel
JMenuBar
JTextComponent
AbstractButton
JTextArea
JTextField
JMenuItem
JButton
JMenu
Class
Abstract Class
If there is a line between two classes, then the lower class is a derived class of the higher class.
This color shading indicates a class that is not used in this text, but is included here for reference. If you have not heard of any of these classes, you can safely ignore them.

Applets do not use the `setVisible` method. Applets are displayed automatically. For this reason, an applet also normally does not have a `main` method. A very simple applet is shown in Display 13.2. When this applet is viewed, it will simply display the text

```
Hello out there!
```

Note that a `JApplet` has a content pane, just as a `JFrame` does, and you add components to the content pane of the `JApplet`, rather than adding them directly to the `JApplet`. As illustrated in Display 13.2, you add a `JLabel` (or other component) to a `JApplet` just as you would add one to a `JFrame`. `JLabel`

Applets do not have titles, so there is no need to use the `setTitle` method in an applet. This is because applets normally are part of a Web-site display, and the display can add any title. As you will see in Section 13.3, the Web display document also takes care of sizing the applet, so you do not give any size instructions for an applet.

DISPLAY 13.2 A Trivial Applet

```
import javax.swing.*;
import java.awt.*;//For Container class
public class HelloApplet extends JApplet
{
    public void init()
    {
        Container contentPane = getContentPane();
        contentPane.setLayout(new FlowLayout());
        JLabel friendlyLabel = new JLabel("Hello out there!");
        contentPane.add(friendlyLabel);
    }
}
```

Resulting GUI (Using an Applet Viewer)

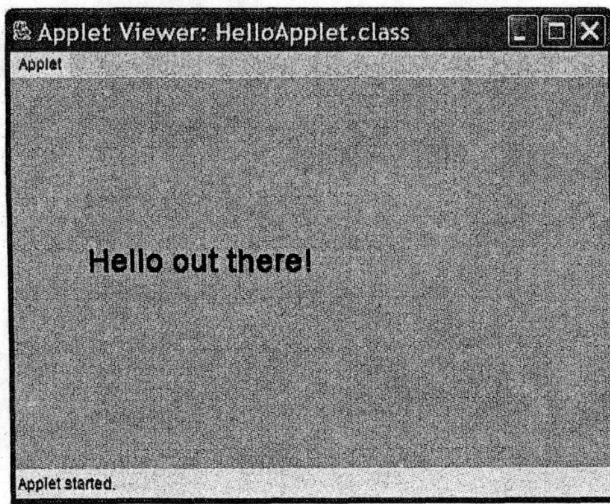

init

Applets do not normally use constructors, but they do use a method named `init` that serves a similar purpose. When defining an applet, you place all the initializing actions—such as setting colors, adding buttons, and adding text fields—in the method named `init`. The `init` method has no parameters.

Applets do not need to be closed with listeners, so they do not include an invocation of `addWindowListener` in their `init` methods. When the Web document is closed, the applet will automatically close.

(Other very simple examples of applets are given in Chapter 1. In Chapter 1, the applets have no layout manager specified. If a `JApplet` has no layout manager specified, it has the `BorderLayout` manager by default. If a component is added without specifying a region, it goes in the region `BorderLayout.CENTER`. In Chapter 1, we did not use any layout manager, in order to keep the examples simple, but now that you understand layout managers, we suggest that you always use an explicit layout manager.)

Quick Reference: The `JApplet` Class

The `JApplet` class is the class normally used to create an applet. This class is in the Swing library, so, when using this class, you use the following `import` statement:

```
import javax.swing.*;
```

Running an Applet

applet viewer

You compile an applet in the same way that you compile all of the other Java classes you have seen. However, you run an applet differently from other Java programs. The normal way to run an applet is as part of a Web-site document. The applet is then viewed through a Web browser. We will discuss this means of viewing an applet in Section 13.3. However, applets can also be viewed using an **applet viewer,** a program designed to run applets as stand-alone programs. If you are using an integrated environment that has a menu command called Run Applet, Run, Execute, or something similar, you can probably use one of these commands to run an applet just as you run an ordinary Java application program. (In the TextPad environment, which comes on the CD included with this book, the command is Run Java Applet on the Tools menu. This environment command will automatically invoke an applet viewer. If a window pops up asking you to choose a file, answer "No.") If this approach does not work, you will need to check with a local expert or else read Section 13.3 for more details on viewing applets.

If you run the applet shown in Display 13.3 in an applet viewer, the result will look similar to the GUI shown in that display.

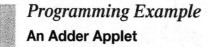

Programming Example

An Adder Applet

Display 13.3 contains an applet that will produce an adding-machine window that is essentially the same as the one we produced in Chapter 12. The details are almost identical to those in the Swing class we defined in Display 12.21. To obtain this adder applet from that Swing class, we simply did the following:

- replaced `extends JFrame` with `extends JApplet`;
- deleted the `main` method;
- replaced the constructor heading with the `init` method heading;
- deleted some lines not needed for an applet. ■

DISPLAY 13.3 An Applet Adding Machine *(Part 1 of 2)*

```
import javax.swing.*;
import java.awt.*;
import java.awt.event.*;

public class AdderApplet extends JApplet
                         implements ActionListener
{
    private JTextField inputOutputField;
    private double sum = 0;

    public void init()
    {
        Container contentPane = getContentPane();
        contentPane.setLayout(new BorderLayout());

        JPanel buttonPanel = new JPanel();
        buttonPanel.setBackground(Color.GRAY);
        buttonPanel.setLayout(new FlowLayout());
        JButton addButton = new JButton("Add");
        addButton.addActionListener(this);
        buttonPanel.add(addButton);
        JButton resetButton = new JButton("Reset");
        resetButton.addActionListener(this);
        buttonPanel.add(resetButton);
        contentPane.add(buttonPanel, BorderLayout.SOUTH);

        JPanel textPanel = new JPanel();
        textPanel.setBackground(Color.BLUE);
        textPanel.setLayout(new FlowLayout());
        inputOutputField =
                      new JTextField("Numbers go here.", 30);
        inputOutputField.setBackground(Color.WHITE);
        textPanel.add(inputOutputField);
        contentPane.add(textPanel, BorderLayout.CENTER);
    }
```

DISPLAY 13.3 An Applet Adding Machine *(Part 2 of 2)*

```
        public void actionPerformed(ActionEvent e)
        {
            if (e.getActionCommand().equals("Add"))
            {
                sum = sum +
                    stringToDouble(inputOutputField.getText());
                inputOutputField.setText(Double.toString(sum));
            }
            else if (e.getActionCommand().equals("Reset"))
            {
                sum = 0;
                inputOutputField.setText("0.0");
            }
            else
                inputOutputField.setText("Error in adder code.");
        }

        private static double stringToDouble(String stringObject)
        {
            return Double.parseDouble(stringObject.trim());
        }
    }
```

Resulting GUI (Using an Applet Viewer)

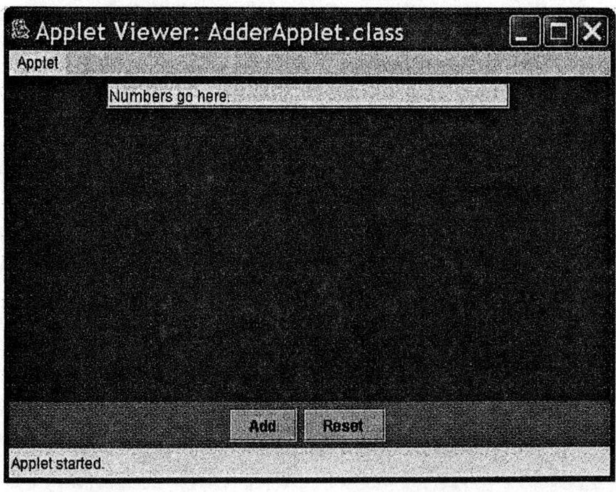

■ Java Tip
Converting a Swing Application to an Applet

It is easy to convert a Swing application to an applet. In most cases, you simply follow these instructions:

1. Derive the class from the class `JApplet` instead of from the class `JFrame`. That is, replace `extends JFrame` with `extends JApplet` on the first line of the class definition.
2. Remove the `main` method. An applet does not need the things that are typically placed in `main`. An applet is automatically made visible, and its size is determined by the applet viewer or by the Web page it is embedded in.
3. Replace the constructor with a method named `init`. The body of the `init` method can be the same as the body of the deleted constructor, but with some items removed, as described in steps 4–6.
4. Delete any invocation of `addWindowListener`. (The applet viewer or the Web page containing the applet will take care of ending the applet. So you do not need any window-listener object, such as an object of the class `WindowDestroyer` given in Chapter 12.)
5. Delete any invocation of `setTitle`. (Applets have no titles.)
6. Delete any invocation of `setSize`. (Sizing is done by the applet viewer or by the Web page in which the applet is embedded.)

For example, we obtained the applet in Display 13.3 from the Swing application in Display 12.21 by following these rules. □

? Self-Test Questions

1. Do you normally include constructors in an applet-class definition?
2. Is it normal for an applet class to have a `main` method?
3. Which of the following methods might you use in an applet? `addWindowListener`; `getContentPane`; `setTitle`; `setSize`.

Adding Icons to an Applet

Display 13.4 illustrates one way to add a picture to an applet. A simplified version of that applet was given in Chapter 1, but we can provide a more complete description of it now that you know more about applets. An icon is simply a picture. It is normally, but not always, a small picture. The easiest way to display an icon in an applet is to place the icon in a `JLabel`. In the applet in Display 13.4, the picture in the file `duke_waving.gif` is displayed as an icon that is part of the `JLabel` named `niceLabel`. The two lines that add the icon are reproduced as follows:

`ImageIcon`

```
ImageIcon dukeIcon = new ImageIcon("duke_waving.gif");
niceLabel.setIcon(dukeIcon);
```

DISPLAY 13.4 An Applet with an Icon

```
import javax.swing.*;
import java.awt.*;

public class DukeApplet extends JApplet
{
    public void init( )
    {
        Container contentPane = getContentPane( );
        contentPane.setLayout(new BorderLayout( ));

        JLabel spacer = new JLabel("              ");
        contentPane.add(spacer, "West");
        JLabel niceLabel = new JLabel("Java is fun!");
        ImageIcon dukeIcon = new ImageIcon("duke_waving.gif");
        niceLabel.setIcon(dukeIcon);
        contentPane.add(niceLabel, BorderLayout.CENTER);
    }
}
```

Resulting GUI[1]

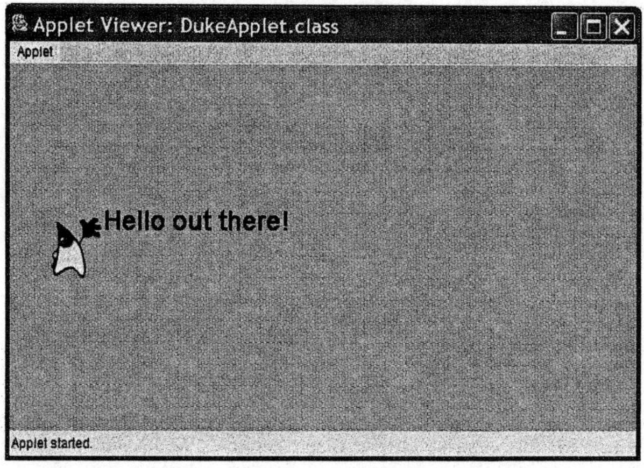

1. Java, Duke, and all Java-based trademarks and logos are trademarks or registered trademarks of Sun Microsystems, Inc., in the United States and other countries.

`ImageIcon` is a class in the Swing library. The label `niceLabel` is created in the normal way that we described in Chapter 12:

```
JLabel niceLabel = new JLabel("Java is fun!");
```

The icon picture is a digital picture in one of the standard formats. The picture—in this case, `duke_waving.gif`—must be converted to an `ImageIcon` before it can be added to a label. This task is done as follows: `new ImageIcon("duke_waving.gif")`. So the following code creates an `ImageIcon` based on the picture `duke_waving.gif` and stores a reference to the icon in the variable `dukeIcon`:

```
ImageIcon dukeIcon = new ImageIcon("duke_waving.gif");
```

The method `setIcon` adds an icon to a label, as in the following statement:

```
niceLabel.setIcon(dukeIcon);
```

If you want the label to have only the icon and no text, then simply use the default constructor when you create the `JLabel`. For example, if we had used

```
JLabel niceLabel = new JLabel();
```

in Display 13.4 instead of

```
JLabel niceLabel = new JLabel("Java is fun!");
```

then the string `"Java is fun!"` would not have appeared in the applet; only the icon would have been displayed.

Chapter 14 contains more material on icons.

Quick Reference: Icons and the Class `ImageIcon`

An **icon** is simply a small picture, although it is not really required to be small. The class `ImageIcon` is used to convert a picture file to a Swing icon.

Syntax:

```
ImageIcon Name_Of_ImageIcon =
        new ImageIcon(Picture_File_Name);
```

The *Picture_File_Name* is a string giving either a relative or an absolute path name to the picture file. (So if the picture file is in the same directory as your applet, you need give only the name of the picture file.)

Example:

```
ImageIcon SmileyFaceIcon =
        new ImageIcon("smiley.gif");
```

FAQ: Who Is Duke?

Duke is the character shown in the applet in Display 13.4. He has become a mascot for the Java language. The Duke icon is used here with permission from Sun Microsystems, Inc.

? Self-Test Questions

4. How do you add an icon based on the digital picture file `smiley.gif` to an applet?
5. When you specify the file for a digital picture, such as `smiley.gif`, as an argument to the `ImageIcon` constructor, can you use a path name?

13.2 INTRODUCTION TO HTML

You shall see them on a beautiful quarto page, where a neat rivulet of text shall meander through a meadow of margin. -Richard Brinsley Sheridan, *The School for Scandal*

hypertext

Documents designed to be read on the Web, or through a Web browser regardless of whether they are on the Web, are typically expressed in a language called **HTML**. HTML stands for **Hypertext Markup Language. Hypertext** is simply text that contains items which you can click, using your mouse, to go to another document. These connections from document to document are called **links**, or **hyperlinks.** The documents themselves are often called **pages,** which is why a person's or a company's main location on the Web is called a **home page.** The terms **HTML document** and **HTML page** mean the same thing and simply refer to a hypertext document created with the HTML language.

home page

HTML is not a full-blown programming language like Java. It is just a collection of simple commands that you can insert into a page of text in order to convert it to something that can be viewed with a Web browser. The commands allow you to insert pictures and hyperlinks into the page. They also allow you to write editing commands that specify a main heading, a subheading, a paragraph beginning, and so forth. In short, most of HTML is simply a language for formatting a manuscript so it can be viewed on the Web.

This is not a book on HTML programming, so we will give you only a small taste of the language. This introduction will allow you to design some very simple documents for the Web (or just for your browser). If you want to become an expert in HTML, you should eventually go on to a book dedicated entirely to that subject.

HTML Basics

Most HTML commands are of the form

```
<Command>
Some text
</Command>
```

For example, the following commands make the phrase "My Home Page" a level 1 heading, which is the largest standard heading:

<h1>

```
<h1>
My Home Page
</h1>
```

Notice that the notation </*Command*>—in this example, `</h1>`—is used to mark the end of the text to which the command applies.

<h2>

You can have smaller heads, called level 2 heads (command `h2`); even smaller heads, called level 3 heads (command `h3`); and so forth.

Remember: HTML Is Not Case Sensitive

We will write our HTML commands in lowercase letters. However, unlike Java, HTML does not distinguish between uppercase and lowercase letters in commands, so the commands, would behave the same if they were expressed in uppercase letters. (Any text to be displayed as text to be read by the person viewing the document will, of course, display uppercase letters in uppercase and lowercase letters in lowercase.)

Some commands do not need to be closed with a command of the form </*Command*>. One such command is

```
<br>
```


This command begins a new line. Another is

```
<p>
```

<p>

which is a command to begin a new paragraph.

Commands in HTML are not absolute commands that determine the exact size of a portion of text, or even the exact line breaks. When you give a command for a level 1 head, you can reasonably assume that it will be bigger than a level 2 head, but the browser will determine the exact size of the text. You can force a line break by inserting the **break command:**

break

```
<br>
```

If you write a large piece of text (or even sometimes a small amount of text), the browser will insert line breaks where necessary in order to fit the text on the screen, using rules that help it determine where such breaks "look good," and it will ignore your line breaks unless they are indicated with the `<br>` command.

You can make some layout specifications. For example, anything between the commands `<center>` and `</center>` will be centered on the page when it is displayed. The following commands will center the level 1 head we discussed earlier:

<center>

```
<h1>
<center>
My Home Page
</center>
</h1>
```

Or, if you prefer, this code can also be written as follows:

```
<center>
<h1>
My Home Page
</h1>
</center>
```

Remember: HTML File Names

An HTML file is a regular text file that you create and edit with a text editor, in the same way that you write a Java program. HTML files should end with `.html`, but otherwise they can be named using the same rules you use to name other files on your system.

Programming Tip
A Simple HTML-Document Outline

comments

Display 13.5 contains an outline for a simple HTML document. That display also illustrates how you write comments in HTML. For example,

```
<!--Beginning of HTML document-->
```

is a comment. A comment begins with `<!--` and ends with `-->`. We have used comments to explain the new HTML commands, but a real document would not have this many comments, nor would it explain basic HTML commands, as we have done here.

<html>

<head>

<title>

The entire document should be enclosed in the pair `<html>` and `</html>`, the first tag at the beginning and the second tag at the end. The head of the document is enclosed in `<head>` and `</head>`. The head is not displayed when the document is viewed, but it does record information that is used by a browser. In our document, it consists only of a title (enclosed in `<title>` and `</title>`). The title is used as a name for the document. For example, a browser will let users set a bookmark at a document so they can return to it at a later time. The bookmark will have the name given in this title. (Some browsers call bookmarks "Favorites.")

<body>

<address>

The part of the document that is displayed on the screen is divided into two parts. The **body** (enclosed in `<body>` and `</body>`) is the real content of the document. The other displayed part is enclosed in `<address>` and `</address>`, and it is optional. It is used to give an e-mail address for contacting the document's owner and usually includes the date that the document was last modified.

Display 13.6 shows a very simple HTML document, and Display 13.7 shows how this document would appear when viewed in a browser. Remember that the exact line breaks, size of letters, and other layout details are determined by the particular browser, so it might look a little different on your browser. The portion that discusses the Sun Microsystems Web site is explained in the next subsection. ○

Inserting Hyperlinks

Well this is all nice, but it would hardly be worth the effort if an HTML document did not also contain some active elements. The key active element is a link that the person viewing the document can click to view another HTML document. The other document may be on the same computer or on a computer thousands of miles away. These links are called **hyperlinks,** or simply **links.**

hyperlink

The syntax for hyperlinks is as follows:

```
<a href="Path_To_Document">
Displayed_Text_To_Click
</a>
```

For example, the following code creates a link to the author's home page:

```
<a href="http://www-cse.ucsd.edu/users/savitch">
Walter Savitch
</a>
```

DISPLAY 13.5 Outline of a Simple HTML Document

```
<html> <!--Beginning of HTML document-->
<head> <!--Begin the document head-->
<title> <!--Begin document title. Used for browser "bookmarks"-->
Title of document.
</title> <!--End document title-->
</head> <!--End the document head-->
<body> <!--Stuff to appear on screen begins here-->
<h1>
First main heading.
</h1>
Maybe some text.
<h2>
First subheading.
</h2>
Probably some text.
<h2>
Second subheading.
</h2>
Probably some text.
<h1>
Second main heading.
</h1>
And then more of the same.
   ...
</body> <!--Regular stuff ends here, but address is displayed-->
<address> <!--Optional, but normally used-->
The e-mail address of the person maintaining the page.
Also, the date of the last time the page was changed.
(You can actually put in whatever you want here, but the
 e-mail address and date are what people expect.)
</address>
</html> <!--End of HTML document-->
```

A real HTML document should not have this many comments.

■ DISPLAY 13.6 A Very Simple HTML Document

```
<html>
<head>
<title>
Java Club Home Page
</title>
</head>
<body>
<h1>
<center>
Java Club
</center>
</h1>

<h2>
Club Purpose
</h2>
<p>
A major goal of the club is to encourage
its members to become good programmers.
<p>
The club provides a setting where people who
like to program in the Java language can meet
and talk with other like-minded programmers.

<h2>
Meeting Times
</h2>
The first Wednesday of each month at 7 PM.
<h2>
Sun Microsystems Java Website
</h2>
<a href="http://java.sun.com">
Click here for the website
</a>
<p>
</body>

<address>
javaclub.somemachine@someschool.edu
<br>
January 1, 2004
</address>
</html>
```

Blank lines are ignored when the document is displayed, but they can make your HTML code easier to read.

Text may have different line breaks when displayed on your browser.

A new paragraph will always produce a line break and some separation.

This code is explained in the subsection entitled "Inserting Hyperlinks."

■ DISPLAY 13.7 Browser View of Display 13.6

Be sure to include the quotation marks as shown. The *Displayed_Text_To_Click* will be displayed and underlined (or otherwise highlighted) by the browser. In this example, if the person viewing the document clicks the text `Walter Savitch`, then the browser will display the author's home page. You can insert this code in any document in any part of the world, and it will take you to La Jolla, California, with a click of your mouse button.

The HTML document in Display 13.6 includes a link to the Java Web site of Sun Microsystems. If you view this HTML document with a browser, it will look approximately like Display 13.7. If the user clicks the text that is underlined, the browser will display Sun Microsystems' Java Web site. (That is, it will display the HTML document on the company's computer that gives information about Java.)

Quick Reference: Inserting a Hyperlink

The command for inserting a hyperlink is as follows:

Syntax:

```
<a href="Path_To_Document">
Displayed_Text_To_Click
</a>
```

It may appear inside any text.

Example:

```
<a href="http://java.sun.com">
Sun Microsystems Java website
</a>
```

The *Path_To_Document* can be either a full or relative path name to an HTML file or a URL to any place on the Web. If the person viewing the document clicks the *Displayed_Text_To_Click*, the document indicated by *Path_To_Document* will be displayed.

FAQ: What Is a URL?

URL

The name of an HTML document on the Web is called a **URL,** which is an abbreviation for **Uniform Resource Locator.** The name is a kind of path name for the World Wide Web, a system that covers the entire globe. The hyperlinks we described in this section are all URLs, such as

```
http://java.sun.com
```

URLs are absolute path names to documents that can be anywhere in the world. You can also use relative path names for links to HTML documents on your own computer.

URLs often begin with `http`, which is the name of the protocol used to transfer and interpret the HTML document (but now we are getting beyond the scope of this book). Most browsers will allow you to omit the `http://` and will fill it in for you.

▲ *Gotcha*

Not Using Your Reload (Refresh) Button

Most browsers keep copies of the most recently used HTML pages. That way, if you want to go back to one of those pages, the browser can recover the pages very quickly. Usually, this is a good thing, since it makes your browser run faster. However, when you are designing and debugging an HTML page, it can be a problem.

Suppose you test an HTML page with your browser and notice something that needs to be fixed. If you change the HTML page to fix the problem and then look again at the page with your browser, you will probably see no change. This situation can occur even if you exit your browser; reenter the browser, starting with some other page; and then jump to the page being fixed. The problem is that, as we said, most browsers keep copies of the most recent pages that were displayed. The browser then reuses those copies instead of loading new versions of the pages.

To ensure that your browser is displaying the most current version of a page, click the button labeled Reload, Refresh, or something similar. This action will cause the browser to reload the page and thereby give you the latest version. △

Remember: Automatic Documentation with `javadoc`

The Java language comes with a program named `javadoc` that can automatically generate documentation for your Java classes. The documentation that is produced by `javadoc` is an HTML document that you read with a browser, just as you do any other HTML document. The program `javadoc` is described in Appendix 9.

Displaying a Picture

We do not need pictures for what we are doing with HTML in this chapter, but you might want to put a picture in your HTML document. The command to insert a picture is as follows:

<img src="*File_With_Picture*">

For example, suppose you have a digital version of a picture in the subdirectory `images`. To be specific, suppose the picture file `mypicture.gif` is in the directory `images`, and `images` is a subdirectory of the directory where the HTML page is. You could add the picture to your HTML document by inserting the following code:

```
<img src="images/mypicture.gif">
```

The picture can be in any directory, but you must give a path that will lead to the picture file. You can use either a full path name or a relative path name (that is, relative to the directory containing the HTML document) to indicate the location of the file with the encoded picture. Most commonly used picture-encoding formats are accepted.

? Self-Test Questions

6. What is the difference between the commands <h2> and <H2>?

7. How do you insert a link to the following home page?

   `http://www.fool.com/`

8. How will the following be displayed by a browser?

```
<p>
A major goal of the club is to encourage
its members to become good programmers.
<p>
The club provides a setting where people who
like to program in the Java language can meet
and talk with other like-minded programmers.
```

   (Where would the line breaks be? Where would the browser add space?)

Programming Tip

HTML Is a Low-Level Language

HTML is a low-level language. HTML for a Web browser is analogous to assembly language for a computer. Most Web-page designers now use a high-level design language that translates into HTML. If you plan to do a lot of Web-page design, you should consider learning one of these languages. Three examples of such languages are Dreamweaver (Macromedia, Inc.), FrontPage (Microsoft Corporation), and GoLive (Adobe Systems Inc.).

13.3 APPLETS IN HTML

Write it here; run it there! -Sounds like somebody's ad copy[2]

In this section, we tell you how to embed an applet in an HTML document so that the document and the applet can be viewed by a Web browser, possibly one halfway around the world.

Placing an Applet in an HTML Document

If you place the following command in an HTML document, the document will display the adder window created by the applet in Display 13.3:

```
<applet code="AdderApplet.class" width=400 height=200>
</applet>
```

This command assumes that the HTML file and the file `AdderApplet.class` are in the same directory (same folder). If they are not in the same directory, then you would use an absolute or relative path name for the file `AdderApplet.class`. An expression such as the one previously displayed is often called an **applet tag.**

applet tag

For example, Display 13.8 contains a sample HTML document that includes the applet given in Display 13.3. When displayed with a browser, this HTML document would look approximately as shown in Display 13.9.

sizing an applet

Notice that when you place an applet in an HTML document, you give the name of the byte-code file that ends in `.class`, rather than the `.java` file or some other file name. Also notice that you specify the width and height of the applet in this command, not within the applet-class definition. The width and height are given in pixels.

Quick Reference: Applets in HTML Documents

You place an applet in an HTML document as shown in the given code. You use the byte-code (`.class`) file of the applet. If the file is not in the same directory (same folder) as the HTML document, you can use either a full or a relative path name to the applet file. The width and height are given in pixels.

2. But I just made it up.

Syntax:

```
<applet code="Name_Of_.class_File" width=Integer height=Integer>
</applet>
```

Example:

```
<applet code="AdderApplet.class" width=400 height=200>
</applet>
```

DISPLAY 13.8 An HTML Document with an Applet

```
<html>
<head>
<title>
Budget Help
</title>
</head>

<body>
<h1>
The Budget Help Home Page
<br>
Helpful Hints for a Balanced Budget
</h1>

<h2>
Pay off your credit cards every month.
</h2>

<h2>
Do not spend more than you earn.
</h2>

<h2>
Here is an adder to help you plan your budget:
</h2>
<applet code="AdderApplet.class" width=400 height=200>
</applet>
<p>
</body>

<p>
<address>
budgethelp@fleeceyou.com
<br>
December 31, 2004
</address>
</html>
```

■ DISPLAY 13.9 Browser View of Display 13.8

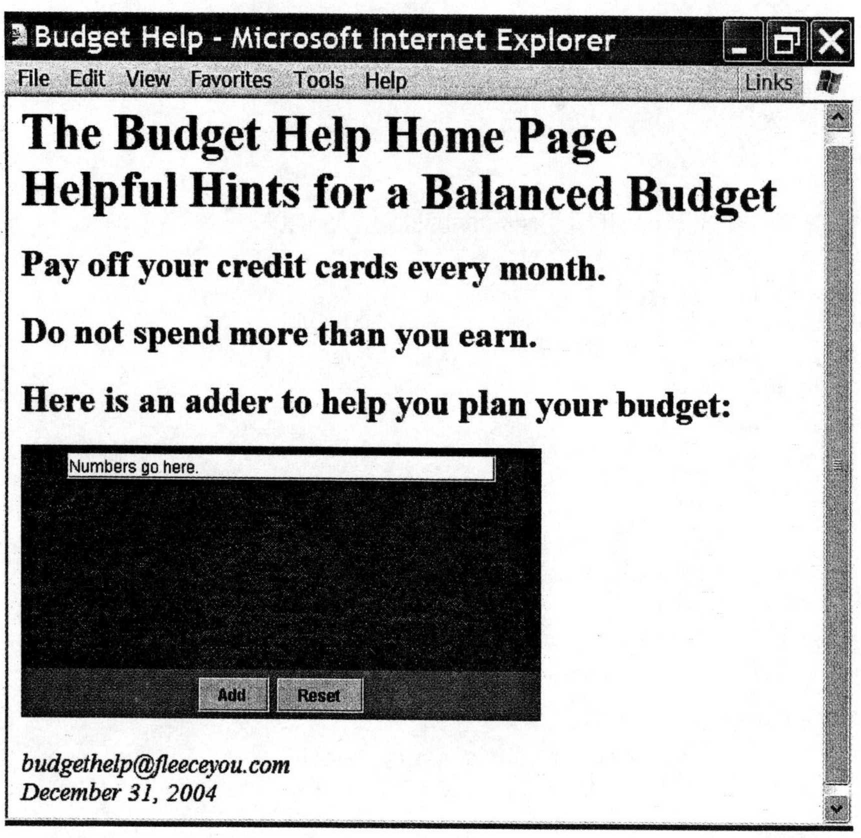

■ **Java Tip**

Applet Viewer Revisited

Even if you have not been able to run an applet viewer from an environment, you can undoubtedly run an applet viewer via a one-line command. For example, you would run the applet in Display 13.3 as follows:

```
appletviewer AdderApplet.html
```

However, if you run an applet via a one-line command in this way, you may need to create an HTML document yourself (named `AdderApplet.html` in this example) and place the applet tag in the HTML document. □

? Self-Test Questions

9. When you list an applet in an HTML document, do you list the `.java` file or the `.class` file?
10. Give the HTML code to insert the applet named `HelloApplet` into an HTML document.

▲ Gotcha
Using an Old Web Browser

Your Web browser must be set up to run applets. Web browsers do not use the same Java interpreter that is used to run regular Java applications. If you have an old Web browser that is not set up for applets or that is set up only for applets created using an earlier version of Java, you may not be able to run applets from an HTML document. This can be the case even if Java applications run fine on your system. In such cases, all you can do is obtain a new browser.

Unfortunately, even obtaining a new browser does not always help, because the Java updates for browsers are typically made much later than the updates for the core Java language. Moreover, if you place an applet in an HTML document and expect other people to view the applet over the Web, then the applet's `.class` file will be sent to other people's computers and run on their browsers. And, of course, you cannot reasonably expect all those other people to have the most recent browser.

If you expect an applet to be widely viewed over the Web, you should test it on a number of different browsers. Testing your applet on Netscape Navigator and Microsoft's Internet Explorer should be sufficient, but you should test it on older versions of these browsers as well as the latest release. If you have trouble getting your applet to work on older browsers, consider using the older `Applet` class as described in the optional subsection "The Older `Applet` Class."

Although you may have problems running your applets on a browser, you should have no such problem running them from the applet viewer, as long as you have a recent version of Java. So you should be able to run and test your applets, even if you cannot run them from an HTML page. However, if they are not ultimately placed in HTML documents, you may as well use regular Swing GUIs derived from `JFrame`. △ applet viewer

---

The Older `Applet` Class *(Optional)*

If you find that your applet does not work on a wide enough array of browsers, try using the older `Applet` class instead of the `JApplet` class. You can usually do this simply by deleting all the `J`s, replacing `JApplet` with `Applet`, `JButton` with `Button`, `JLabel` with `Label`, and so forth. This approach will require the following `import` statements: `Applet`

```
import java.awt.*;
import Java.awt.event.*;
import java.applet.*;
```

And you may as well delete the following `import` statement:

```
import javax.swing.*;
```

You also need to make another, slightly more complicated alteration. Unlike a `JApplet`, an `Applet` has no content pane. So you use `add` with the applet itself rather than using a content pane, and in general, whatever you did to the content pane of a `JApplet`, you need to do directly to the `Applet`. For example, if the method `init` contains the line

```
getContentPane( ).add(friendlyLabel);
```

in the `JApplet`, then to convert it to an `Applet`, you need to replace this statement with

```
add(friendlyLabel);
```

For most simple applets, these changes will produce an applet that will run on older as well as newer browsers. However, there are things you can do with a `JApplet` that you cannot do with the older `Applet` class. For example, the class `Applet` cannot easily accommodate icons, so your applets should not contain icons when you use the `Applet` class. In Chapter 14, we discuss menus. You can use menus with a `JApplet`, but not with an `Applet`, so you must use buttons instead.

Extra code on CD

We have followed these rules to produce applets based on the `Applet` class instead of the `JApplet` class for the applets in Displays 13.2 and 13.3. The results are in the files `OlderHelloApplet.java` and `OlderAdderApplet.java` on the accompanying CD.

Quick Reference: The `Applet` Class *(Optional)*

The class `Applet` is an older applet class that was used to produce applets before the `JApplet` class came on the scene. Applets produced using the class `Applet` cannot have as many features as those produced with the class `JApplet`. However, they will work on a wider range of browsers. So if you expect your applets to be viewed by a wide array of users, it might be prudent to use the class `Applet`, rather than the class `JApplet`. For very simple applets, it is easy to convert a `JApplet` to an `Applet`. The details are given in the optional subsection "The Older `Applet` Class." The `Applet` class requires the following `import` statement:

```
import java.applet.*;
```

Applets and Security

Suppose somebody on the Web reads your HTML page and that HTML page contains an applet. That applet's byte-code is run on the reader's browser, which is on the reader's computer. So your applet can be a program that runs on other people's computers. More frightening, other people's applets can run on your computer. Moreover, you do not know that an HTML page contains an applet until you load it into your browser, and then it is too late to reject the applet. At that point, it is already stored on your computer.

Whenever somebody else's program runs on your computer, there are serious security concerns. Will the program leave a virus on your computer? Will it read confidential information from your files? Will it change and thus corrupt your operating system? Applets are designed so that they cannot (or at least cannot easily) do any of these things. Applets cannot run any of your programs, and they cannot read or write to files on your computer (unless the applet originated on your computer). But be warned: There are programs other than applets that can be run through your browser and that can gain access to things on your computer—things that you may have thought were private. Commercially available antivirus and other protection software can help to guard your computer against such invasive programs.

? Self-Test Questions

11. For the subsection "The Older `Applet` Class *(Optional)*": A `JApplet` has an `init` method. Does an `Applet` have an `init` method?
12. For the subsection "The Older `Applet` Class *(Optional)*": A `JApplet` has a content pane. Does an `Applet` have a content pane?

CHAPTER SUMMARY

- Applets are Java programs designed to be placed in and run from a Web-site document.
- Applets are similar to Swing GUIs derived from the class `JFrame`.
- An applet is normally a derived class of the class `JApplet`.
- An applet normally has no `main` method and no constructors. However, the method `init` serves the same purpose as a constructor for an applet.
- An applet's `init` method does not include any invocations of `addWindowListener`, `setTitle`, or `setSize`.
- Documents designed to be read across the World Wide Web or through a Web browser are typically written in a language called HTML. HTML stands for Hypertext Markup Language. Applets can be embedded in and run from HTML documents.

✔ Answers to Self-Test Questions

1. Applet classes do not usually use constructors. However, they do use a method named `init` that serves a similar purpose.
2. Applet classes do not normally have a `main` method.
3. You are very likely to use `getContentPane` when defining an applet. You would not normally use `addWindowListener`, `setTitle`, or `setSize`, because an applet does not have a title, and its size and closing are handled by the applet viewer or the Web document in which the applet is embedded. (It is possible to use them in certain kinds of components that might be added to an applet, but that is not what we are emphasizing in this question.)
4. You create a label (with or without text) by using a constructor for the class `JLabel`. You create the icon from `smiley.gif` by using a constructor for the

class `ImageIcon`. You add the icon to the label with the method `setIcon`. For example, the following code might be used in the `init` method of an applet:

```
JLabel niceLabel = new JLabel();
ImageIcon smileyFaceIcon = new ImageIcon("smiley.gif");
niceLabel.setIcon(smileyFaceIcon);
getContentPane().add(niceLabel);
```

5. You may use a relative or absolute path name when specifying the digital picture file.
6. None. HTML is not case sensitive.
7.

```
<a href="http://www.fool.com/">
Anything you want to say goes here.
</a>
```

8. A line break and some extra space will be added at each <p>. The line breaks in the text will be ignored, and the browser will insert line breaks where necessary to fit the text in the browser window.
9. The `.class` file.
10.

```
<applet code="HelloApplet.class" width=400 height=200>
</applet>
```

The width and height can, of course, be set to values other than 400 and 200, respectively.

11. An `Applet` has an `init` method just as a `JApplet` does.
12. An `Applet` does not have a content pane.

Programming Projects

1. Design an HTML home page for yourself. Use your imagination to put in whatever you would like people to know about you or that you think they should know about you. Some possibilities are your name, your occupation or class schedule, where you go to school or work, your hobbies, your favorite quotation, how to reach you by e-mail, or anything else you want to say. Note that your home page, like any home page, will consist of several files, each of which contains HTML documents. The hyperlinks allow the person viewing the document to move from one HTML document to another by clicking a mouse button. *Variation*: If you are in a class, ask your instructor if you need to include an applet on your home page.

   Remember, anything you place on your home page can be viewed by anybody in the world. Include only information that you do not mind being made public.
2. Convert the Swing application in Display 12.19 to an applet, and place it in an HTML document.
3. Every first-year electrical engineering student learns that two resistors (a resistor is a common type of electrical component) can be connected in either of two configurations, series or parallel, and that there are simple formulas to calculate the

equivalent resistance of both configurations (the value of a single resistor that can replace the two). If $R1$ and $R2$ are the two resistor values, then

$$\text{Series resistance} = R1 + R2, \text{ and}$$

$$\text{Parallel resistance} = (R1 * R2) / (R1 + R2).$$

Write an applet that provides a windowing interface to let a user enter two resistor values and choose which configuration to calculate. Include two text fields (label them `"Resistor 1"` and `"Resistor 2"`) to read in the two values, two buttons (label them `"Series"` and `"Parallel"`) to select the configuration, and another text field (label it `"Equivalent Resistance"`) to display the calculated value and indicate which configuration was selected. For example, if the user enters `100` for $R1$ and `50` for $R2$ and clicks the `"Series"` button, then the message would read `"Series Equivalent = 150"`. If the user enters the same values and clicks the `"Parallel"` button, then the message would read `"Parallel Equivalent = 33.3"`. Put the applet in a Web page that explains the calculations.

4. Modify the GUI calculator program from Programming Project 7 in Chapter 12 to run as an applet. If you have not already done this project as a GUI, do it now, but do it as an applet.

5. (The Swing part of this exercise is quite straightforward, but you do need to know a little about how to convert numbers from one base to another.) Write an applet that converts numbers from base-10 (ordinary decimal) notation to hexadecimal (base-16) notation. The program uses Swing to do input and output via an applet interface. The user enters a base-10 integer numeral in one text field and clicks a button labeled `"Convert"`. The equivalent hexadecimal numeral then appears in another text field. Be sure that the two fields are labeled. Include a `"Clear"` button that clears both text fields.

6. Rewrite the program in Display 12.19 so that it is an applet and so that it has all of the following changes:

   i. The class name is `MemoApplet`.

   ii. There are six buttons instead of five, and they are arranged as follows:

Save Memo 1	Save Memo 2	Clear
Get Memo 1	Get Memo 1	Exit

   The buttons are still at the bottom of the GUI (applet), with the text area above them. (*Hint*: Use a `GridLayout` manager on the button panel.)

   iii. When the user saves the text as memo 1, the text area changes so that it says `"Memo 1 saved."`, and when the user saves the text as memo 2, the text area changes to `"Memo 2 saved."` (See Self-Test Exercise 43 of Chapter 12 for a hint.)

   iv. The text area has line wrap, so that if more characters are entered than will fit on the line, the extra characters automatically go on the next line.

7. Do Programming Project 4 of Chapter 9, but write it as an applet.

8. Do Programming Project 7 of Chapter 9, but write it as an applet.

Appendices

APPENDIX 1

Keywords

Keywords are also called *reserved words*. You may not redefine any of the keywords given in this appendix. Their meanings are determined by the Java language and cannot be changed. In particular, you cannot use any of these keywords for variable names, method names, or class names.

```
abstract
assert*

boolean
break
byte

case
catch
char
class
const
continue

default
do
double

else
extends

false*
final
finally

float
for

goto

if
implements
import
inner*
instanceof
int
interface

long

native
new
null*

package
private
protected
public

return

short
static
strictfp
super
switch
synchronized

this
throw
throws
transient
true*
try

void
volatile

while
```

* According to the Sun documentation, these are not considered keywords. However, some authorities list them as keywords. For safety, this book considers them to be keywords, and you should as well.

APPENDIX 2

Precedence Rules

This appendix describes the rules that Java uses to determine the order in which operations are performed when evaluating an expression. In this list, operators on the same line are of equal precedence. As you move down the list, the operators in each line are of lower precedence than the ones on the previous line. When the computer is deciding which of two operations to perform first and the order is not dictated by parentheses, then it performs the operation of higher precedence before the operation of lower precedence. Some operators have equal precedence, and then the order of operations is determined by the sequence of the operators. Binary operators of equal precedence are performed in left-to-right order. Unary operators of equal precedence are performed in right-to-left order.

Highest Precedence

The dot operator, array indexing, and function call `.`, `[ ]`, and `( )`

The unary operators (+, −, ++, − −, `!`, and ~[1]), and type casts `(`*Type*`)`

The binary operators `*`, `/`, and `%`

The binary operators + and −

The binary operators (shift operators)[1] <<, >>, and >>>>

The binary operators <, >, <=, >=, and `instanceof`

The binary operators == and `!=`

The binary operator &

The binary operator (xor)[1] ∧

The binary operator |

The binary operator &&

The binary operator ||

The ternary operator (conditional operator) `?:`

The assignment operators =, *=, /=, %=, +=, −=, <<=, >>=, >>>>=, &=, ∧=, and |=

Lowest Precedence

---

1. Not discussed in this book.

APPENDIX 3

Unicode Character Set

The characters shown in this table are a subset of the Unicode character set known as the ASCII character set. The numbering is the same whether the characters are considered to be members of the Unicode character set or of the ASCII character set. Character number 32 is the blank. Only the printable characters are shown in the table.

<table>
<tr><td>32</td><td></td><td>56</td><td>8</td><td>80</td><td>P</td><td>104</td><td>h</td></tr>
<tr><td>33</td><td>!</td><td>57</td><td>9</td><td>81</td><td>Q</td><td>105</td><td>i</td></tr>
<tr><td>34</td><td>"</td><td>58</td><td>:</td><td>82</td><td>R</td><td>106</td><td>j</td></tr>
<tr><td>35</td><td>#</td><td>59</td><td>;</td><td>83</td><td>S</td><td>107</td><td>k</td></tr>
<tr><td>36</td><td>$</td><td>60</td><td><</td><td>84</td><td>T</td><td>108</td><td>l</td></tr>
<tr><td>37</td><td>%</td><td>61</td><td>=</td><td>85</td><td>U</td><td>109</td><td>m</td></tr>
<tr><td>38</td><td>&</td><td>62</td><td>></td><td>86</td><td>V</td><td>110</td><td>n</td></tr>
<tr><td>39</td><td>'</td><td>63</td><td>?</td><td>87</td><td>W</td><td>111</td><td>o</td></tr>
<tr><td>40</td><td>(</td><td>64</td><td>@</td><td>88</td><td>X</td><td>112</td><td>p</td></tr>
<tr><td>41</td><td>)</td><td>65</td><td>A</td><td>89</td><td>Y</td><td>113</td><td>q</td></tr>
<tr><td>42</td><td>*</td><td>66</td><td>B</td><td>90</td><td>Z</td><td>114</td><td>r</td></tr>
<tr><td>43</td><td>+</td><td>67</td><td>C</td><td>91</td><td>[</td><td>115</td><td>s</td></tr>
<tr><td>44</td><td>,</td><td>68</td><td>D</td><td>92</td><td>\</td><td>116</td><td>t</td></tr>
<tr><td>45</td><td>-</td><td>69</td><td>E</td><td>93</td><td>]</td><td>117</td><td>u</td></tr>
<tr><td>46</td><td>.</td><td>70</td><td>F</td><td>94</td><td>^</td><td>118</td><td>v</td></tr>
<tr><td>47</td><td>/</td><td>71</td><td>G</td><td>95</td><td>_</td><td>119</td><td>w</td></tr>
<tr><td>48</td><td>0</td><td>72</td><td>H</td><td>96</td><td>`</td><td>120</td><td>x</td></tr>
<tr><td>49</td><td>1</td><td>73</td><td>I</td><td>97</td><td>a</td><td>121</td><td>y</td></tr>
<tr><td>50</td><td>2</td><td>74</td><td>J</td><td>98</td><td>b</td><td>122</td><td>z</td></tr>
<tr><td>51</td><td>3</td><td>75</td><td>K</td><td>99</td><td>c</td><td>123</td><td>{</td></tr>
<tr><td>52</td><td>4</td><td>76</td><td>L</td><td>100</td><td>d</td><td>124</td><td>|</td></tr>
<tr><td>53</td><td>5</td><td>77</td><td>M</td><td>101</td><td>e</td><td>125</td><td>}</td></tr>
<tr><td>54</td><td>6</td><td>78</td><td>N</td><td>102</td><td>f</td><td>126</td><td>~</td></tr>
<tr><td>55</td><td>7</td><td>79</td><td>O</td><td>103</td><td>g</td><td></td><td></td></tr>
</table>

APPENDIX 4

SavitchIn

```
import java.io.*;
import java.util.*;

/**
 Class for simple console input.
 A class designed primarily for simple keyboard input of the
 form "one input value per line". If the user enters an improper
 input, i.e., an input of the wrong type or a blank line, then
 the user is prompted to reenter the input and given a brief
 explanation of what is required. Also includes some additional
 methods to input single numbers, words, and characters, without
 going to the next line.
*/
public class SavitchIn
{
    /**
     Reads a line of text and returns that line as a String
     value. The end of a line must be indicated either by a
     new-line character '\n' or by a carriage return '\r'
     followed by a new-line character '\n'. (Almost all systems
     do this automatically. So you need not worry about this
     detail.) Neither the '\n' nor the '\r', if present, are
     part of the string returned. This class will read the rest
     of a line if the line is already partially read.
    */
    public static String readLine()
    {
        char nextChar;
        String result = "";
        boolean done = false;

        while (!done)
        {
            nextChar = readChar();
            if (nextChar == '\n')
               done = true;
            else if (nextChar == '\r')
            {
                //Do nothing.
                //Next loop iteration will detect '\n'.
            }
            else
               result = result + nextChar;
        }

        return result;
    }
```

```
/**
 Reads the first string of nonwhitespace characters on
 a line and returns that string. The rest of the line
 is discarded. If the line contains only whitespace,
 the user is asked to reenter the line.
*/
public static String readLineWord()
{
    String inputString = null,
           result = null;
    boolean done = false;

    while(!done)
    {
        inputString = readLine();
        StringTokenizer wordSource =
                          new StringTokenizer(inputString);
        if (wordSource.hasMoreTokens())
        {
            result = wordSource.nextToken();
            done = true;
        }
        else
        {
            System.out.println(
              "Your input is not correct. Your input must");
            System.out.println(
             "contain at least one nonwhitespace character.");
            System.out.println(
                             "Please try again. Enter input:");
        }
    }

    return result;
}

/**
 Precondition: The user has entered a number of type int
 on a line by itself, except that there may be
 whitespace before and/or after the number.
 Action: Reads and returns the number as a value of type
 int. The rest of the line is discarded. If the input is
 not entered correctly, then in most cases, the user will
 be asked to reenter the input. In particular, this
 applies to incorrect number formats and blank lines.
*/
public static int readLineInt()
{
    String inputString = null;
    int number = -9999;//To keep the compiler happy.
                     //Designed to look like a garbage value.
    boolean done = false;
```

```
    while (! done)
    {
        try
        {
            inputString = readLine();
            inputString = inputString.trim();
            number = Integer.parseInt(inputString);
            done = true;
        }
        catch (NumberFormatException e)
        {
            System.out.println(
                    "Your input number is not correct.");
            System.out.println(
                    "Your input number must be");
            System.out.println(
                    "a whole number written as an");
            System.out.println(
                     "ordinary numeral, such as 42");
            System.out.println("Minus signs are OK,"
                     + "but do not use a plus sign.");
            System.out.println("Please try again.");
            System.out.println("Enter a whole number:");
        }
    }

    return number;
}

/**
 Precondition: The user has entered a number of type long
 on a line by itself, except that there may be whitespace
 before and/or after the number.
 Action: Reads and returns the number as a value of type
 long. The rest of the line is discarded. If the input is
 not entered correctly, then in most cases, the user will
 be asked to reenter the input. In particular, this
 applies to incorrect number formats and blank lines.
*/
public static long readLineLong()
{
    String inputString = null;
    long number = -9999;//To keep the compiler happy.
                  //Designed to look like a garbage value.
    boolean done = false;

    while (! done)
    {
        try
        {
            inputString = readLine();
            inputString = inputString.trim();
```

```
                number = Long.parseLong(inputString);
                done = true;
            }
            catch (NumberFormatException e)
            {
                System.out.println(
                        "Your input number is not correct.");
                System.out.println(
                            "Your input number must be");
                System.out.println(
                            "a whole number written as an");
                System.out.println(
                             "ordinary numeral, such as 42");
                System.out.println("Minus signs are OK,"
                              + "but do not use a plus sign.");
                System.out.println("Please try again.");
                System.out.println("Enter a whole number:");
            }
        }

        return number;
    }

    /**
     Precondition: The user has entered a number of type
     double on a line by itself, except that there may be
     whitespace before and/or after the number.
     Action: Reads and returns the number as a value of type
     double. The rest of the line is discarded. If the input
     is not entered correctly, then in most cases, the user
     will be asked to reenter the input. In particular, this
     applies to incorrect number formats and blank lines.
    */
    public static double readLineDouble()
    {
        String inputString = null;
        double number = -9999;//To keep the compiler happy.
                     //Designed to look like a garbage value.
        boolean done = false;

        while (! done)
        {
            try
            {
                inputString = readLine();
                inputString = inputString.trim();
                number = Double.parseDouble(inputString);
                done = true;
            }
            catch (NumberFormatException e)
            {
```

```
                System.out.println(
                        "Your input number is not correct.");
                System.out.println(
                        "Your input number must be");
                System.out.println(
                         "an ordinary number either with");
                System.out.println(
                          "or without a decimal point,");
                System.out.println("such as 42 or 9.99");
                System.out.println("Please try again.");
                System.out.println("Enter the number:");
            }
        }

        return number;
    }

    /**
     Precondition: The user has entered a number of type float
     on a line by itself, except that there may be whitespace
     before and/or after the number.
     Action: Reads and returns the number as a value of type
     float. The rest of the line is discarded. If the input is
     not entered correctly, then in most cases, the user will
     be asked to reenter the input. In particular,
     this applies to incorrect number formats and blank lines.
    */
    public static float readLineFloat()
    {
        String inputString = null;
        float number = -9999;//To keep the compiler happy.
                      //Designed to look like a garbage value.
        boolean done = false;

        while (! done)
        {
            try
            {
                inputString = readLine();
                inputString = inputString.trim();
                number = Float.parseFloat(inputString);
                done = true;
            }
            catch (NumberFormatException e)
            {
                System.out.println(
                        "Your input number is not correct.");
                System.out.println(
                        "Your input number must be");
                System.out.println(
                         "an ordinary number either with");
```

```
                System.out.println(
                          "or without a decimal point,");
                System.out.println("such as 42 or 9.99");
                System.out.println("Please try again.");
                System.out.println("Enter the number:");
            }
        }

        return number;
    }

    /**
     Reads the first nonwhitespace character on a line and
     returns that character. The rest of the line is
     discarded. If the line contains only whitespace, the
     user is asked to reenter the line.
    */
    public static char readLineNonwhiteChar()
    {
        boolean done = false;
        String inputString = null;
        char nonWhite = ' ';//To keep the compiler happy.

        while (! done)
        {
            inputString = readLine();
            inputString = inputString.trim();
            if (inputString.length() == 0)
            {
                System.out.println(
                         "Your input is not correct.");
                System.out.println(
                         "Your input must contain at");
                System.out.println(
                         "least one nonwhitespace character.");
                System.out.println("Please try again.");
                System.out.println("Enter input:");
            }
            else
            {
                nonWhite = (inputString.charAt(0));
                done = true;
            }
        }

        return nonWhite;
    }

    /**
     Input should consist of a single word on a line, possibly
     surrounded by whitespace. The line is read and discarded.
     If the input word is "true" or "t", then true is returned.
     If the input word is "false" or "f", then false is
```

```
 returned. Uppercase and lowercase letters are considered
 equal. If the user enters anything else (e.g., multiple
 words or different words), the user is asked
 to reenter the input.
*/
public static boolean readLineBoolean( )
{
    boolean done = false;
    String inputString = null;
    boolean result = false;//To keep the compiler happy.

    while (! done)
    {
        inputString = readLine( );
        inputString = inputString.trim( );
        if (inputString.equalsIgnoreCase("true")
               || inputString.equalsIgnoreCase("t"))
        {
            result = true;
            done = true;
        }
        else if (inputString.equalsIgnoreCase("false")
                    || inputString.equalsIgnoreCase("f"))
        {
            result = false;
            done = true;
        }
        else
        {
            System.out.println(
                     "Your input is not correct.");
            System.out.println("Your input must be");
            System.out.println("one of the following:");
            System.out.println("the word true,");
            System.out.println("the word false,");
            System.out.println("the letter T,");
            System.out.println("or the letter F.");
            System.out.println(
                     "You may use either upper-");
            System.out.println("or lowercase letters.");
            System.out.println("Please try again.");
            System.out.println("Enter input:");
        }
    }

    return result;
}
/**
 Reads the next input character and returns that character.
 The next read takes place on the same line where this
 one left off.
*/
```

```
public static char readChar( )
{
    int charAsInt = -1; //To keep the compiler happy.
    try
    {
        charAsInt = System.in.read( );
    }
    catch(IOException e)
    {
        System.out.println(e.getMessage( ));
        System.out.println("Fatal error. Ending program.");
        System.exit(0);
    }

    return (char)charAsInt;
}

/**
 Reads the next nonwhitespace input character and returns
 that character. The next read takes place immediately
 after the character read.
*/
public static char readNonwhiteChar( )
{
  char next;

  next = readChar( );
  while (Character.isWhitespace(next))
      next = readChar( );

  return next;
}

/**
 The methods given next are not used in the text, except
 for a brief reference in Chapter 2. No program code uses
 them. However, some programmers may want to use them.
*/

/**
 Precondition: The next input in the stream consists of
 an int value, possibly preceded by whitespace, but
 definitely followed by whitespace.
 Action: Reads the first string of nonwhitespace characters
 and returns the int value it represents. Discards the
 first whitespace character after the word. The next read
 takes place immediately after the discarded whitespace.
 In particular, if the word is at the end of a line, the
 next read will take place starting on the next line.
 If the next word does not represent an int value,
 a NumberFormatException is thrown.
*/
```

```
public static int readInt() throws NumberFormatException
{
    String inputString = null;
    inputString = readWord();
    return Integer.parseInt(inputString);
}
/**
 Precondition: The next input consists of a long value,
 possibly preceded by whitespace, but definitely
 followed by whitespace.
 Action: Reads the first string of nonwhitespace characters
 and returns the long value it represents. Discards the
 first whitespace character after the string read. The
 next read takes place immediately after the discarded
 whitespace. In particular, if the string read is at the
 end of a line, the next read will take place starting on
 the next line. If the next word does not represent a long
 value, a NumberFormatException is thrown.
*/
public static long readLong()
                    throws NumberFormatException
{
    String inputString = null;
    inputString = readWord();
    return Long.parseLong(inputString);
}
/**
 Precondition: The next input consists of a double value,
 possibly preceded by whitespace, but definitely
 followed by whitespace.
 Action: Reads the first string of nonwhitespace characters
 and returns the double value it represents. Discards the
 first whitespace character after the string read. The
 next read takes place immediately after the discarded
 whitespace. In particular, if the string read is at the
 end of a line, the next read will take place starting on
 the next line. If the next word does not represent a
 double value, a NumberFormatException is thrown.
*/
public static double readDouble()
                    throws NumberFormatException
{
    String inputString = null;
    inputString = readWord();
    return Double.parseDouble(inputString);
}
/**
 Precondition: The next input consists of a float value,
 possibly preceded by whitespace, but definitely
 followed by whitespace.
```

```
 Action: Reads the first string of nonwhitespace characters
 and returns the float value it represents. Discards the
 first whitespace character after the string read. The
 next read takes place immediately after the discarded
 whitespace. In particular, if the string read is at the
 end of a line, the next read will take place starting on
 the next line. If the next word does not represent
 a float value, a NumberFormatException is thrown.
*/
public static float readFloat()
                     throws NumberFormatException
{
    String inputString = null;
    inputString = readWord();
    return Float.parseFloat(inputString);
}

/**
 Reads the first string of nonwhitespace characters and
 returns that string. Discards the first whitespace
 character after the string read. The next read takes
 place immediately after the discarded whitespace. In
 particular, if the string read is at the end of a line,
 the next read will take place starting on the next line.
 Note that if it receives blank lines, it will wait until
 it gets a nonwhitespace character.
*/
public static String readWord()
{
    String result = "";
    char next;

    next = readChar();
    while (Character.isWhitespace(next))
         next = readChar();

    while (!(Character.isWhitespace(next)))
    {
        result = result + next;
        next = readChar();
    }

    if (next == '\r')
    {
        next = readChar();
        if (next != '\n')
        {
            System.out.println("Fatal error in method "
                 + "readWord of the class SavitchIn.");
```

```
            System.exit(1);
        }
    }

    return result;
}

/**
 Precondition: The user has entered a number of type byte
 on a line by itself, except that there may be whitespace
 before and/or after the number.
 Action: Reads and returns the number as a value of type
 byte. The rest of the line is discarded. If the input is
 not entered correctly, then in most cases, the user will
 be asked to reenter the input. In particular, this applies
 to incorrect number formats and blank lines.
*/
public static byte readLineByte()
{
    String inputString = null;
    byte number = -123;//To keep the compiler happy.
                //Designed to look like a garbage value.
    boolean done = false;

    while (! done)
    {
        try
        {
            inputString = readLine();
            inputString = inputString.trim();
            number = Byte.parseByte(inputString);
            done = true;
        }
        catch (NumberFormatException e)
        {
            System.out.println(
                    "Your input number is not correct.");
            System.out.println(
                    "Your input number must be a");
            System.out.println(
                    "whole number in the range");
            System.out.println("-128 to 127, written as");
            System.out.println(
                    "an ordinary numeral, such as 42.");
            System.out.println("Minus signs are OK,"
                         + "but do not use a plus sign.");
            System.out.println("Please try again.");
            System.out.println("Enter a whole number:");
        }
    }

    return number;
}
```

```
/**
 Precondition: The user has entered a number of type short
 on a line by itself, except that there may be whitespace
 before and/or after the number.
 Action: Reads and returns the number as a value of type
 short. The rest of the line is discarded. If the input is
 not entered correctly, then in most cases, the user will
 be asked to reenter the input. In particular, this applies
 to incorrect number formats and blank lines.
*/
public static short readLineShort()
{
    String inputString = null;
    short number = -9999;//To keep the compiler happy.
                    //Designed to look like a garbage value.
    boolean done = false;

    while (! done)
    {
        try
        {
            inputString = readLine();
            inputString = inputString.trim();
            number = Short.parseShort(inputString);
            done = true;
        }
        catch (NumberFormatException e)
        {
            System.out.println(
                    "Your input number is not correct.");
            System.out.println(
                    "Your input number must be a");
            System.out.println(
                    "whole number in the range");
            System.out.println(
                    "-32768 to 32767, written as");
            System.out.println(
                    "an ordinary numeral, such as 42.");
            System.out.println("Minus signs are OK,"
                         + "but do not use a plus sign.");
            System.out.println("Please try again.");
            System.out.println("Enter a whole number:");
        }
    }

    return number;
}

public static byte readByte() throws NumberFormatException
{
    String inputString = null;
    inputString = readWord();
```

```
        return Byte.parseByte(inputString);
    }

    public static short readShort( ) throws NumberFormatException
    {
        String inputString = null;
        inputString = readWord( );
        return Short.parseShort(inputString);
    }

    //The next class was intentionally not used in the code for
    //other methods, so that somebody reading the code could
    //more quickly see what was being used.
    /**
     Reads the first byte in the input stream and returns that
     byte as an int. The next read takes place where this one
     left off. This read is the same as System.in.read( ),
     except that it catches IOExceptions.
    */
    public static int read( )
    {
        int result = -1; //To keep the compiler happy
        try
        {
            result = System.in.read( );
        }
        catch(IOException e)
        {
            System.out.println(e.getMessage( ));
            System.out.println("Fatal error. Ending program.");
            System.exit(0);
        }
        return result;
    }
}
```

APPENDIX 5

Protected and Package Modifiers

In this text, we always use the modifiers `public` and `private` before instance variables and method definitions. Normally, these are the only modifiers you need, but there are two other possibilities that fall in between the two extremes of `public` and `private`. In this appendix, we discuss the modifier `protected` as well as the restriction that applies when you use no modifier at all.

If a method or instance variable is modified by `protected` (rather than `public` or `private`), then it can be directly accessed inside of its own class definition, and it can be directly accessed inside of any class derived from it. Moreover, if marked `protected`, then it can also be directly accessed in any method definition for any class in the same package. That is the extent of the access; the protected method or instance variable cannot be directly accessed in any other classes. Thus, if a method is marked `protected` in class *A*, and class *B* is derived from class *A*, then the method can be used inside any method definition in class *B*. However, in a class that is not in the same package as class *A* and is not derived from class *A*, it is as if the `protected` method were `private`.

The modifier `protected` imposes a peculiar sort of restriction, since it allows direct access to any programmer who is willing to go through the bother of defining a suitable derived class. Thus, it is like saying, "I'll make it difficult for you to use this item, but I will not forbid you to use it." In practice, instance variables should never be marked `protected`. On very rare occasions, you may want to have a method marked `protected`. However, if you want an access level that is intermediate between `public` and `private`, the access described in the next paragraph is often a preferable alternative.

You may have noticed that, if you forget to place one of the modifiers `public` or `private` before an instance variable or method definition, your class definition will still compile. If you do not place any of the modifiers `public`, `private`, or `protected` before an instance variable or method definition, then the instance variable or method can be directly accessed inside the definition of any class in the same package, but not outside of the package. This type of access is called **package access**, or **default access.** You use package access when you have a package of cooperating classes that act as a single encapsulated unit. Note that package access is more restricted than `protected` access and that package access gives more control to the programmer defining the classes. If you control the package directory, then you control who is allowed package access.

APPENDIX 6

The DecimalFormat Class

An object of the class DecimalFormat has a number of different methods that can be used to produce numeral strings in various formats. In this appendix, we describe some uses of one of these methods, named format. The general approach to using the DecimalFormat class is as follows:

Create an object of the class DecimalFormat, using a String pattern:

Syntax:

DecimalFormat *Variable_Name* = DecimalFormat(*Pattern*);

Example:

```
DecimalFormat formattingObject = new DecimalFormat("000.000");
```

The method format of the class DecimalFormat can then be used to convert a number of type double to a corresponding numeral String.

Syntax:

Decimal_Format_Object.format(*Double_Expression*)
produces a numeral string corresponding to the *Double_Expression*.
The *Decimal_Format_Object* is typically a *Variable_Name*.

Examples:

```
System.out.println(formattingObject.format(12.3456789));
String numeral = formattingObject.format(12.3456789);
```

Assuming that the object formattingObject is created as shown previously, the output produced by the foregoing println statement is

```
012.346
```

The format of the string produced is determined by the *Pattern* string that was used as the argument to the constructor that created the object of the class DecimalFormat.

For example, the pattern "00.000" means that there will be two digits before the decimal point and three digits after the decimal point. Note that the result is rounded when the number of digits is less than the number of digits available. If the format pattern is not consistent with the value of the number, such as a pattern that asks for two digits before the decimal point for a number like 123.456, then the format will be violated so that no digits are lost.

You can create patterns such as "#0.##0", in which the character '0' stands for a compulsory digit and the character '#' stands for an optional digit. Examples of patterns are shown in Display A6.1.

Percent Notation

The character '%' placed at the end of a pattern indicates that the number is to be expressed as a percentage. The '%' causes the number to be multiplied by 100 and have a percent sign (%) appended to it.

DISPLAY A6.1 Demonstration of the DecimalFormat Class *(Part 1 of 2)*

```
import java.text.*;

public class DecimalFormatDemo
{
    public static void main(String[] args)
    {
        DecimalFormat twoDigitsPastPoint = new DecimalFormat("0.00");
        DecimalFormat threeDigitsPastPoint =
                         new DecimalFormat("00.000");

        double d = 12.3456789;
        System.out.println(twoDigitsPastPoint.format(d));
        System.out.println(threeDigitsPastPoint.format(d));

        double money = 12.8;
        System.out.println("$" + twoDigitsPastPoint.format(money));
        String numberString = twoDigitsPastPoint.format(money);
        System.out.println(numberString);

        DecimalFormat percent = new DecimalFormat("0.00%");

        double fraction = 0.734;
        System.out.println(percent.format(fraction));

        DecimalFormat eNotation1 =
           new DecimalFormat("#0.###E0");//1 or 2 digits before point
        DecimalFormat eNotation2 =
           new DecimalFormat("00.###E0");//2 digits before point

        double number = 123.456;
        System.out.println(eNotation1.format(number));
        System.out.println(eNotation2.format(number));

        double small = 0.0000123456;
        System.out.println(eNotation1.format(small));
        System.out.println(eNotation2.format(small));
    }
}
```

■ DISPLAY A6.1 **Demonstration of the `DecimalFormat` Class** *(Part 2 of 2)*

Sample Screen Dialog

```
12.35
12.346
$12.80
12.80
73.40%
1.2346E2
12.346E1
12.346E-6
12.346E-6
```

Scientific Notation (E-Notation)

E-notation is specified by including an `'E'` in the pattern string. For example, the pattern `"00.###E0"` approximates the specification of two digits before the decimal point, three or fewer digits after the decimal point, and at least one digit after the `'E'`, as in `12.346E1`. As you can see by the examples of E-notation in Display A6.1, the exact details of what E-notation string is produced can be a bit more involved than our explanation so far. Here are a couple more details:

> The number of digits indicated after the `'E'` is the minimum number of digits used for the exponent. As many more digits as are needed will be used.
>
> The **mantissa** is the decimal number before the `'E'`. The minimum number of significant digits in the mantissa (that is, the sum of the number of digits before and after the decimal point) is the *minimum* of the number of digits indicated before the decimal point plus the *maximum* of the number of digits indicated after the decimal point. For example, `12345` formatted with `"##0.##E0"` is `"12.3E3"`.

To see how E-notation patterns work, it would pay to play with a few cases, and in any event, do not count on a very precisely specified number of significant digits.

APPENDIX 7

The `Iterator` Interface

The `Iterator` interface is designed to be implemented in conjunction with classes whose objects are collections of elements. In a good implementation, repeated execution of the method `next` would produce all elements in the collection. The `Iterator` interface might be implemented by the collection class itself or by another class whose objects are iterators for the collection class. The `Iterator` interface specifies the following three methods:

```
/**
 Returns the next element. Throws a
 NoSuchElementException if there is no next element.
**/
public Object next();

/**
 Returns true if there is an element left for next to return.
*/
public boolean hasNext();

/**
 Removes the last element that was returned by next.
 Throws an UnsupportedOperationException if the remove
 method is not supported by this Iterator. Throws an
 IllegalStateException if the next method has not yet
 been called or if the remove method has already been
 called after the last call to the next method.
*/
public void remove();
```

All the exception classes mentioned are derived classes of `RunTimeException`, so an object of any of these exception classes need not be caught or declared in a `throws` clause.

The `Iterator` interface is in the package `java.util`. So when defining a class that implements the `Iterator` interface, the file should contain the following `import` statement:

```
import java.util.*;
```

A sample implementation of the `Iterator` interface is given in the answer to Self-Test Question 23 in Chapter 10.

APPENDIX 8

Cloning

clone

A **clone** of an object is (or at least should be) an exact copy of the object. The emphasis here is on both *exact* and *copy.* A clone should look as though it has the exact same data values as the object being copied, and it should be a true copy and not simply another name for the object being copied. In Section 5.6, entitled "Information Hiding Revisited," we discussed some of the problems involved in making copies of an object. You should read that section before reading this appendix.

A clone is made by invoking the method named `clone`. The method `clone` is invoked in the same way as any other method. The heading for the method `clone` is as follows:[1]

```
public Object clone( )
```

Although the method `clone` returns a copy of an object of some class, it always returns it as an object of type `Object`. So you normally need a type cast. For example, consider the class `PetRecord` in Display 5.20 of Chapter 5. After you make suitable additions to the class definition, you can make a copy of an object of type `PetRecord` as follows:

```
PetRecord original = new PetRecord("Fido", 2, 5.6);
PetRecord extraCopy = (PetRecord)original.clone( );
```

Be sure to notice the type cast `(PetRecord)`.

The foregoing invocation of `clone` (or any invocation of `clone`) will not work unless the class implements the `Cloneable` interface. Thus, in order to make the preceding code work, you must do two things. First, you must change the beginning of the class definition for `PetRecord` to the following:

```
public class PetRecord implements Cloneable
```

Second, you must add a definition of the method `clone` to the class definition. In the case of the class `PetRecord`, the method `clone` would be defined as shown in Display A8.1.

extra code on CD

On the accompanying CD, we have included a copy of the class `PetRecord` that includes the definition of the method `clone` from Display A8.1.

Note that the `Cloneable` interface and `clone` method behave in more complicated ways than most interfaces and inherited methods. Although the class `Object` has a method named `clone`, it is not inherited automatically. You must include `implements Cloneable` in the definition of the class, and you must include a definition of `clone`, even if it is defined as in Display A8.1, which, in effect, simply says that the method `clone` behaves as it would if it were inherited in the normal way.

If the instance variables are all of types whose objects cannot be changed by their methods, such as the primitive types and the type `String`, then the definition of `clone` shown in Display A8.1 will work fine. In that definition, the method `clone` invokes the version of

1. In the class `Object`, the method `clone` is `protected`, not `public`, but it normally makes more sense to make it `public` in the classes you define.

DISPLAY A8.1 Implementation of the Method `clone` (Simple Case)

```
public Object clone()
{
    try
    {
        return super.clone();//Invocation of clone in class Object
    }
    catch(CloneNotSupportedException e)
    {//This should not happen.
        return null; //To keep the compiler happy.
    }
}
```

Works correctly if each instance variable is of a primitive type or of the type `String`. Does not work correctly in most other cases.

`clone` in the class `Object`,[2] which simply makes a bit-by-bit copy of the memory used to store the calling object's instance variables. The `try-catch` blocks are required because the method `clone` can throw the exception `CloneNotSupportedException` if the class does not implement the `Cloneable` interface. Of course, in these classes, we are implementing the `Cloneable` interface, so the exception will never be thrown, but the compiler will still insist on the `try-catch` blocks. There is a bit of detail to worry about here, but as long as each instance variable is either of a primitive type or of type `String`, the definition of `clone` in Display A8.1 will work just fine and can simply be copied unchanged into your class definition.

If your class has instance variables of a class type (other than a class whose objects cannot change, like `String`), then the definition of `clone` in Display A8.1 is legal, but it probably does not do what you want a `clone` method to do. If the class contains an instance variable of some class type, the clone produced will have a copy of the instance variable's memory address, rather than a copy of the instance variable's data. For a class that cannot be changed, like `String`, this condition is not a problem. For most other classes, this condition would allow access to private data in the way we described in Section 5.6, entitled "Information Hiding Revisited." When defining a `clone` method for a class that has instance variables of a class type (other than the type `String` or a similar unchangeable class type), your definition of `clone` should make a clone of each instance variable of a changeable class type. Of course, this task requires that those class types for the instance variables have a suitable `clone` method themselves. The way to define such a `clone` method is illustrated in Display A8.2. Let's go over some of the details in the definition of that `clone` method.

---

2. If your class is a derived class of some class (other than `Object`), we are assuming that the base class has a well-defined `clone` method, since `super.clone` will then refer to the base class.

DISPLAY A8.2 Outline of a Class with Cloning

```
public class Neighbor implements Cloneable
{
    private String name;
    private int numberOfChildren;
    private PetRecord pet;

    public Object clone()
    {
        try
        {
            Neighbor copy = (Neighbor)super.clone();
            copy.pet = (PetRecord)pet.clone();
            return copy;
        }
        catch(CloneNotSupportedException e)
        {//This should not happen.
            return null; //To keep the compiler happy.
        }
    }

    public PetRecord getPet()
    {
        return (PetRecord)pet.clone();
    }

      <There are presumably other methods that are not shown.>
}
```

The following line makes a bit-by-bit copy of the memory used to store the calling object's instance variables:

```
Neighbor copy = (Neighbor)super.clone();
```

This sort of copy works fine for the instance variable `numberOfChildren`, which is of the primitive type `int`. It is also satisfactory for the instance variable `name` of type `String`. However, the value it gives to the instance variable `copy.pet` is the address of the `pet` instance variable of the calling object. It does not, as yet, give `copy.pet` the address of a *copy* of the calling object's `pet` instance variable. To change the value of `copy.pet` so that it names a copy of the calling object's `pet` instance variable, the `clone` method definition goes on to do the following:

```
copy.pet = (PetRecord)pet.clone();
```

APPENDIX 9

Javadoc

The Java language comes with a program named `javadoc` that will automatically generate HTML documents that describe your classes. This documentation tells somebody who uses your program or class what she or he needs to know in order to use it, but omits all the implementation details, such as the bodies of all method definitions (both public and private), all information about private methods, and all private instance variables.

`javadoc` is normally used on packages, although it can also be used on single classes. Packages are discussed in Chapter 5. You need to have access to an HTML browser (a Web browser) so that you can view the documents produced by `javadoc`. However, you do not need to know very much HTML in order to use `javadoc`. Chapter 13 contains more HTML instruction than you need to know for this purpose.

In this appendix, we will first discuss how you should comment your classes so that you can get the most value out of `javadoc`. We will then discus the details of how you run the `javadoc` program.

Commenting Classes for Use with `javadoc`

To get a more useful `javadoc` document, you must write your comments in a particular way. All the classes in this book have been commented for use with `javadoc`.

The program `javadoc` will extract the heading for your class as well as the headings for all public methods, public instance variables, and certain comments. No method bodies and no private items are extracted.

For `javadoc` to extract a comment, the comment must satisfy two conditions:

1. The comment must *immediately precede* a public class definition or a public method definition (or other public item).
2. The comment must use the /* and */ style, and the opening /* must contain an extra *. So the comment must be marked by /** at the beginning and */ at the end.

All of the /* and */ style comments in this book are of this form. Note that both // style comments and comments preceding any private items will not be extracted.

You can insert descriptions of parameters and the value returned by a method into the comment preceding the method. The following code illustrates how this operation is done:

```
/**
 Computes the total cost of multiple identical items.
 @param number number of items purchased
 @param price cost of one item
 @return total cost of number items at price for one
*/
public static double cost(int number, double price)
{
    return number*price;
}
```

Note that each @ **tag** is on a line by itself. The following are some of the @ tags allowed:

```
@param Parameter_Name Parameter_Description
@return Description_Of_Value_Returned
@throws Exception_Type Explanation
```

If an @ tag is included for an item, `javadoc` will extract the explanation for that item and include it in the documentation.

You can also insert HTML commands in your comments so that you gain more control over `javadoc`, but that is not necessary and may not even be desirable. HTML commands can clutter the comments, making them harder to read when you look at the source code.

Running `javadoc`

To run `javadoc` on a package, you must be in the directory (folder) that *contains* the package directory, not in the package directory itself. To phrase it another way, you must be one directory above the directory that contains the class (or classes) for which you want to generate documentation. Then all you need to do is give the following command:

```
javadoc -d Document_Directory Package_Name
```

The *Document_Directory* is the name of the directory in which you want `javadoc` to place the HTML documents it produces.

The accompanying CD has a package named `javadocsample`, which contains the two classes `Person` and `Student` from Chapter 7. It also contains the result of running the following command (look in the subdirectory `ap09`):

```
javadoc -d javadocsampledocs javadocsample
```

You can also run the `javadoc` program on a single class file. For example,

```
javadoc SavitchIn.java
```

The result of running `javadoc` on the file `SavitchIn.java` is in the file `SavitchIn.html` on the accompanying CD.

You can link to another set of Java documents so that your HTML documents include live links to standard classes and methods. The syntax is as follows:

```
javadoc -link Link_To -d Document_Directory Package_Name
```

Link_To is either a path to your local version of the Java documentation or the URL of the Sun Web site with standard Java documentation. As of this writing, that URL was

```
http://java.sun.com/j2se/1.4/docs/api/
```